Principles of Law for Managers

There are legal implications about most aspects of an organization's activity, whether it enters into a contract with a supplier, a customer or an employee or engages in competition with another company. This text looks at all the aspects of law that are relevant to a manager's work, explaining the core issues and illustrating them with case studies. Avoiding the intricacies of legal terminology and extensive case histories, *Principles of Law for Managers* explains in simple terms the legal consequences of management decisions.

Topics covered include

- business organization and finance
- workforce
- health and safety
- environment
- products
- intellectual property
- UK and EC competition

Each chapter offers strategies for managers, key learning points and exercises as well as lists of useful books and addresses, providing a basis for managers to gain an understanding of the way law works in order to run their business successfully.

Anne Ruff is Principal Lecturer in Law at Middlesex University Business School. The contributors are also all based at Middlesex University.

Routledge series in the principles of management
Edited by Joseph G. Nellis

The Routledge series in the principles of management offers stimulating approaches to the core topics of management. The books relate the key areas to strategic issues in order to help managers solve problems and take control. By encouraging readers to apply their own experiences, the books are designed to develop the skills of the all-round manager.

Principles of operations management
R.L. Galloway

Principles of marketing
G. Randall

Principles of applied statistics
M. Fleming and J. Nellis

Principles of accounting and finance
P. Sneyd

Principles of human resource management
D. Goss

Principles of Law for Managers

Edited by Anne Ruff

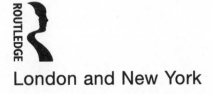

London and New York

First published 1995
by Routledge
11 New Fetter Lane, London EC4P 4EE

Simultaneously published in the USA and Canada
by Routledge
29 West 35th Street, New York, NY 10001

© 1995 Anne Ruff

Typeset in Times by
J&L Composition Ltd, Filey, North Yorkshire

Printed and bound in Great Britain by
T.J. Press (Padstow) Ltd, Padstow, Cornwall

British Library Cataloguing in Publication Data
A catalogue record for this book is available from the British Library

Library of Congress Cataloguing in Publication Data
Principles of law for managers/edited by Anne Ruff.
   p.   cm. — (The Routledge series in the principles of management)
Includes bibliographical references and index.
ISBN 0–415–07378–2
1. Executives–Legal status, laws, etc.–Great Britain. 2. Business
law–Great Britain. I. Ruff, Anne R. II. Series.
KD665.B86P75 1995
349.41′024658–dc20   94–37890
[344.10024658]   CIP

Contents

Figures, tables and boxes

FIGURES

TABLES

BOXES

Contributors

Brenda Barrett MA, PhD, Barrister at Law is Professor of Law at Middlesex University. Professor Barrett has regularly given papers on aspects of occupational health and safety at national and international conferences, as well as for many years teaching postgraduate students in Personnel Management. She has published widely on occupational health and safety and on employers' liability. Her research work has included many industry based projects in the areas of safety and environmental management.

Penny Childs BA (Hons), LLM is Principal Lecturer and Deputy Head of the Law School at Middlesex University. An experienced manager in her own right, she has taught extensively at degree and postgraduate level. Her areas of expertise include environmental law, criminal law, the law of tort and information technology law.

Stephen Homewood BA (Hons), Barrister, ACIArb is Senior Lecturer in Law at Middlesex University and Course Leader of the CPE (FT). A member of the UK Environmental Lawyers Association and a Fellow of the Institute of Arbitrators, he has for many years taught Public Law and more recently Environmental Law. Recent publications include an article 'Enforcing Environmental Law', co-authored with David Lewis, which was published in the Environmental Law Journal.

Penelope Kent LLB (Hons), LLM, Solicitor is Principal Lecturer in Law at Middlesex University. She has taught European Community Law on a range of undergraduate and postgraduate programmes including the MBA and the LLB. She has written *European Community Law* (2nd edition pending) which is a comprehensive guide to the principles of EC law. Her work as a legal trainer has encompassed both public and private sector organizations.

Malcolm Leder LLB (Hons), Solicitor is Professor of Consumer Law and Head of the Law School at Middlesex University. He regularly contributes to consumer publications and is co-author of *Consumer Law* (4th edition pending). He is a consultant to both consumer organizations and well-known manufacturers and retailers. He has extensive experience of teaching postgraduate management students and of leading training workshops for managers in industry and commerce. He has judicial experience as a part-time Chairman of Social Security Appeal Tribunals.

David Lewis LLB (Hons), MA, MIPM is Reader in Employment Law at Middlesex University. Apart from teaching on a wide range of degree and postgraduate management courses, as well as being a regular contributor to specialist commercial seminars, he has considerable experience as a consultant in employment law. He is the author of *Essentials of Employment Law* (currently in its 4th edition) and joint author of *Discipline* in the IPM's 'Law at Work' series. He is currently a member of the Executive Committee of the Industrial Law Society and of the editorial committee of the Industrial Law Journal.

Elvira Rubin LLB (Hons), Barrister is Senior Lecturer in Law at Middlesex University. After working in the travel business in Germany, the USA and Japan as well as in London, she qualified as a lawyer. She has considerable experience of teaching Company and Commercial Law to English and European business students and is undertaking research on the consequences of Spain's membership of the European Community on Spanish company law.

Anne Ruff, Barrister at Law, is an experienced lecturer, administrator and author. She has taught the law of contract to both undergraduate and postgraduate students. Her publications include *Commercial and Industrial Law* (3rd edition).

John Weldon LLB (Hons), LLM is Senior Lecturer in Law and Programme Leader of the LLB degree and Law Set at Middlesex University. He has a long-standing interest in and experience of Intellectual Property Law. He teaches this subject on the undergraduate programme and has developed a successful course on design management. Currently he is developing a Postgraduate Certificate in Intellectual Property for lawyers practising in Malaysia and elsewhere.

Series editor's preface

In recent years there has been a dramatic increase in management development activity in most Western countries, especially in Europe. This activity has extended across a wide spectrum of training initiatives, from continuing studies programmes of varying durations for practising managers to the provision of courses leading to the award of professional and academic qualifications. With regard to the latter the most prominent developments have been in terms of the Master of Business Administration (MBA) and Diploma in Management (DMS) programmes, particularly in the UK where virtually every university now offers some form of post-graduate and/or post-experience management qualification.

However, the explosion of formal management training programmes such as the MBA and DMS has tended to be in advance of suitably tailored management textbooks. Many of the core functional areas of these programmes have had to rely on some of the more specialized and thus more narrowly focused textbooks, which are more appropriate for undergraduate requirements. They have generally not provided a suitable balance between academic rigour and practical, business-related relevance. The Routledge series covering the principles of management has been specifically developed to service the needs of an expanding management audience. The series deals with the full range of core subjects as well as many of the more popular elective courses that one would expect to find in most MBA and DMS programmes. Many of the books will also be attractive to those students taking professional exams, for example in accountancy, banking, etc., as well as managers attending a wide range of development courses. Each book in the series is written in a concise format covering the key principles of each topic in a pragmatic style which emphasizes the balance between theory and application. Case studies, exercises, and references for further reading are provided where appropriate.

It gives me pleasure to express my thanks to the staff of Routledge for the commitment and energy which they have devoted to the development of this series, and in particular to Francesca Weaver who has skilfully steered each book through the minefield of production from beginning to end. I would also like to express my gratitude to my secretary Christine Williams for maintaining her joviality throughout the development of the 'Principles' series.

Joseph G. Nellis
Cranfield School of Management

Chapter 1

Introduction

Anne Ruff

WHY DO MANAGERS NEED TO KNOW ABOUT THE LAW?

The answer is so that they can be more efficient and more effective in their job. Law impinges on many aspects of a manager's role. Specialist managers, such as personnel managers, sales managers, or production managers will need to be familiar with the detail of particular areas of law. Knowledge of the law will enable managers to develop their analytical skills so that the legal dimensions of a problem can be identified and resolved as part of the overall management solution. A manager's social skills of persuading, negotiating and leading will be enhanced by an understanding of the legal issues involved. Managers should be aware of and familiar with basic legal principles so that at the very least they can effectively communicate when necessary with the enterprise's lawyer! Ignorance of the law is no defence in court, and nor is it likely to be much of a defence at work.

An effective manager must:

- know about most aspects of the enterprise's business
- have the skills necessary for decision-making, communicating, handling employees and customers, selling
- be able to plan, organize, co-ordinate and control the enterprise.

The law is particularly concerned with:

- the organization and financing of an enterprise
- the relationship between the enterprise and its employees
- health and safety in the workplace
- the impact of the enterprise and its product on the environment
- the enterprise's liability for its products
- protecting the enterprise's interests in its ideas and products
- preventing unfair competition between enterprises.

In order to make the best decisions, handle employees and customers, effectively sell the product profitably, plan future developments and organize the enterprise, the successful manager should, at the very least, be aware of the legal aspects of the particular situation. Unwittingly falling foul of the law can be expensive.

HOW TO USE THIS BOOK

This book is an introduction to law especially written for managers. The authors have adopted a case study approach to law and have tried to relate the content of each chapter to experiences commonly encountered by managers.

Chapter 1

This chapter:

- explains the structure and purpose of the book and how to make the best use of the material
- makes a few points about legal terminology
- considers the two main functions of the law
- describes the sources of English law
- explains the key concepts in English law.

This chapter should be used as a quick reference point when reading the later chapters. It provides a brief overview of the whole legal process.

Chapters 2–8

These chapters examine areas of English law which are of particular relevance to managers. Each of these chapters follows a common structure. After a brief introduction a practical example is highlighted in order to illustrate the types of legal problems which can arise in the context of the content of the chapter. This example is referred to and developed as appropriate in the remainder of the chapter. Chapter 2 describes the different ways in which an enterprise can be legally organized and a case history provides the factual background. In Chapter 3 four short case illustrations are used, indicating the wide-ranging nature of the legal problems which can arise in the relationship between the enterprise and its workforce. Chapters 4–8 use one or more case studies to set the scene, provide a reference point and illustrate the complex legal issues which can affect managers. These case studies are based either on a legal case or on a typical factual scenario.

The selected case is followed by the core of the chapter which is a description and analysis of the relevant law. You should treat this section as a guide to the motorways of the law with some discussion of the legal A roads. The legal B roads and footpaths are generally ignored. However, by concentrating on a particular case you are shown how the main legal principles operate in a detailed factual context.

This is followed by a section entitled 'strategies for managers' which discusses the practical implications of the law for managers to help them avoid or at least reduce the risk of legal liability. Then there is a list of key learning points which set out briefly the basic information which managers need to know.

Finally there are some exercises. The aim of these is to encourage you to find out how the enterprise where you work deals with the legal issues raised in the chapter. You might also be able to find out why the enterprise responds in a particular way. It might not always be easy to find out such information, but that in itself will tell you something about the enterprise. Doing these exercises will also help you to understand the practical implications of the law in the context of your own employment.

At the end of each chapter there is an information section which will help you to carry out more detailed research. A list of legal references, usually case names and law report details, is given together with the names of relevant journals and books and a list of useful addresses and telephone numbers.

Chapter 9

This chapter stresses the importance of the European Union for future legal developments, both because of the single market and because of the policy of harmonizing the relevant laws of member states. Likely developments in the subject matter covered in each of the previous chapters are noted. Finally, there is a review of the basic strategies which managers should encourage their enterprises to adopt.

LEGAL TERMINOLOGY

Why is the term 'enterprise' used throughout the book? We used this term because it covers all types of organizations which employ managers. It has no specific legal meaning unlike other more limited terms. We intend it to cover private and public sector organizations, as well as profit-making as opposed to charitable organizations. It should be noted, however, that we do not look at the legal issues specific to public sector or charitable organizations. 'Enterprise' covers the smallest organizations such as the sole trader, through partnerships, to private and public companies and multi-national organizations. It covers organizations which manufacture, distribute and sell goods as well as those which provide services.

As you will see, the sources of English law are cases and legislation. In this book we have only occasionally referred to specific cases (for example, *Lambert* v *Lewis* (1982))[1] because it would be inappropriate in a book written for managers rather than for lawyers. We have given the names of key pieces of legislation such as the Consumer Protection Act 1987 or the EC Framework Directive on health and safety. Occasionally a specific section or part of an Act is referred to either because it is particularly important or in order to identify it clearly.

The meaning of words and their application to specific facts is at the heart of the law. Words in common use often have a more precise meaning to the lawyer. Other words are used which are unfamiliar to the general reader. Readers should not be put off by legal jargon, but think of it as a form of shorthand. We have attempted to minimize its use, but sometimes it is necessary to use particular words in order to state a particular legal principle accurately and briefly.

THE FUNCTION OF THE LAW

Most people think of the law in the context of the courts punishing offenders or resolving disputes. However, as well as its dispute resolution function the law also has a planning function which can help to avoid disputes arising in the first place. If a dispute does arise then it may be preferable not to use the law to resolve it but to use an alternative method of dispute resolution.

The planning function of the law

Planning is one of the basic functions of a manager. Knowledge of the law can help a manager to plan wisely by ensuring that:

- the enterprise is organized in the most appropriate legal form
- its staffing policies satisfy the legal requirements
- it complies with legal requirements in its operation
- the product meets the required legal standards
- the enterprise prevents the unauthorized use of its trade secrets
- it does not adopt unfair trading practices.

Ensuring compliance with the law can not only avoid accidents but can minimize the risk of time-consuming and costly disputes which could threaten the viability of the enterprise.

All enterprises operate within some form of legal framework, whether the enterprise is a sole trader, a partnership or a limited company. Managers should be aware of the legal framework of the enterprise in which they work. If the aim is to expand or even to contract the enterprise, managers should consider what sort of legal framework is most appropriate to the new commercial context. The advantages and disadvantages of the different legal frameworks should be considered, together with financial and other commercial factors.

The great majority of enterprises need to recruit and keep employees, as well as occasionally needing to dismiss an employee or reduce the size of the overall workforce. In order to achieve and maintain a good relationship with its employees and to avoid costly disputes, an enterprise should organize its personnel procedures in accordance with the legal requirements.

An employer is also responsible for ensuring that the workplace is safe for employees and for visitors. Again it is preferable to avoid accidents and to minimize legal liability by ensuring that the workplace is organized so that it complies with the law. The enterprise should, for the same reasons, also aim to avoid damaging the environment, and ensure that its operation complies with the law.

Enterprises exist to sell a product or provide a service. Managers are usually responsible for ensuring that their part of the business plan is successfully implemented. The cost of the product needs to be estimated. Certain costs can be accepted by the producer or passed on to the pur- chaser, and this decision must be reflected in any contract terms. The specification of the product should also be stated clearly in any contract. The product must satisfy the legal requirements as to quality and to safety.

The success of many enterprises is often connected with possession of valuable information about the product or processes used in providing a service, or of a recognized name or motif. In many cases such confidential information can by careful planning be legally protected from unauthorized use by other enterprises. Unauthorized use of information could seriously erode the profitability of the enterprise. In addition where an enterprise holds personal data on computer, management systems must be set up to ensure that the data is kept and used in accordance with the legislative requirements.

The enterprise must sell its goods or services. Both the United Kingdom law and the law of the European Union (known, confusingly, as European Community law) uphold the principle of free competition. Therefore any agreements between enterprises to share out a market or fix a minimum price, or any national law which in effect prevents an enterprise from trading in another state, may well be invalid.

Dispute resolution and the law

It is always preferable to avoid litigation. It is time-consuming and expen- sive, and it is unlikely to make commercial sense to sue a good and reliable supplier or customer of long standing. In addition, litigation provides a public airing of a dispute which may not be in the best interests of either party. However, even with perfect planning, disputes can and do arise. The great majority, probably well over ninety per cent, are unlikely to get to court, although lawyers will often be involved in the resolution of the dispute. If an enterprise is involved in a breach of the criminal law, however, then there is less opportunity for an informal resolution of the matter with the prosecuting authority, whether it is the Crown Prosecution Service (CPS), the Health and Safety Executive or the trading standards department of the local authority.

Larger enterprises will often have their own legal department which will initially advise managers on particular problems and may refer more complex cases to a specialist firm of solicitors. Smaller enterprises are likely to have a firm of solicitors which they use as and when necessary. Solicitors may refer the case to a barrister for an opinion on the legal issues. This is done for a variety of reasons such as where the solicitor does not have the necessary expertise, or where it is more economic for the solicitor to get a barrister to do the research. Enterprises cannot normally approach a barrister direct; they must go through a solicitor.

If a dispute concerns a civil matter then it will be dealt with in the civil courts. Examples of such cases would be a claim for compensation by one enterprise against another for breach of contract, or for the supply of defective goods, or for breach of copyright, or an application for an injunction to prevent an ex-employee working for another company and divulging trade secrets.

The legal process: civil courts

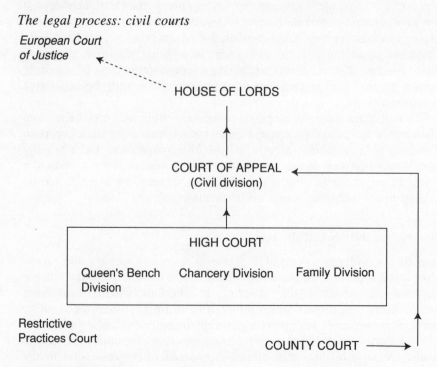

Figure 1.1 Civil courts

Cases are normally started in the county court or one of the three divisions of the High Court. The jurisdiction of a county court is limited geographically and to a certain extent financially. Usually the court has jurisdiction if the defendant lives in its area. The county court can hear claims in contract, tort, and the recovery of debts, as well as disputes over land, and bankruptcy proceedings. The county court tries cases arising out of contract or tort claims of up to £50,000. Cases where the claim is between £25,000 and £50,000 will be heard in the High Court if, for example, it is a test case, or raises questions of general public interest or is particularly complex. If the claim is for more than £50,000 the case will normally be heard in the High Court. Cases are usually heard by a circuit judge. However, where the claim is for £5,000 or less then the case is heard by a district judge. In practice district judges deal mainly with bankruptcy, insolvency, financial and property matters, which also fall within the jurisdiction of the county court, as do family cases and some claims for under £1,000. An advantage of using the small claims jurisdiction (i.e. for claims under £1,000) is that if the claimant loses the case they will not be liable to pay the other person's legal costs. This jurisdiction, which is a form of arbitration, is also available, if both parties agree, where the claim is for more than £1,000. Normally there is no jury in the county court.

If the case is not appropriate for the county court, then it will be started in the High Court which has three divisions. Normally the cases are heard by a single judge. The Queen's Bench Division hears cases on many commercial matters such as breach of contract and the tort of negligence. There is a specialist Commercial Court within the division and the aim of this court is to provide a forum in which there is familiarity with the subject matter of commercial and mercantile disputes. Examples of the type of cases heard by the court include banking and international credit, international trade, and arbitration disputes. The court is also concerned with providing speedy and efficient procedures for resolving disputes without unnecessary formality.

The Chancery Division of the High Court will hear, for example, cases involving land worth more than £30,000, bankruptcy, partnership disputes and cases involving patents, trade marks, registered designs or copyright. There is a Patents Court within the division. The third division of the High Court, the Family Division, as its name implies, hears matrimonial matters and child care cases.

If a litigant is unhappy with the decision of the county court or High Court then an appeal may lie to the Court of Appeal (civil division) and then in limited circumstances to the House of Lords.

If the case concerns the interpretation of European Community law then the House of Lords must refer the case to the European Court of Justice for an authoritative interpretation. Lower courts have the option of referring the case to the European Court of Justice.

The Restrictive Practices Court has a very limited jurisdiction which is mainly concerned with the legality of agreements which attempt to restrict free competition between manufacturers and suppliers of goods and services (see Chapter 8).

The legal process: criminal courts and tribunals

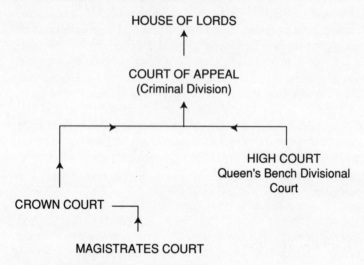

Figure 1.2 Criminal courts

If the case is a criminal one, such as a prosecution for breach of health and safety regulations, or supplying goods with a false trade description, or insider dealing, then the case will start in the magistrates' court. If the offence is classified as a summary offence then the trial will also take place in that court. If the offence is more serious and is classified as an indictable offence, then the trial will take place in the Crown Court. Certain middle-ranking offences can be tried in either court.

Appeals against the decision of a magistrates' court normally go to the Crown Court. Appeals against the decision of the Crown Court will normally go to the Court of Appeal. An appeal can be brought against conviction or against sentence. Enterprises are most likely to receive fines, but in certain circumstances it is possible for the sentence to be one of imprisonment, which in the case of a limited company would be served usually by the responsible company directors. An appeal from the Court of Appeal lies to the House of Lords, but only on a point of law of general public importance.

Apart from courts, legal disputes may be resolved in tribunals. Where new legal rights have been established in the last forty years or so then government has frequently provided that any disputes concerning those rights should be heard by a tribunal rather than a court. The advantages of tribunals were thought to be that they were quicker, cheaper, informal and specialist. Industrial tribunals which hear employment cases such as unfair dismissal and redundancy claims, as well as race and sex discrimination claims, are an example of such tribunals (see Chapter 3). However, there are currently delays of at least six months before a case is heard. The law has become so complex that employers often employ lawyers to represent them and the tribunals have become much more formal than originally intended. Employees are not eligible for legal aid and so are often not represented.

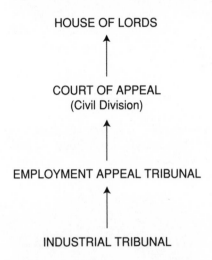

HOUSE OF LORDS

COURT OF APPEAL
(Civil Division)

EMPLOYMENT APPEAL TRIBUNAL

INDUSTRIAL TRIBUNAL

Figure 1.3 Employment tribunals

An industrial tribunal is composed of a legally qualified chairman and two lay people representing respectively employers' associations and trade unions. An appeal against the tribunal's decision can be made to the Employment Appeal Tribunal (EAT) on a question of law and then to the Court of Appeal and the House of Lords.

Alternative methods of resolving disputes

Going to court to resolve a dispute can be time-consuming, expensive, confrontational, stressful, legalistic and very public. Therefore it is often preferable to resolve a dispute between enterprises using a method which is quicker, cheaper, aimed at resolving problems, private and with experts in the subject-matter of the dispute rather than having lawyers decide the issues. It seems likely that in the future mediation or conciliation or arbitration will be more frequently used as methods of settling disagreements.

Arbitration is often used as a means of resolving a dispute arising out of a contract. In particular arbitration is common in the construction industry and in shipping disputes. London is an international centre for arbitration and many disputes are settled according to English law although the contract and the parties may have little or no connection with England. Arbitration arises as a result of agreement between the parties. They will choose the arbitrator, and the terms of reference. The arbitrator will normally be an expert in the subject-matter of the dispute. The parties will agree to be bound by the arbitrator's decision, although it is possible to appeal to a court against the arbitrator's decision in certain circumstances. A form of arbitration is available in the county court.

In employment disputes, whether between employers and employees or between employers and trade unions, the Advisory, Conciliation and Arbitration Service (ACAS) acts as a conciliator, that is, it attempts to facilitate a resolution of the dispute.

SOURCES OF ENGLISH LAW

The first thing to note is that English law applies to Wales but does not automatically apply to the rest of the United Kingdom, that is Scotland and

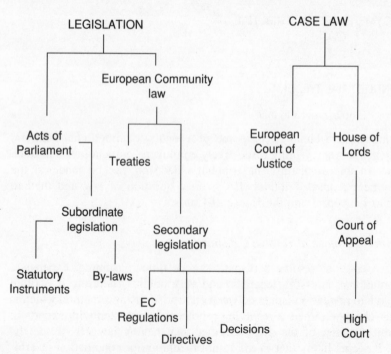

Figure 1.4 Sources of English law

Northern Ireland. In particular the criminal legal system in Scotland is different from that in England. However, almost all of the law in this book is applicable to the whole of the United Kingdom.

Central and local government produce a vast amount of documentation, guidelines, circulars, policy documents, Green Papers, White Papers, Bills, Actions, Orders in Council, and Statutory Instruments. The courts decide hundreds if not thousands of cases each day. The United Kingdom is a member of the European Union which in turn produces documentation and judicial decisions. Two problems arise from this mass of material. First which material is law and so binding, and which is advice or merely the basis for discussion? Second, how do you keep up to date with changes in the law? The second part is discussed in Chapter 9.

There are two main sources of English law today: legislation and case law, also known as judicial precedent. In the past there were two other sources: custom and law books written by eminent lawyers, but they are now of little importance in practice. A major development in the last twenty years has been the impact of European Community law which takes priority over all conflicting domestic law of member states including that of the United Kingdom.

Legislation

United Kingdom legislation

Acts of Parliament are the major source of new domestic law. Changes in the law or the introduction of new law will usually be put into effect by an Act of Parliament. An Act of Parliament is also called a statute.

The normal procedure is for a government department to draft a Bill. This is discussed by, and must be approved by, the two Houses of Parliament which are the House of Commons and the House of Lords. The Bill must then receive the Royal Assent, that is the approval of the monarch, in order to become an Act of Parliament. An Act does not necessarily have legal effect from the moment it receives the Royal Assent. It is not uncommon for complex legislation to come into effect in stages.

English legislation is usually drafted in a detailed and precise form. Broad brush statements of principle are normally avoided. The approach of the courts when interpreting legislation is to concentrate on the words used in the Act and to interpret them fairly restrictively. The courts will not normally look at the reason why the legislation was introduced and approved. Acts are sub-divided into sections and, where the Act is complex, sections are often grouped into Parts.

Subordinate legislation

Subordinate legislation is usually created under powers delegated by Parliament. It is often concerned with detailed provision such as the maximum limits for compensation for unfair dismissal, the date on which certain sections of an Act come into force, or the implementation of European Community law. A complex Act may make provision for the Secretary of State to draft and implement detailed provisions to give effect to the principles set out in the Act. This is normally done by way of a statutory instrument (SI) which has to be approved by Parliament or, in certain circumstances, by the Privy Council. Documents such as departmental circulars, guidance notes and policy statements are not sources of law, although they may be of considerable practical importance. Local government is also able to draw up by-laws under delegated powers.

European Community law

European Community law became part of English law by virtue of the European Communities Act 1972. The three main sources of EC law are:

● treaties
● secondary legislation, in particular regulations and directives
● decisions of the European Court of Justice.

Treaties

The fundamental principles of EC law are to be found in the various EEC treaties starting with the European Economic Community Treaty (1957) also known as the Treaty of Rome and, since 1993, as the European Community (EC) Treaty, which was modelled on the European Coal and Steel Community Treaty (1951), and continuing with the Single European Act (1986) and the Treaty on European Union (TEU) (which came into force on 1 November 1993) otherwise known as the Maastricht Treaty. The treaties were initially concerned with the economic goal of creating a single market in Europe by, for example, ensuring that competition was not distorted. However, they were also concerned with wider social goals such as improving employment opportunities for workers, as well as providing a framework for political co-operation in the 1986 Act. The European Union is concerned with matters outside the scope of this book, namely a common foreign and security policy as well as justice and home affairs. Unlike United Kingdom legislation, EC legislation tends to be expressed in broad general principles. The European Court of Justice when interpreting EC legislation is concerned with giving effect to the purpose of the legislation rather than giving effect just to the words used in the legislation.

The importance of EC law and policy to managers cannot be under-estimated. As will be seen it affects to a greater or lesser extent the content of each of the chapters in this book.

The institutional framework of the EC is set out in the EC Treaty. Although the framework has evolved over the years, the four central institutions provided for in the foundation treaties are still amongst the most important.

The European Parliament   518 members have been directly elected by citizens of the member states since 1979. Forty nine new MEPs will be added to this total, eighteen from the former East Germany. The European Parliament (EP) sits in Luxembourg or Strasbourg. It does not make EC law. Its functions are chiefly supervisory and advisory. It must be consulted by the Council of Ministers about certain proposed legislation. The EP must approve the budget proposed by the Commission and agreed by the Council. Its powers in relation to both the Council of Ministers and the Commission have been increased by the Maastricht Treaty and now include the power to veto certain legislation.

The Council of Ministers   This consists of the relevant Ministers from the member states. Thus if the subject under discussion is agriculture then the Agriculture Ministers of the twelve member states will be present. The council is primarily a political body, but it also has the power to approve or reject secondary legislation, such as regulations and directives. The Council of Ministers should be distinguished from the European Council, a summit meeting of heads of state or government, held at least once a year to provide a continuing political stimulus to integration.

The Commission   While the Commission resembles a civil service it also has executive and supervisory functions. It is based in Brussels. There are seventeen Commissioners nominated by the member states, with France, Germany, Italy, Spain and the United Kingdom nominating two each. The Commission puts forward proposals to the Council of Ministers, it drafts the EC budget proposal, it attempts to ensure that member states comply with EC law, it is responsible for the implementation of policy, and it negotiates with other states or international bodies on behalf of the Community.

The European Court of Justice and the Court of First Instance   The main task of the European Court of Justice (ECJ) is to ensure that the courts of member states consistently interpret and apply EC law. Most cases are referred to it by courts in member states, but the Commission can also take a member state to court where it considers that the state is not complying with EC law. The ECJ sits in Luxembourg. It consists of thirteen judges, one from each member state and a President, together with six advocates-general who present submissions and recommendations to the court in a particular case. An advocate-general's recommendations are often followed by the ECJ. Since 1988 a Court of First Instance (CFI) has been established to hear specific types of cases including some involving competition law and staffing disputes. Appeals from the CFI may be heard by the ECJ.

Secondary legislation

The second source of EC law is to be found in its secondary legislation. There are three obligatory types: regulations, directives and decisions. Regulations once approved by the Council of Ministers are normally automatically part of the United Kingdom law. Directives on the other hand are binding on the United Kingdom and other member states but usually only become part of the law of each state when approved, for example, by the House of Commons or the House of Lords. However, if the member state has not incorporated, or has only partially incorporated, the directive into its domestic law then in certain circumstances an individual will still be able to argue successfully that the directive is part of the domestic law and the courts must give effect to it. Decisions of the EC institutions are binding on the parties to whom they are addressed. Appeals against competition decisions are heard by the CFI.

Direct effect and the supremacy of EC law over national law

The early case law of the ECJ made it clear that EC law can be directly effective. This means that it takes effect in each member state without the need to pass an implementing statute, giving individuals the right to rely on it before the national courts. The ECJ has also held on a number of occasions that directly effective EC law takes precedence over conflicting national law. Most of the key provisions of the EC Treaty, such as those relating to the single market, are directly effective.

Case law

One of the chief characteristics of the English legal system which distinguishes it from other legal systems is that decisions in particular cases are a source of law. If an English court has made a decision on a particular point of law such as the meaning of a phrase in a statute, then if the point comes before a court again it must follow the earlier court's decision. This is known as the doctrine of binding precedent. For such a system to work it is necessary to have a hierarchy of courts (see Figures 1.1 to 1.4 above). The courts at the top of the hierarchy are binding on the lower courts. In practice it is the decisions of the House of Lords and the Court of Appeal which are legally influential, although decisions of the High Court can be if they are accepted and followed by the higher courts. The decisions of the House of Lords are binding on all lower courts. The Court of Appeal is bound by decisions of the House of Lords and usually by its own previous decisions. The Court of Appeal's decisions are binding on all lower courts.

In addition to having a hierarchy of courts it is necessary to have a system of law reporting. This is because if the decisions of the court are a source of law, it is essential that there is a detailed record not just of the decision but also the reasoning behind the decision, for it is the reasoning that must be adopted and applied to the facts of subsequent cases.

The English system of law reports might appear disorganized to the outsider. There are no official law reports as such, although the courts prefer the reports produced by the Incorporated Council of Law Reporting. There is no requirement that every decision of even the higher courts should be reported. Important Court of Appeal decisions occasionally get overlooked for a couple of years or more. There are general law reports which cover a broad spectrum of cases, such as the Weekly Law Reports or the All England Law Reports, and there are specialist law reports such as Simon's Tax Cases or the Industrial Relations Law Reports. In addition newspapers such as *The Times*, *The Independent*, *The Guardian* and *The Daily Telegraph* carry their own law reports.

The English common law system whose rules of law historically developed case by case was exported to many colonies and is the system still to be found in a large number of Commonwealth countries as well as in the USA. The importance of cases as a source of law has declined in England during the last hundred years, as major reforms and innovations have usually been implemented by legislation. However, case law still remains an important source of law. The tort of negligence, for example, is a judicial creation first formulated in 1932. In civil law systems, such as those in continental Europe, cases although influential are not a source of law. This different approach to cases and the role of the courts has been highlighted by the United Kingdom's membership of the European Community.

The European Court of Justice has tended to adopt a civil law approach to the interpretation of legislation, which places more emphasis on the purpose behind the legislation rather than narrowly interpreting and giving effect to the words of the legislation. The decisions of the ECJ on the interpretation and application of EC law are binding on all the courts of all the member states, including the UK. Nevertheless, the ECJ is not bound by its own previous decisions and is free to depart from those decisions in the light of new circumstances.

MAJOR CONCEPTS IN ENGLISH LAW

There are certain fundamental areas of English law whose concepts permeate most branches of English law. The four areas of law whose principles are of great relevance to managers and to the remainder of this book are:

- law of contract
- law of tort
- law of property
- criminal law.

Law of contract

The law of contract is concerned with legally enforceable agreements. We all enter into contracts every day. Buying a cup of coffee creates a contract, as does having your hair cut. Equally the multimillion pound purchase of a company will be legally encapsulated in a contract. The law of contract is relevant to most of the chapters in this book. A contract underpins the creation of a company or a partnership, the purchase of shares in a company, the relationship between an employer and employee, the buying and selling of goods and services, and agreements between businesses which try to restrict the activities of competitors. The first thing to note is that to be legally enforceable a contract does not usually have to be signed. It does not usually even have to be in writing.

Pre-requisites for determining the existence of a contract

The crucial requirement is that there must be an agreement between the parties. In legal jargon there has to be an offer and an acceptance. For example, Oliver offers to buy a cup of coffee which is advertised on Nicholas's menu as costing fifty pence. Nicholas accepts Oliver's offer and agrees to provide him with a cup of coffee for fifty pence. If Nicholas had run out of coffee he could inform Oliver and in effect reject Oliver's offer.

In addition to there being agreement between the parties, the terms of the agreement must be reasonably clear if the court is to enforce them. If there is any ambiguity or uncertainty then the court will not usually fill in the gaps with what it considers to be reasonable terms.

It is presumed that the parties in a commercial situation intend the agreement to be legally binding. This presumption can be rebutted. In *Kleinwort Benson* v *Malaysian Mining Corp. Berhad* (1989)[2] a bank lent a company approximately £8 million on the basis of a letter of comfort provided by the parent company. The court held that such a letter did not amount to a legally binding promise and the company was unable to recover the money it was owed.

One more essential requirement is consideration. This means that if a promise is to be enforced by the courts, the person trying to enforce the promise must have given something of economic value, however small, in exchange for the promise. If Chris promises to give Steve £1 million and Steve does not promise to give Chris something in return then it is very unlikely that Steve can enforce such a promise.

Managers need to be aware of certain legal problems which arise in the context of reaching agreement. In particular these relate to the use of standard form contracts, and to work starting while negotiations continue. These problems usually arise because the parties are much more concerned with the commercial realities than with the legal niceties of contracting.

Standard form contracts

These are frequently used because it is much more efficient where an enterprise enters into hundreds if not thousands of standard transactions. Problems arise where either or both parties to the transaction use standard forms which state different things and nobody has noticed until things start to go wrong.

For example, in *Butler Machine Tool Co.* v *Ex-cell-o Corp. (England)* (1979)[3] a company (the sellers) stated in a letter that it could provide a machine to another company (the buyers) on certain standard terms. One of these terms was a price escalation clause. The buyers placed an order by letter but on different terms and conditions which did not include a price escalation clause. At the bottom of the letter was a tear-off slip which the sellers signed and returned to the buyers. The slip stated that the sellers accepted the buyers' terms. However, the sellers had also written that the order was in accordance with their first letter, which included a price escalation clause. The price of the machine increased by thousands of pounds between the date of the agreement and its delivery. Did the buyers have to pay the increased price? In this case the court said that the price escalation clause was not a term of the contract, but such cases do depend on the precise facts. Therefore, it is essential that managers read the small print and clarify any ambiguities before becoming legally bound if they wish to avoid being caught out.

Continuing negotiations

If commercial pressures require that work is started on a project then sometimes the legal requirements are overlooked, again to the financial detriment of the business.

For example, in *British Steel Corp.* v *Cleveland Bridge & Engineering*

Co. (1984)[4] one company (the buyers) asked another company (the sellers) to supply them with steel nodes for a building which the buyers were erecting for a third party. There were lengthy discussions over the specifications and terms of the contract, both parties having their own standard terms which conflicted on crucial matters. During the negotiations the buyers issued a letter of intent asking the sellers to start work while the final details were being worked out between them. All the nodes except one were delivered, but the parties were still negotiating over the terms including one relating to liability for late delivery. The sellers had not been paid for any of the nodes delivered so they refused to hand over the last one. There was then a steel strike and the last node could not be delivered for another four months. The sellers then claimed that there was no contract but that they were entitled to be paid a reasonable price for the nodes supplied. The buyers claimed that there was a contract and that they were entitled to damages for late delivery of the last node. The damages claimed were more than the total reasonable price claimed by the sellers. The court held that on the facts there was no legally binding contract and so the sellers were entitled to be paid a reasonable price for the nodes supplied. This case indicates that by failing to enter a contract the buyers were unable to impose obligations on the sellers regarding, for example, the date of delivery, or the quality of the product.

What are the remedies for breach of contract?

The first thing to note is that usually only parties to a contract can sue or be sued on the contract. This is known as the doctrine of privity of contract and distinguishes contractual rights from tortious and property rights. If Oliver buys a cup of coffee from Nicholas for Simon which has ground glass in it causing Simon to be ill, then Simon is unable to sue Nicholas for breach of contract because Simon was not a party to the contract which was made between Oliver and Nicholas. Simon will probably have a remedy against the manufacturer of the coffee under the tort of negligence, and may have a similar remedy against Nicholas.

One major exception to the doctrine of privity is the concept of agency. For example, if Simon had asked Oliver to buy a cup of coffee for him from Nicholas, then Oliver could be acting as Simon's agent and the contract for the cup of coffee is made between Simon and Nicholas. This is particularly relevant where a limited company or a partnership enters into a contract (see Chapter 2).

If there is a breach of contract what can the innocent party do? There are two options available if the breach is serious. The first is to treat the contract as terminated by the breach and claim damages if loss has been suffered. The second is to continue with the contract and claim damages. If the breach is not serious then only the second option is available (see Chapter 6 and also Chapter 3).

The first option is not dependent on a court order, and is sometimes used by parties to a contract who have entered into a bad bargain, for example where the market price of goods has fallen between the date of the contract and the date of the delivery of the goods. However, this can be risky. For example, in *Cehave* v *Bremer, The Hansa Nord* (1976)[5] sellers supplied citrus pellets some of which on delivery were found to be damaged by overheating. The buyers rejected all the shipment and claimed back the price paid (£100,000) from the sellers. The shipment was then sold on the open market and the buyers bought it for £30,000. The buyers were not entitled to recover the £100,000 from the sellers because the breach was not sufficiently serious to entitle them to treat the contract as at an end and to reject the goods. The buyers were only entitled to recover damages to compensate them for the defective pellets.

The innocent party will be able to recover damages for any foreseeable loss arising from the breach of contract. This will normally include loss of profits or other losses made, for example, on a sub-contract. The aim of damages in the law of contract is to put the innocent party in the position in which they would have been if the contract had been performed properly. There are two methods of calculating the amount of damages recoverable based on the difference in value or the cost of cure (see Chapter 6). In all cases the innocent party is under an obligation to mitigate or minimize their loss. This could even include buying the goods at a higher price from the original seller who was in breach if the seller was the only available source of the goods!

Law of tort

Tort means wrong or harm. The law of tort is primarily concerned with compensating individuals by awarding them damages where they have suffered loss or injury or damage because of the actions of another person. In certain circumstances it is possible to obtain an injunction, that is, a court order. For example, an employer could obtain such an order prohibiting a competitor from employing the employer's ex-employee where the ex-employee had access to the employer's trade secrets. The law of tort imposes obligations on us all and on particular categories of individuals, whereas the obligations imposed by contract are usually those agreed to by the parties to the contract. Under the law of tort no one, for example, should:

- intentionally damage another person's goods
- interfere with another person's commercial interests (see Chapter 7)
- libel or slander another person

- trespass on another person's land
- use any land owned in such a way that it causes a nuisance to the owner of neighbouring property (see Chapter 5)
- behave in a negligent way so that damage is caused to another person or to their property (see Chapters 4, 5 and 6)
- commit a breach of statutory duty (see Chapter 4).

The tort of negligence is the most important tort in practice today. It is wide-ranging and in particular is relevant to the liability of a manufacturer, or supplier, or retailer for harmful products and processes which cause injury to employees, or customers, or neighbours (see Chapters 4, 5 and 6). The tort of negligence is a relatively new development having been formulated by the House of Lords in 1932 in the snail in the ginger-beer bottle case (*Donoghue* v *Stevenson*).[6] In this case a customer purchased some ginger-beer in an opaque bottle from a café owner. The ginger-beer was drunk by a friend who discovered what she thought to be a decomposed snail in the bottle. This caused her to suffer a stomach upset as well as shock. The friend could not sue the retailer for breach of contract because there was no contract between them. The purchaser could sue the retailer for breach of contract but had not suffered any injury so would only have been able to recover nominal damages. The House of Lords held that the friend could sue the manufacturer and introduced the neighbour principle into English law. The essence of this principle is that every individual must take reasonable care to avoid doing acts or omissions which would harm their neighbour. A neighbour is anyone whom it is reasonably foreseeable might be harmed by the act or omission.

Initially this principle was limited to manufacturers of goods and their ultimate consumers. Over the following sixty years it has expanded to apply, for example, to injuries suffered in traffic accidents, negligence by members of the professions, negligent design or erection of a building as well as liability for inaccurate statements. Normally, for liability in the tort of negligence to arise there has to be some physical injury to a person or to their property. This should be contrasted with the law of contract where the loss that is suffered is normally just financial or economic loss. Occasionally the same set of facts creates liability in contract and in tort. Usually it is preferable to sue for breach of contract, partly because it is more difficult to prove negligence.

Employers, whether sole traders, partnerships or limited companies will be liable for the torts of their employees if they are committed during the course of their employment. This is known as vicarious liability. Thus, if a van driver negligently drives a van and injures a pedestrian the employer will be vicariously liable to the pedestrian. The van driver will also be liable, but in practice an employee is unlikely to be sued because the employee rarely has enough money to pay any damages.

Law of property

Rights in contract and tort are enforceable against another individual, that
is the other party to the contract or the person who committed the tort. A
right in property often gives an individual a right in the property itself
which is normally enforceable against anybody else. In English law
property is classified as follows:

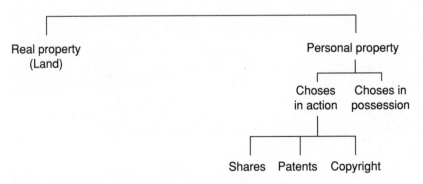

Figure 1.5 Classification of property in English law

This book is concerned with personal property rather than real property. *Choses in possession* means actual objects which are tangible and
can be used, such as a computer or a filing cabinet. There are a variety of
different rights which can exist over such items. You may own these
items because you have purchased them outright. Alternatively you may
hire them which only gives you the right to them in accordance with the
hire contract, the hirer remains the owner of the goods. You may merely
be looking after them for someone else but you will still have an
obligation to take care of them. In certain circumstances the person in
possession of goods may have a right to keep them, such as the unpaid
seller of goods.

Choses in action means a right which can be enforced by legal action.
For example, if you own shares in a company you will be given a share
certificate which is a piece of paper of little intrinsic value. However, the
certificate is valuable because it shows that you are the owner of the shares
and it gives you the right to sell the shares and ultimately your right to the
value of the shares can be enforced in the courts (see Chapter 2). Similarly
patents and copyrights are examples of intellectual property which is an
increasingly important area of property law (see Chapter 7). The software
on your computer will be purchased by you subject to the copyright of the
software company.

Criminal law

Criminal law is not just concerned with crimes of violence or crimes against property. It is also used by the state to punish enterprises which engage in business practices considered to be reprehensible. Therefore an enterprise may, for example, find itself taken to court for breach of the health and safety at work regulations (see Chapter 4), or for breach of environmental laws (see Chapter 5) or for selling goods with a false trade description (see Chapter 6). Most but not all criminal offences are defined by statute. Some, for example assault, are also a tort.

The statute creating the offence will sometimes make the employer, whether a sole trader, a partnership or a limited company, liable for an offence committed by employees in the course of their employment. Most criminal prosecutions are brought by the Crown Prosecution Service. However, the type of offences of concern to managers are more likely to be prosecuted by a relevant inspectorate such as the Health and Safety Inspectorate. Normally the prosecution has to prove beyond reasonable doubt that the essential elements of the offence have been committed and that the accused had the necessary guilty mind, that is the intention to commit the offence. In certain circumstances the guilty mind of the employee can be attributed to a limited company and the company is criminally liable.

The punishment for this type of criminal offence is likely to be a fine but imprisonment is usually an option available to the courts.

CONCLUSION

The law is like an octopus. Its tentacles creep into the most unexpected places. The effective manager should be aware of the legal ramifications of a particular decision or strategy and tailor it to comply with the law. This book is aimed at helping such a manager navigate a safe passage.

NOTES: CASE REFERENCES

1 *Lambert* v *Lewis* [1982] AC 225; [1981] 2 WLR 713.
2 *Kleinwort Benson* v *Malaysian Mining Corp. Berhad* [1989] 1 WLR 379; [1989] 1 All ER 785.
3 *Butler Machine Tool Co.* v *Ex-cell-O Corp. (England)* [1979] 1 WLR 401; [1979] 1 All ER 965.
4 *British Steel Corp.* v *Cleveland Bridge of Engineering Co.* [1984] 1 All ER 504.
5 *Cehave* v *Bremer, The Hansa Nord* [1976] QB 44; [1975] 3 All ER 739.
6 *Donoghue* v *Stevenson* [1932] AC 562; [1932] All ER Rep 1.

JOURNALS

Business Law Review.
New Law Journal.

FURTHER READING

Berlins, M. and Dyer, C. (1989) *The Law Machine*, Harmondsworth: Penguin.
Bevan, A. (1992) *Alternative Dispute Resolution*, London: Sweet & Maxwell.
Steiner, J. (1994) *Textbook on EC Law*, London: Blackstone Press.
Walker, R.J. and Ward, R. (1993) *The English Legal System*, London: Butterworths.

USEFUL ADDRESSES

The Law Society
113 Chancery Lane
London WC2A 1PL   Tel. no. 0171 242 1222

The General Council of the Bar
3 Bedford Row
London WC1R 4DB   Tel. no. 0171 242 0082

Central Office of the Industrial Tribunals
Southgate Street
Bury St Edmunds
Suffolk IP33 2AQ   Tel. no. 01284 762300

The Advisory, Conciliation and Arbitration Service (ACAS)
Clifton House
83–118 Euston Road
London NW1 2RB   Tel. no. 0171 396 5100

The Chartered Institute of Arbitrators
24 Angel Gate
City Road
London EC1V 2RS   Tel. no. 0171 837 4483

The European Commission Information Office
8 Storey's Gate
London SW1P 3AT   Tel. no. 0171 973 1992

The European Parliament Information Office
2 Queen Anne's Gate
London SW1H 9AA   Tel. no. 0171 222 0411.

Chapter 2

Enterprise structures, finance and the law

Elvira Rubin

The organization and legal liabilities of an enterprise and its managers will depend to a certain extent upon whether it is a company, a partnership or a sole trader. This chapter explains the nature of these legal structures and the advantages and disadvantages of each of them. Limited companies are looked at in more detail because they are subject to the most legal regulation.

The following topics are considered in the context of each type of enterprise:

- the legal requirements for setting up the enterprise
- how money can be raised
- legal areas of management
- what happens on insolvency

CASE HISTORY

Richard Branson has an enviable record as a businessman and entrepreneur. He has used a variety of legal structures according to the commercial requirements of the particular enterprise.

He started his business career as a sole trader publishing a student magazine. He then turned his business into a number of private limited companies. In 1986 he converted some of these companies into a public limited company. In 1989 he re-registered as a private limited company.

INTRODUCTION

This chapter looks at the legal framework within which enterprises such as Branson's are organized and indeed reorganized.

Managers need to be aware of the different forms of legal organization because they give rise to different rights and liabilities. The amount of capital needed and the preferred degree of control over the enterprise will influence which type of business organization to choose. Legal rules exist

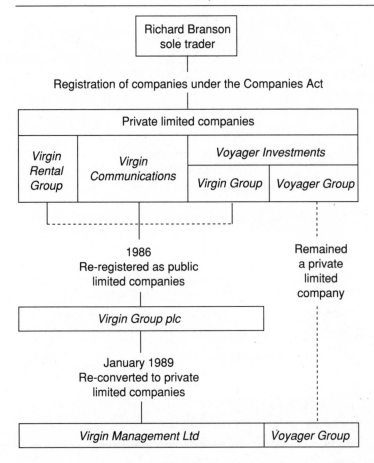

Figure 2.1 Development of Richard Branson's business enterprises

which are intended to protect the interests of those investing in, trading with and working within a particular level organization. Legal rules also ensure that the interests of those involved in the insolvency and/or liquidation of a business are adequately safeguarded.

There is a considerable amount of domestic legislation and case law as well as European Community Law in this area. EC law is intended to bring into line the different national laws of the member states. In most situations, ignorance of the law is no defence.

In addition there are self-regulatory guidelines such as:

- the Listing Rules of the Stock Exchange
- the City Code on Takeovers and Mergers.

TYPES OF BUSINESS ORGANIZATIONS

These are:

- sole trader
- partnership
- limited company
- European economic interest grouping.

Managers need to be aware of the different types of business organizations because of the legal consequences that will flow from either establishing or joining one particular type of enterprise.

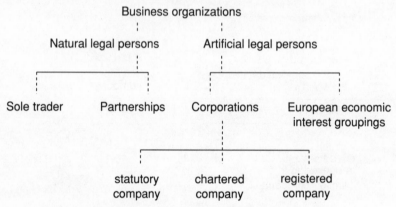

Figure 2.2 Different types of business organizations

The sole trader

A new enterprise is usually started by an individual working as a sole trader. This is the easiest but also the most hazardous way to venture into the commercial world. Some enterprises always remain organized on this basis but some, such as Richard Branson's, do not. Managers need to be aware of the legal position of the sole trader whether they are employed by or do business with them.

This section will look at the following issues:

- the legal position of the sole trader
- setting up the enterprise
- who may become a sole trader?
- how can money be raised for the enterprise?
- the management of the enterprise
- what happens on insolvency?
- how to expand the enterprise.

The legal position of the sole trader

Sole traders and their enterprises are not legally distinct but are subject to the ordinary civil and criminal law. This means that the sole trader is personally vulnerable. They alone bear the responsibility for all of the debts and liabilities of the enterprise. They can lose personal assets such as their house. In order to have some protection against possible bankruptcy or loss, sole traders may transfer some of their personal assets to other people such as members of their family, or into a trust. Such steps may however be set aside by the courts and should only be taken with legal advice. On the positive side, as the sole provider of capital the sole trader is entitled to all of the profits.

Since July 1992 it has been possible for sole traders to set up as a single member private limited company, limiting their personal liability.[1] This has the advantage of allowing the sole trader still to be totally in control of the enterprise, while at the same time limiting liability.

Setting up the enterprise

No minimum capital requirements and no legal formalities need be observed, although licences are required to operate certain businesses, such as food production.

The name of the enterprise may simply be that of the entrepreneur or any other name chosen at random, so long as its use is legal and does not confuse the public. If the name is chosen at random, all business correspondence, orders, receipts etc., must state the name of the owner of the enterprise and an address in Great Britain, for formal communication. The name must also be prominently displayed at the business premises.

The accounts need not be in a particular format and there is no need to disclose financial records to anyone but the Inland Revenue.

Who may become a sole trader?

There are no legal limitations other than the requirements under the law of contract that individuals should have capacity to enter into contracts. This would, for example, make it difficult for a person under eighteen to become a sole trader, because normally only adults can enter into legally binding contracts.

How can money be raised for the enterprise?

If the sole trader does not have sufficient funds of their own they may try to borrow from a bank or from relatives, or friends. A bank may grant a loan against personal security such as the sole trader's house or on the basis of a properly prepared business plan. The government may also be of assistance with a number of business start-up schemes.

The management of the enterprise

The management is entirely in the sole trader's hands which means that business decisions can be reached quickly, but lack of expertise may lead to miscalculations and financial loss. The sole trader also carries the unforeseeable risks such as fire, theft, burglary, natural disasters, etc. which may be insured against, but only at a cost which the enterprise may not be able to bear. Sole traders can recruit employees to lighten their workload.

What happens on insolvency?

Sole traders will be insolvent when they are no longer able to pay debts as they fall due. If the sole trader is made bankrupt, the court may appoint a receiver to take control of the sole trader's property. Creditors usually appoint a trustee in bankruptcy who will realize the assets and pay the creditors in a prescribed order. The assets do not include tools or similar items which are needed for employment and personal effects like clothes and household items. The bankruptcy order may then either be discharged automatically or by the court. An insolvent person or undischarged bankrupt may come to a voluntary arrangement with their creditors, for example to pay them ten pence in every pound.

How to expand the enterprise

If the business venture proves successful then the question of expansion arises. The sole trader might need more expertise and/or capital. The two main options are setting up a partnership or a limited company. Richard Branson decided to set up a limited company, which is more usual where the enterprise is a commercial venture. A partnership is more commonly set up where the enterprise is based on professional skills.

PARTNERSHIP

A partnership usually consists of between two and twenty partners each of whom bring skills and capital into the enterprise. Generally each partner is responsible for the activities of the partnership and personally liable for the partnership debts jointly with the co-partners.

This section will look at the following issues:

- the nature of a partnership
- setting up a partnership

- the partnership agreement
- insolvency
- why a partnership rather than a limited company?

Nature of a partnership

There are two types of partnership:

- general
- limited.

General partnership

A general partnership is an unincorporated association of persons 'carrying on a business in common with a view to profit'. The number of partners is limited to twenty; however certain professions, such as solicitors and accountants, may form a partnership with more than twenty partners. The partners collectively are called the 'firm'. The position in law of the partners is similar to that of the sole trader. Since the partnership does not have a legal existence of its own, it does not acquire a separate legal personality. Therefore the partners are jointly and/or individually liable for all the debts and other legal obligations of the partnership. They are also responsible for any torts committed in the normal course of the business and can incur criminal liability. The partners may sue and be sued in the name of the firm.

Limited partnership

The Limited Partnership Act 1907 introduced the concept of a limited partnership, which enables a partner to join the partnership solely to invest money. The principles of the general partnership apply, with two very important exceptions, which are that:

- the 'silent partner' is not entitled to take part in the management and
- the liability of the 'silent partner' is limited to the amount of capital contributed.

Any 'silent partner' who becomes involved in the management of the partnership will lose this protection and become as vulnerable as the general partners. There must always be at least one general partner in a limited partnership.

Setting up a partnership

A partnership is governed by the Partnership Act 1890 and based on a contract. Normally only adults may become partners. There are no formal legal requirements for the formation of a partnership. It may be created orally or in writing and the existence of a general partnership may even be implied in law.

Prospective partners are advised to draw up a partnership agreement with the help of a solicitor in order to avoid later unpleasant and costly conflicts.

The partnership agreement: general

This regulates not only the setting up, but also the management and dissolution of the partnership.

A partnership agreement usually contains clauses dealing with the following matters.

Nature and place of business

The nature of the business should be clearly specified, the place of business must be clearly stated and any property should be held in the name of the partnership or the name(s) of one or more of the partners.

Name of the firm

The name of the firm may simply be that of one or all of the partners, or any other name chosen at random (see 'Setting up the enterprise' on p. 27). The partnership may be called 'Smith, Brown & Co.', but never '& Co. Ltd'. The name and address of the owners must be displayed at the business premises and on business stationery.

Duration of the partnership

The commencement date and duration of the partnership should be stated.

Capital of the partnership

The amount of capital contributed by each partner should be stated and whether interest on the capital should be paid before or after distribution of net profits.

The partners themselves provide the funds. Additional capital may be raised out of profits, or by way of loans or possibly through government schemes.

Distribution of profits

If the partners are to be paid a salary, that must be expressly stated in the agreement.

The bank account

The agreement should name the bank and stipulate in particular who is authorized to sign cheques.

The partnership agreement: management of the partnership

The role of manager may be assigned to one or more partners. Any limitations on the partners' authority, such as not being able to contract on behalf of the business, must be stated in the agreement.

The relationship between the partners is based on mutual trust and good faith. In particular each partner:

- should keep the others informed about the affairs of the business
- should observe confidentiality
- should account to the partners for benefits obtained from the firm's business, which have not been approved by the other partners
- should not compete with the firm without permission

Accounts

Proper accounts should be kept and annual balance sheets provided. It is worth noting that there is no legal requirement for them to be published.

Arbitration

An arbitration clause may be inserted, so that any disputes can be settled in private without a public hearing in court.

The partnership agreement: termination and variation

Dissolution

The partnership will automatically be dissolved by the retirement, death, bankruptcy of any of the partners, unless a clause preserving the continuation of the business has been inserted.

Dissolution can also be triggered in other circumstances, for example, by an expiry of the term or purpose of the partnership, or by an order of the court.

Variation

The agreement may be varied with the consent of all of the partners.

Insolvency

Basically the same rules apply to an insolvent partnership as to an insolvent sole trader. Insolvency is the inability of the partnership to pay the debts, when due.

If the partnership is insolvent, then the partnership will be wound up. If the partnership and one or all of the partners are insolvent, then a claim exists against the partnership, the bankrupt partner and the solvent co-partners.

Why a partnership rather than a limited company?

There are many reasons why an enterprise might prefer to be a partnership. These include:

- certain professional bodies, such as the Law Society, do not allow their members to limit their liability
- no legal formalities to be complied with in setting-up
- no minimum capital requirements
- no disclosure of accounts
- tax reasons
- no requirement to file documents with the Registrar of Companies.

LIMITED COMPANIES: GENERALLY

Much of the remainder of the chapter concentrates on limited liability companies. Such companies are subject to detailed legal regulation concerning:

- formation
- management
- shareholders
- company capital
- changes in organizational structure
- liquidation of the company.

THE LIMITED COMPANY

Richard Branson, having successfully set up a business as a sole trader, formed three private limited companies, one of which, *Voyager Investments*, had two subsidiaries, *Virgin Group* and *Voyager Group*. Why did Richard Branson form a limited company rather than a partnership?

The major disadvantage of the partnership, which is the unlimited liability of the partners, may be overcome by forming a limited liability company by registration under the Companies Act 1985. The price to be paid for this advantage is:

- increased legal formalities
- publication of accounts, which allows the public, including competitors, to study the financial situation of the enterprise and possibly gain a competitive advantage
- administrative expense
- the management is no longer in the hands of the investors of capital, i.e. the shareholders, unless they are also directors.

The word 'company' in this context refers to a corporation, which is an artificial legal person,[2] distinct from its members and which continues in existence until dissolved. The English legal system permits a number of ways of creating a corporation.

The registered limited company, created under the Companies Act 1985, is the most widely used in practice and of the four types of business organizations listed at the beginning of this chapter, is the one subject to the most legal regulation.

As an 'artificial' legal person, a company can:

- own property
- open a bank account in its own name
- employ people
- enter into contracts
- lend and borrow money
- sue and be sued.

It is owned by the shareholders and acts through human agents, namely the board of directors or other corporate officers.

In practice companies limited by shares are the most important. Companies limited by guarantee are not suited for commercial purposes. Unlimited companies have the advantage of not being required to publish

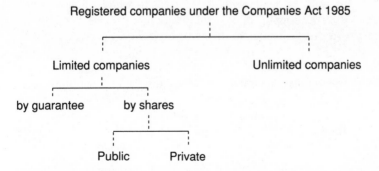

Figure 2.3 Classification of registered companies

their accounts, which makes such companies attractive to professional people, but have the disadvantage of unlimited liability.

In companies limited by shares the liability of the members is limited to the full nominal value on their shares. The phrase 'limited liability company' is often misunderstood. The company is fully liable to the extent of all its assets. It is the liability of the shareholders that is limited.

Companies limited by shares may be 'private' or 'public' companies, depending upon how they raise their money.

The two main types of companies limited by shares and registered under the Companies Act 1985 are:

- private companies
- public companies

The private company

When the sole trader, such as Richard Branson, or the partnership needs to expand, this type of business organization is most frequently chosen, because of the benefits it confers, namely:

- separate legal personality
- limited liability
- no limit on the number of shareholders
- easy transfer of shares
- possible tax advantages.

The company must have at least one director and one company secretary, who does not need special qualifications. A sole director may not simultaneously function as the secretary, and an auditor must be appointed.

There are no minimum capital requirements. Theoretically it would be possible to incorporate a private single member company with one share of a nominal value of one penny. Other limited companies need at least two shareholders, holding one share each. The extent to which such a private company can raise additional capital in the future is restricted, because it is not allowed to offer its securities to the general public. A private company may commence trading once it has received its certificate of incorporation from the Registrar of Companies.

Recently advantageous accountancy exemptions have been introduced for small and medium sized companies. Small companies may file 'abbreviated accounts', thus maintaining much of their confidentiality. Medium companies may only abbreviate their profit and loss account. The shareholders of these companies must, however, be presented with a full account.

The public company

The basic difference between a private company and a public company is that the shares of a public company can be traded on the Stock Exchange. The public company may offer its securities to the general public, either on the listed or unlisted securities market, which enables the company to raise substantial amounts of capital.

The fundamental rules relating to a public company require that:

1 Its name must be followed by the words 'public limited company' or 'plc' or the Welsh equivalent. A private company's name must end with the word 'limited' or 'Ltd'.
2 The minimum number of shareholders is two, with no upper limit.
3 There are at least two directors.
4 There is a qualified company secretary.
5 There is also a professionally qualified auditor(s).
6 The minimum authorized share capital is £50,000, of which at least one-quarter must be paid on issue; the remainder may be called up later. In addition to a certificate of incorporation, a trading certificate is required to commence trading and borrowing.

A private company may re-register as a public company when its capital requirements can no longer be privately satisfied. In 1986 Richard Branson re-registered three of his companies as public limited companies under the umbrella of *Virgin Group plc*. When Anita Roddick planned the expansion of The Body Shop, the necessary funds could not be supplied by private investors.

Similarly a public company may re-register as a private company when it no longer wants to be subject to the strict rules of the Stock Exchange. For example, in 1989 Richard Branson re-registered the Virgin Group as private companies. A public company must re-register when the share capital falls below the authorized minimum of £50,000.

Forming a limited company

This section looks at the legal and financial aspects of setting up a limited company, in particular:

● the promoter and pre-incorporation contracts
● registration of the company
● off-the-shelf companies
● the Memorandum of Association
● the Articles of Association
● consequences of incorporation.

The promoter and pre-incorporation contracts

When the owners of a business decide to incorporate, they are regarded as the 'promoters' of the company. The promoter will usually be personally liable on contracts entered into on behalf of the company before the company is actually incorporated.

Registration of the company

A number of documents must be delivered to the Registrar of Companies, including the Memorandum of Association (see below) and the Articles of Association (see below).

The costs of registration include a registration fee and legal and other professional fees.

Once the certificate of incorporation is issued, the new legal personality is born. Public companies also need a 'trading certificate', which is a statement from the Registrar of Companies concerning the statutory capital requirements of such companies, in order to commence business and to borrow money.

Off-the-shelf companies

Besides creating a company through registration it is also possible to buy one ready made, 'off-the-shelf', from an enterprise, which creates and deals in companies. These companies are kept dormant until purchased.

The Memorandum of Association

This document defines the constitution and powers of the company. It should contain certain clauses dealing with the following matters.

Name of the company

A private company's name must end with the word 'Limited', such as *Virgin Group Limited*, or 'Ltd' and that of a public company with 'public limited company' or 'plc', such as *Virgin Group plc*.

Public company

If the company is a public company, the Memorandum must state that it is a public company.

Location

The Memorandum must state the location of the registered office of the company.

The objects of the company

This clause specifies the activities that the company may engage in now or in the future. Until recently if the company strayed beyond these activities, the transaction was considered *ultra vires* (outside its powers) and void. However, recent legislation introduced a major change to the doctrine of *ultra vires*.[3] A company can now adopt an objects clause, stating that the purpose of the company is that of a 'general commercial company'.

The validity of a transaction with a third party, e.g. a contract with another business, can no longer be questioned because of any lack of corporate or directors' capacity or powers based on the company's constitution. However, the *ultra vires* doctrine still has some effect in relation to the internal affairs of the company.

Limitation of liability

There must be a clause stating that the liability of the shareholders is limited.

Capital clause

The amount of the nominal or authorized share capital must be stated and how it is divided into shares of a fixed amount.

Association clause

The subscribers to the memorandum are listed and a declaration made that they desire to be formed into a company and take up the indicated number of shares.

Here is an extract from the Memorandum of Association of one of Richard Branson's companies.

Memorandum of Association
of
Virgin Atlantic Airways Limited

1 The name of the Company is 'Virgin Atlantic Airways Limited'.
2 The Company is to be a private company.
3 The registered office of the Company will be situated in England.
4 The objects for which the Company is established are:

(a) To carry on the business or businesses of operating and flying or otherwise utilizing or turning to account by all and any lawful means whatsoever aircraft of all types and descriptions, including, but without in any way limiting the nature of the Company's activities, . . . purchase and hire of aeroplanes, hovercraft, sea planes, flying boats, airships, balloons, parachutes, gliding machines and other machines or apparatus designed for aerial transport; . . .

(b) To carry on any other trade or business whatever which can in the opinion of the Board of Directors be advantageously carried on in connection with or ancillary to any of the businesses of the Company.

(c) To do all such other things as may be deemed incidental or conducive to the attainment of the Company's objects or any of them.

5 The liability of the Members is limited.
6 The share capital of the Company is £100,000 divided into 100,000 shares of £1 each.

[The memorandum is then signed, dated and attested.]

Box 2.1 Memorandum of Association of Virgin Atlantic Airways Ltd

The Articles of Association

The Articles deal with the internal management of the company such as issue and transfer of shares, borrowing powers, meetings of shareholders and voting rights, dividends, appointment and powers of directors etc. A company may adopt the Articles as given in the Companies Act 1985, but it is advisable to draft them individually, in order to meet the specific needs of a company.

Consequences of incorporation

Once the certificate of incorporation has been issued, a new legal person has come into being and the most important principle of English company law takes effect, namely, that of the 'separate legal personality' of the company. The 'veil of incorporation' is dropped and hides the identity of the incorporators and the members of the company.

Case illustration

Salomon v. A. Salomon & Co. Ltd (1896)[4]

Mr Salomon, having conducted his bootmaking business as a sole trader, decided to incorporate and formed a limited company by the process of registration. He, his wife and his five children (the minimum number of shareholders was seven for a private company until 1907, and until 1980 for a public company), who were at all times fully informed of the intended arrangement, were the subscribers to the Memorandum of Association. He then sold his business to this company for £39,000 approximately. Part of the purchase price were fully paid up shares, one to each member of his family with the remainder to Mr Salomon himself. Another part of the purchase price remained outstanding as a debt owed by the company. This was secured by way of debentures issued to Mr Salomon, giving him a floating charge over the assets of the company. He thereby became a secured creditor of the company. The company later went into liquidation with insufficient assets to pay all the creditors. The trade creditors claimed that the whole arrangement was a sham, arguing that the company and Mr Salomon were the same, that therefore the debentures were invalid, and that they were entitled to the available assets.

  The House of Lords decided that Mr Salomon and the company were two different persons, that the company was not the agent of the subscribers to the memorandum, and that the debentures were valid. Therefore Mr Salomon, as a secured creditor of the company, was entitled to be repaid ahead of the trade creditors who in fact received nothing.

Box 2.2 Salomon v Salomon (1896)

Once a company is incorporated it becomes solely responsible for its actions, exercised by humans on its behalf. The legal effect of this change must be fully understood, especially where former sole traders or partners are concerned. From a practical point of view, nothing has changed. They still conduct the affairs of the business as before, but with one most important difference. Whereas once they owned all the assets, now they are usually the company's directors, but all they own are shares in the company. The company itself is the owner of all the assets and is responsible, for example, for insuring the company's assets.

There are, however, exceptions to the principle of the separate legal personality. Judicial decisions have established that the 'corporate veil' can be lifted in the interest of justice or fairness. Basically it is not permissible to hide behind the corporate identity to evade legal obligations such as taxes, performance of contracts, or to act fraudulently, etc.[5] A number of statutory provisions also have the effect of 'lifting the veil'.

The management of the company

The day to day management of the company is carried out by the board of directors. The shareholders have a residual and concurrent management function which is exercisable at the General Meeting.

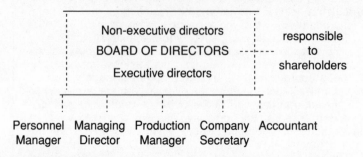

Figure 2.4 Example of management structure

The board of directors develops the general business policy for the company. The Articles usually grant them the full power of management with the power to delegate to a managing director or executive directors, who implement the business policy. The authority of the board may be limited in specific areas, such as borrowing on behalf of the company. Board meetings are held as specified in the Articles. The directors choose one of their number as chairman, who usually has the casting vote. The Articles also fix the required quorum, that is the number of directors needed to be present to validate the decision taken.

The shareholders at the General Meeting of shareholders:

- elect the board of directors
- can make alterations to the constitution of the company
- can decide on the winding-up or re-construction of the company
- can commence litigation if the directors fail to do so
- can approve certain transactions by the directors.

Ultimately, the power of management lies with the directors and dissatisfied shareholders may elect either to remove the directors or to sell their shares. In addition external authorities such as:

- the DTI (the Department of Trade and Industry)
- the Secretary of State for Trade and Industry
- the Director General of Fair Trading

- the EU Commission
- debenture holders

may intervene in the company's management in certain circumstances.[6]

The directors of the company

The directors have a crucial role in the management of a company. Therefore it is important to know:

- who is a director
- who can be appointed as a director
- what information a director must disclose to the company
- when directors can be paid a salary
- when directors can be dismissed
- the implications of trading by directors
- the duties owed by directors
- how these duties are enforced.

Who is a director?

Anybody 'occupying the position of a director', that is, functioning as a director, may be deemed to be a director, regardless of title. This may also cover 'shadow directors', that is, persons whose instructions are followed by the directors, but does not include persons merely giving professional advice, such as lawyers or accountants. The number of directors is usually fixed by the Articles, although private companies must have at least one director and public companies at least two.

The directors may function in three ways:

- as the board of directors collectively they are the policy makers
- as the agents of the company they can bind the company
- as executive directors they are employees of the company and carry out the policy decisions of the board.

Who can be appointed as a director?

The first directors are appointed on incorporation and subsequent directors are normally appointed at the AGM (Annual General Meeting). The following persons are normally disqualified from directorship:

- persons over the age of 70 may not be directors of public companies or their subsidiaries
- undischarged bankrupts
- persons convicted of certain offences
- persons subject to a court disqualification order

- a director who has been found guilty of serious offences in connection with the company
- a director who has been found liable for 'wrongful' or 'fraudulent' trading (see below).

Anyone involved in the management of a company while disqualified is personally liable for all relevant debts incurred.

What information must a director disclose to the company?

Directors must inform the company of their holdings of shares in or debentures of the company or any company within the group of companies. Unless expressly required to do so, directors do not have to own their company's securities.

When can directors be paid a salary?

Directors are not usually paid simply for being directors. It is therefore usual practice for directors to have a contract of employment with the company, so that they can be paid a salary.

When can directors be dismissed?

The shareholders may, by simple majority, remove a director from office before his term has expired if they are not satisfied by his performance. Such a removal may amount to a breach of the director's contract of employment and the director would then be entitled to compensation.

Directors normally retire by rotation but may be re-elected. Companies are required to keep a register of the particulars of directors and company secretaries.

Trading by directors

Transactions by directors with the company   Directors can trade with the company. However, the law has created a number of safeguards, to prevent directors from using information and opportunities acquired by virtue of their position for their personal advantage.

Transacting business on behalf of the company   The directors can enter into *contracts* on behalf of the company either in writing or under the company's common seal. A contract can also be entered into on behalf of the company by an authorized agent of the company.

The directors and the company can also be liable for *tortious* and *criminal* acts.

The directors may be *personally liable* to the company if they have been acting negligently in performing their duties (see below). The *company* may be vicariously liable for the wrongful acts of its employees while acting in the course of their employment (see Chapter 1).

In certain circumstances directors can be criminally liable. However, to be guilty of a crime the accused must normally have the necessary mens rea, that is, the guilty mind. A company can have a guilty mind if it can be shown that the 'persons entitled to represent and direct the mind of the company' have been actively involved. By definition this would include only the board of directors or senior management.[7] It has been established that a company is legally capable of manslaughter. The difficulty in proving this was demonstrated in the case against the management of P & O European Ferries (Dover) Ltd in connection with the ferry disaster at Zeebrugge.[8]

The directors' duties

The directors, as agents of the company, must follow a code of conduct established by Acts of Parliament, case law and extra legal regulations. The directors owe a number of duties to:

- the company itself
- the shareholders as a whole
- the employees
- the creditors (to a certain degree).

There are six main types of duty.

Common law duty of care and skill under the tort of negligence (see Chapter 1)

Case illustration

Dorchester Finance Co. Ltd v *Stebbing* (1977)[9]

The three directors of Dorchester Finance Co., a moneylending company, were Stebbing, Parsons and Hamilton. They never held any board meetings and two of the directors left the running of the company entirely to Stebbing who held blank cheques on the company's account, signed by these two directors, to use in any way he liked. Stebbing lent the company's money to various companies in disregard of the statutory controls on moneylending, thus rendering these loans unenforceable.

All three directors were held liable to the company for their negligence.

Box 2.3 Dorchester Finance Co. Ltd v *Stebbing* (1977)

Equitable and fiduciary duties   For example, a director must not make a secret profit out of his position and a director must not compete with his company.

Case illustration

Industrial Development Consultants Ltd v *Cooley* (1972)[10]

Mr Cooley was the managing director of *Industrial Development Consultants Ltd* and as such he tried to secure a contract for his company with the *Eastern Gas Board*. He learned that the *Gas Board* did not like the set-up of his company but would deal with him personally. Mr Cooley resigned from his company and obtained the contract for himself.

He was held accountable to the company for any profits he made, because his personal interest was in direct conflict with his pre-existing and continuing duty as a managing director of *Industrial Development Consultants Ltd.*

Box 2.4 Industrial Development Consultants v *Cooley* (1972)

Duty of disclosure under the Companies Act 1985   This requires a director to disclose any shareholdings in the company and any interests in contracts with the company.

Duty to employees under the Companies Act 1985 to consider the interests of the employees   This is a very limited requirement compared with other European Union countries where it is common to have active worker participation at board level.

Duties under the Insolvency Act 1986   These are wider than the common law duty (see above). The directors owe duties to creditors and to the company itself. Two *civil* liabilities were created. Directors are obliged to minimize any potential loss to creditors and can be liable for *wrongful trading* if they allow the company to continue trading when there is no reasonable prospect of avoiding insolvent liquidation. Directors can also be held liable for *fraudulent trading* if they knowingly allow the company to continue trading when the company cannot pay its debts and has no prospects of doing so in the future.

If the director is found to have wrongfully or fraudulently traded, then the director can be required to contribute personally to the assets of the company.

The Companies Act 1985 also imposes *criminal* liability for *fraudulent trading*, whether the company is in liquidation or not.

Duty not to participate in insider dealings   Insider dealing in the shares of public companies became a criminal offence in the UK under the Companies Act 1980. The relevant provisions were then replaced by the Company Securities (Insider Dealing) Act 1985.[11] The Community Directive on Insider Trading (89/592/EEC) was finally given effect in the UK by Part V of the Criminal Justice Act 1993 which repeals the 1985 Act in its entirety. The Criminal Justice Act 1993 has broadened insider liability.

The securities covered by the 1993 Act include not only corporate securities but also government stock. 'Insiders' are not just persons 'connected' with a company, but also those who have 'access' to 'inside information'.

It is an offence for directors and other persons to deal and encourage others to deal in securities on a regulated market, based on 'inside information' and to disclose 'inside information'.

'Inside information' is specific or precise unpublished information which relates to particular securities and to particular issuers of securities and which, if made public, would have a significant effect on the price of the securities.

Information is made public 'if it is published in accordance with the rules of a regulated market for the purpose of informing investors and their professional advisers'. 'Inside information' does not cover mere rumour or mere speculation.

Directors of *private* companies are not subject to these criminal provisions. However, they could be liable for breach of one of their other duties if they participate in insider dealing.

Enforcement of directors' duties

The directors' duties are enforced by the company itself as the 'proper plaintiff', since it has a separate legal personality. The company's position should reflect the view of the majority shareholders.[12] Minority shareholders are however protected by a number of common law and statutory provisions.

The contractual liability of a limited company

Entering into a contract

The company, as an 'artificial legal person', can only enter into contracts through humans acting as its authorized *agents*. These agents can be directors, but frequently are other employees, including managers.

The authority of such persons, acting on behalf of the company, is determined by the ordinary rules of the law of agency. The company, as the principal, will be bound by the acts of its agents, if the agents acted under actual, implied, usual or apparent authority.[13] Managers who are authorized to enter into certain contracts are agents. An agent dealing with a third party on behalf of his principal, warrants that he has the necessary authority to do so and he will bind his principal, the company. Should he, however, act without authority, then the agent will be in 'breach of his warranty of authority' and will become personally liable under the contract and the company is not liable at all, unless the company ratifies the contract.

Liability to third parties

Even if the company has exceeded its powers, or the directors lacked the capacity to enter into the agreement, then if a party who enters into a contract with the company acts in good faith, that is, acts 'genuinely and honestly in the circumstances of the case', the transaction is normally enforceable. However if such a party does not act in good faith, the company may be able to avoid the transaction, or there may not be a contract with the company at all. Nevertheless, the company can if it wishes, ratify the contract.

The shareholders

The role of the shareholder depends on the type of company in which they have invested.

The shareholders of large public companies have no direct say in the management of the company. Their contribution of money is purely for investment purposes. There are, however, certain decisions which can only be made by the shareholders in general meeting, such as the alteration of the Articles or Memorandum.

The shareholders of small private companies are often actively involved in the management of the company, because they are also the directors of the company.

What is a share?

In the legal sense a share is intangible property, a 'chose in action'. This means that the share certificate has no intrinsic value. Its value is determined by the share of the company's assets that it represents. It is an interest in the company.

Shareholders receive dividends which are a distribution of a company's profits and are usually declared by the company in general meeting. No dividend may exceed the amount recommended by the directors.

What rights do shareholders have?

They have the right to:

- vote at shareholders' meetings
- receive dividends when declared
- receive a share of the surplus assets on winding-up.

There are three types of shareholder meetings:

- Annual General Meetings (AGM)
- Extraordinary meetings
- Class meetings for particular classes of shareholders.

Every company must hold at least one Annual General Meeting, normally called by the directors with twenty one days' notice. Should the directors fail to do so, any member of the company may ask the Department of Trade and Industry to do so or two or more shareholders may call a meeting.

There are detailed legal procedural requirements relating to:

- notice of meetings
- proxy voting
- quorum
- voting procedure
- resolutions.

Private companies may dispense with the statutory requirement to hold meetings.

The capital of the company

One of the main reasons for establishing a company is to raise money. A company can raise money in two main ways: namely by issuing shares and by raising loans.

A company's capital is the money available for use in the business. Part of the capital is provided by the shareholders of the company subscribing for shares, or by lenders providing loan capital when, for example, taking debentures. The use of share capital and, to a lesser extent, loan capital is regulated by law, because it is a security for creditors in the event of a winding-up of the company.

Share capital

Private companies usually obtain their capital from private investors, banks or financial institutions through the issue of shares.

Public companies may offer their shares in a variety of ways to the

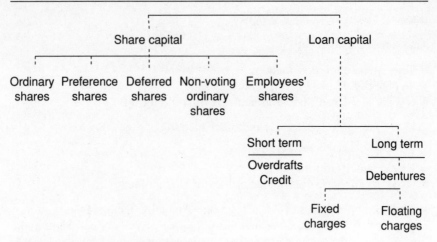

Figure 2.5 Types of company capital

general public. A public company's shares can be sold on the Stock Exchange, if the company is listed on the Stock Exchange.

In order for a company to be listed:

● it must have been trading for at least three years
● the minimum market value of the shares must be £700,000 and debt securities £200,000
● at least 25 per cent of the issued shares must be held by the public.

Smaller unlisted public companies can sell their shares on the:

● Unlisted Securities Market (USM), established in 1980, or
● Over the Counter Market (OTC), which is for smaller companies.

The markets in securities are regulated by the Financial Services Act 1986.

The Act greatly improved the system of control over the investment industry in general. Only authorized persons may now give financial advice and trade in companies' securities. The Act has also established a new legal framework for companies seeking a listing on the Stock Exchange and for offering unlisted securities to the public. There is also improved protection for investors.

Loan capital

Companies often borrow money to finance their activities. These loans may be short term in the form of overdrafts or credit, or long term in the form of debentures.

The difference between share capital and loan capital is that share capital gives a right in the company, whereas loan capital gives a right against the company and the company's property. These rights are based on the contractual relationship arising with the loan arrangement and can be exercised by the creditor when the loan is not repaid in time. Creditors have priority over shareholders as far as their interest payments are concerned and in case of the liquidation of the company.

Both trading and non-trading companies are usually able to borrow money. The main method by which a company can arrange for long-term borrowing is by the issue of debentures.

A *debenture* is the document by which a company acknowledges a debt. Debentures may be issued either individually (like for a bank loan or overdraft) or in a series. Debentures of public companies may be traded on the Stock Exchange. Therefore, the document offering the debentures for sale to the public is a prospectus and subject to the provisions of the Financial Services Act 1986 and the rules of the Stock Exchange.

Security for a debt is usually advisable. In connection with debentures this security is called a 'charge', which gives the lender a right over the company's assets under the charge.

The Companies Act 1989 has introduced a new system for the registration of certain charges. If there is more than one charge over the company's assets there are detailed rules establishing which charge takes priority.

Changes in the organization of the company

There can be a variety of reasons for such changes and they can be carried out in a variety of ways. The law is particularly concerned with three types of organizational change.

Reconstruction

Reconstruction of a company may be a purely internal affair such as a reorganization of the share or loan capital, or it may involve the transfer of the company's assets to a new company with basically the same shareholders. Reconstruction is normally used to come to a compromise or arrangement with the members or creditors. The procedure is different for the reconstruction of insolvent companies where the court is heavily involved, and where a company is being voluntarily wound-up, which may be done without sanction of the court.

Amalgamation

Amalgamation is a merger of two or more companies, by which company A acquires the assets or shares of company B and the shareholders of company B are issued the appropriate number of shares in company A.

In both reconstruction and amalgamation the shareholders and creditors have agreed to the measures to be taken.

Take-over

Here company A attempts to take over 'target' company B by a take-over bid, offering to buy the shares of the shareholders of company B. In most instances the board of directors of company B is not in favour of the take-over.

A take-over is governed by legal and extra-legal rules such as:

- the Companies Act 1985, making it possible to buy out compulsorily the shares of the minority who have not agreed to accept the offer
- the City Code on Takeovers and Mergers, protecting the rights of the shareholders of the target company
- the Monopolies and Mergers Commission, in case of a potential monopoly
- the European Commission may become involved as well, should there be a European dimension.

Liquidation

A company may cease trading. It can continue to exist legally but not practically. However, its existence may be legally terminated or liquidated in a variety of ways. The method used depends upon the reason for the liquidation. *Winding-up* is the usual method of liquidating a company's assets. However, the Financial Services Act 1986 has introduced two alternatives to a winding-up for an insolvent company:

- voluntary arrangements
- administration orders.

All operations connected with insolvency must be carried out by authorized insolvency practitioners.

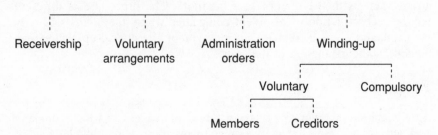

Figure 2.6 Methods of dealing with companies in financial difficulties

Receivership

This is a method of enforcing a debenture against a company when it is in default, or there is some other breach of the loan arrangement. Debenture holders or the court can appoint a receiver to sell the assets of the company. Receivership often results in the liquidation of the company.

Insolvent companies

A company in serious financial difficulties will be deemed insolvent when it is unable to pay its debts when due. The Financial Services Act 1986 has introduced the following two alternatives to a winding-up.

Voluntary arrangements

A proposal may be made by the directors, the administrator or liquidator for a scheme or an arrangement with the company's creditors, who agree to accept a lesser sum than the amount owed them by the company.

Administration orders

The purpose of such an order is to obtain a breathing space from the creditors demanding payment, in order to save the company or to realize its assets most advantageously. The order can be applied for individually or jointly by the directors, and/or creditors.

Winding-up

A company may be dissolved or wound up in the following circumstances:

- if registered for illegal purposes, at the instance of the Attorney-General
- during a reconstruction or amalgamation
- it no longer carries on its business
- on a winding-up.

Winding-up can be voluntary or compulsory.

Voluntary winding-up

This can be done in two ways.

A member's voluntary winding-up   A still solvent company may be voluntarily wound up. This is possible even where a company is in financial difficulties, so long as the directors can make a statutory declaration that the company will be able to pay its debts within a stated period, which is usually twelve months.

A liquidator will be appointed by the members to wind up the affairs of the company and distribute any surplus assets. If the liquidator considers that the company will be unable to pay its debts in full there will be a creditors' voluntary winding-up.

A creditors' voluntary winding-up   A creditors' meeting will be called at which a liquidator may be appointed and the directors' powers will cease. Again after a final meeting with the liquidator the company will be dissolved.

Winding-up by the court (compulsory winding-up)

The court may order the winding-up of a company for a number of reasons, the main one being its inability to pay its debts when due. An application to the court is made by either the company, the directors, the creditors or by all of them. When the winding-up order is issued, all legal action against the company is stayed. A liquidator or official receiver is appointed who must, in the case of an insolvent company, investigate the affairs of the company and establish the reason for the company's failure.

Case illustration

Re Produce Marketing Consortium Ltd (No.2) (1989)[14]

The two directors of the company continued to carry on the company's business of importing fruit when they ought to have known that insolvent liquidation was unavoidable.

The liquidator of the company obtained an order from the court that they were held liable to contribute £75,000 to the assets of the company because of their intimate knowledge of the company's business and because they let the company's indebtedness increase. Liability arose not only for the factual knowledge which the directors ought to have had, but also for facts which they ought to have ascertained.

Box 2.5 Re Produce Marketing Consortium (No. 2) (1989)

Once a winding-up order is obtained, the assets of the company are distributed in prescribed order and any surplus goes to the members.

EUROPEAN ECONOMIC INTEREST GROUPING (EEIG)

This type of business organization was introduced in 1985 by an EC Council Regulation to promote cross-frontier co-operation between

European enterprises. The UK implemented the Council Regulation in 1989.[15]

The typical activities that an EEIG might undertake are:

- joint research and development
- marketing
- exchange of information
- providing specialised services.

These activities must however be connected with the economic activities of its members.

Membership is open to:

- companies or firms
- nationalized industries
- local authorities
- co-operatives.

These organizations must have been formed according to their national laws and must have their registered office and/or central administration in the EU. In the UK a number of firms of solicitors have made use of this new organization.

In the UK an EEIG was given 'legal personality' and consequently is a body corporate, something like an 'incorporated partnership', with unlimited liability.

The management is in the hands of one or more natural persons, apppointed either by the contract or the members. Disqualification from management is dependent on national law. The authority of the manager(s) is based on principles of agency law. The aim is to protect third parties acting in good faith.

In the UK if an EEIG becomes insolvent, it is treated as an 'unregistered company' and is subject to the provisions of the Insolvency Act 1986.

STRATEGIES FOR MANAGERS

The management of any type of business organization must be aware of the legal consequences of commercial activities. This is as true of small firms as of a multinational company.

All those engaged in the management of any business should concentrate on undertaking only those jobs associated with management and delegate any other tasks to other employees.

Therefore managers at all levels need to know who reports to whom, who is legally authorized to do what, and who may be liable for what and to whom, if the limit of that authority is exceeded.

The level of management is generally divided into three groups, i.e. top, middle and lower management. The extent of authority and responsibility will depend on the relevant level.

Managers need to be aware of the legal structure of both the enterprise in which they work and the enterprise with which they do business. The financial vulnerability of sole traders should be recognized and management systems could be introduced which provide for prompt debt recovery and, where appropriate, for personal guarantees or for credit rating checks to be made. A sole trader should always be careful not to be financially overstretched.

If a manager is working within a partnership then, if a written partnership agreement does not exist, it is advisable that one is drawn up with the assistance of a solicitor. This will ensure that the rights and responsibilities of the partners are clearly defined. Individual partners should be made aware of the extent of their authority to enter into agreements on behalf of the partnership since if they exceed their authority they may be personally liable. The partnership should not inadvertently give the impression that a partner's authority is wider than it actually is, since the partnership could then be bound by any contract entered into by that partner. The advantage of trading with a partnership is that the partners are liable for its debts. However, this is only of value if the partners have personal assets which will cover the debts.

The management of companies lies in the hands of the board of directors, developing the general business policy. The execution of that policy is usually delegated to a managing director or to individual directors/managers, responsible for specific aspects of the business. The degree of responsibility and authority of managers will obviously decrease with the lower levels of management.

Those in charge of devising the business strategy and acting on behalf of the company are in most circumstances responsible for the activities of the company and may incur personal liability for the actions taken. Such individuals should be provided with necessary information to ensure that:

- they are at all times aware of any limitations imposed on their authority, especially when entering into loan arrangements or contracts on behalf or with the company
- they are aware of the degree of loyalty and commitment they owe to the company
- they are at all times informed of the financial situation of the company
- all necessary documents and information are properly filed with the Registrar of Companies and within the prescribed time
- they only use the company's capital as permitted by law
- they observe the rules relating to issues of shares and debentures and the distribution of profits.

It is also advisable to have one or more independent non-executive directors on the board of directors and to hold regular board meetings with clearly defined agendas.

Generally conversion to any other type of business organization should only be undertaken on professional advice, especially with regard to loss of control over the business and tax implications. Up to date legal information should be available so that managers are aware of current legal requirements, both civil and criminal, including those under EC law.

Managers are strongly advised to take advantage of the help and advice, which is often free, available from various government offices, such as the DTI, OFT, etc. Banks and professional bodies often hold short courses in order to keep business managers up to date with important legal and commercial developments.

The cost of professional consultation is almost always justified because it can avoid serious legal problems.

Whenever possible, staff should be given the opportunity to obtain further training, so that they may serve their enterprise more efficiently, by operating within the legal framework, and thus contribute effectively to the growth of the business.

KEY LEARNING POINTS

- **All enterprises operate either as a sole trader, a partnership, a limited company or an EEIG.**
- **No formal requirements have to be satisfied in order to set up in business as a sole trader or a partnership; whereas legal formalities have to be complied with in order to set up a limited company.**
- **Sole traders and partners normally have unlimited liability for the debts of their business. The directors of a limited company are normally only liable up to the value of their shares.**
- **Sole traders' businesses and partnerships do not have a separate legal personality from that of the individual sole trader and partners. However, the limited company does have a separate legal personality which means that it has legal rights and liabilities separate from those of the directors.**
- **The activities of a partnership are regulated by the partnership agreement. The activities of a limited company are mainly regulated by the Memorandum of Association and the Articles of Association.**
- **Directors of companies are subject to stringent legal rules.**
- **An insolvent sole trader may be made bankrupt and a receiver appointed, or the trader may come to an arrangement with their creditors. Similarly an insolvent partnership may be dissolved and**

the individual partners may be declared bankrupt if they cannot pay their debts. There are a variety of procedures for dealing with an insolvent company including winding it up.

EXERCISES

1   Do you work for a sole trader, a partnership or a limited company or an EEIG? Would there be any advantages or disadvantages in changing the legal status of the enterprise?

2   If you work in a partnership, is there one partner responsible for the management of the partnership? Try to find out the extent of each partner's authority to act on behalf of the partnership. If you act on behalf of the partnership, are you clear as to the extent of your authority to act? If not, try to clarify your position.

3   If you work in a limited company, is it a private or public company? Are the business activities of your company covered by the objects clause of the company? As a manager in your company, what are you authorized to do on behalf of the company? If you exceed this authority will you, or will the company be liable for your actions?

4   What are the advantages and disadvantages of doing business with a sole trader, a partnership, a private company, a public company or an EEIG?

NOTES: CASE REFERENCES ETC

1 Council Directive 89/667/EEC on Single Member Private Limited Companies, implemented by the Companies (Single Member Private Limited Companies) Regulations 1992, SI 1992 No. 1699.
2 *Salomon* v *A Salomon & Co. Ltd* [1897] AC 22; [1897] 66 LJ Ch 35.
3 Companies Act 1985, ss. 35, 35A, 35B.
4 As footnote 2 above.
5 *Gilford Motor Co. Ltd* v *Horne* [1933] Ch 935.
6 *Maxwell* v *Department of Trade and Industry* [1974] QB 523; [1974] 2 WLR 338.
7 *Tesco Supermarkets Ltd* v *Nattrass* [1972] AC 153; [1971] 2 WLR 1166.
8 *R* v *P & O European Ferries (Dover) Ltd* (1990) 93 Cr App R 72; [1991] Crim LR 695.
9 *Dorchester Finance Co. Ltd* v *Stebbing* [1977] Ch 407; [1989] 3CLC 498.
10 *Industrial Development Consultants* v *Cooley* [1972] 1 WLR 443; 2 All ER 162.
11 *Attorney-General's Reference (No. 1 of 1988)* [1989] AC 971; [1989] 2 WLR 729; [1989] 2 All ER 1.

12 *Foss* v *Harbottle* (1843) 2 Hare 461; (1843) 67 ER 189.
13 *Freeman & Lockyer* v *Buckhurst Park Properties (Mangal) Ltd* [1964] 2 QB 480; [1964] 2 WLR 618.
14 *Re Produce Marketing Consortium Ltd (No. 2)*,[1989] BCLC 520.
15 Council Regulation 2137/85 on the European Economic Interest Grouping, implemented by the European Economic Interest Grouping Regulations 1989, SI 1989 No. 638.

JOURNALS

Company Lawyer.
Business Law Review.
European Business Law Review.

FURTHER READING

The Committee on the Financial Aspects of Corporate Governance (1992), *The Cadbury Code.*
The Department of Trade and Industry and the Central Office of Information (1993), *Company Law Harmonisation.*
Card & James (1994) *Law for Accountancy Students*, London: Butterworths.
Davies, D. (1994) *Finance and Accounting for Managers*, Institute of Personnel and Development.
Farrar, J.H. (1993) *Farrar's Company Law*, London: Butterworths.
Gower, L.C.B. (1992) *Gower's Principles of Modern Company Law*, London: Sweet & Maxwell.
Keenan, D. (1993) *Smith & Keenan's Company Law for Students*, London: Pitman Publishing.
Morse, G. (1991) *Partnership Law*, London: Blackstone Press.
Steiner, J. (1994) *Textbook on EC Law*, London: Blackstone Press.
Stone, R. (1994) *Law of Agency*, Cavendish Publishing.

USEFUL ADDRESSES

Registrar of Companies
Companies House
Crown Way
Maindy
Cardiff CF4 3UF   Tel no. 01222 388588

London Chamber of Commerce
33 Queen St
London EC4R 1BX   Tel no. 0171 248 4444

Department of Trade and Industry
Companies' Division
10–18 Victoria Street
London SW1H ONN   Tel no. 0171 215 5000

Office of Fair Trading
Field House
Bream's Buildings
London EC4A 1HA   Tel no. 0171 242 2858

The European Commission Information Office
8 Storey's Gate
London SW1P 3AT   Tel no. 0171 973 1992.

Chapter 3

The enterprise and its workforce

David Lewis

This chapter seeks to identify a number of the most important areas in which disputes may arise between employers and employees at the workplace, and in which managers are likely to be involved and may be required to take decisions. Case illustrations are used throughout this chapter to set the scene for each area and to show how an enterprise can resolve a particular problem in a practical context. The themes that the chapter will cover are:

- the law relating to recruitment
- types of employment contracts and their contents
- anti-discrimination legislation and maternity rights
- termination of employment
- ACAS and industrial tribunals
- strategies for managers.

THE LAW RELATING TO RECRUITMENT

Case illustration

The managing director of *Minor Holdings plc*, which currently employs fifty people, wishes to introduce new criteria for recruiting staff. He maintains that the most productive employees are black, able-bodied, middle aged, male union members with no criminal convictions.

Box 3.1 Minor Holdings plc

The managing director needs to be advised about the legal implications of selecting staff in accordance with his stated criteria.

What are the legal constraints imposed on employers at the hiring stage?

Sex and race discrimination

The Sex Discrimination Act (SDA) 1975 and the Race Relations Act (RRA) 1975 make it unlawful to discriminate in any of the following ways when offering employment:

- in the arrangements made for the purpose of determining who should be offered employment
- in the terms on which employment is offered
- by refusing or deliberately omitting to offer employment.

It is equally unlawful to refuse to employ a person simply because they have given evidence in connection with proceedings, or have brought, or are about to bring proceedings against a previous employer under the Equal Pay Act (EPA) 1970, the SDA 1975 or the RRA 1975.

It is important to note that the titles of the SDA 1975 and the RRA 1975 do not fully reflect the matters that they cover. The SDA 1975, for example, also outlaws discrimination against married persons on the grounds of marital status, while 'racial grounds' include discrimination on grounds of colour, nationality, and ethnic or national origins.

Can discrimination on grounds of race or sex ever be lawful?

In certain limited circumstances sex or race discrimination at the recruitment stage is permitted by law, if there is a *genuine occupational qualification* (GOQ). In the case of discrimination on grounds of sex, there are several types of GOQ, of which the most important are as follows:

- the essential nature of the job demands a particular physiology (excluding physical strength): for example, when acting a particular role
- the job needs to be held by a particular sex in order to preserve decency or privacy: for example, searching for security purposes
- the nature of the establishment demands a person of a particular sex because it is an establishment for persons requiring specialized care or attention: for example, in a single sex institution
- the job holder provides personal services which can most effectively be provided by a person of a particular sex: for example, in a team of social workers providing specialized services.

The only GOQs allowed for under the RRA 1975 are:

- where discrimination is necessary in order to provide authenticity in the provision of food and drink, in entertainment or in modelling

- where the job holder provides personal welfare services which can be most effectively provided by a person of a particular racial group.

Finally, it should be noted that an employer cannot rely on the existence of a GOQ if the organization already has sufficient workers capable of carrying out those duties whom it would be reasonable to employ in that way.

On the enforcement of rights under the SDA 1975 and RRA 1975, see p. 71.

Discrimination on the grounds of union membership or non-membership

Section 137 of the Trade Union and Labour Relations (Consolidation) Act (TULRCA) 1992 makes it unlawful to refuse employment to people because (a) they are or are not members of a trade union, or (b) they refuse to accept a requirement that they become a member or cease to be a member, or a requirement that they suffer deductions if they fail to join. People are deemed to have been refused employment with an employee if that employer:

1 refuses or deliberately omits to entertain the application or enquiry, or
2 causes the applicant to withdraw or cease to pursue the application or enquiry, or
3 refuses or deliberately omits to offer employment, or
4 makes an offer of employment the terms of which are such as no reasonable employer who wished to fill the post would offer, (and which is not accepted)
5 makes an offer of employment but withdraws it or causes the applicant not to accept
6 offers a job subject to the condition that the applicant becomes or ceases to become a union member and the applicant refuses the offer on the grounds that he or she is unwilling to accept the condition.

If *job advertisements* might reasonably be understood as indicating that employment is only open to people who are or are not union members, or that there is a requirement applying to the post of the sort mentioned in s. 137 of TULRCA 1992, then if people who do not meet the relevant condition are refused employment it will be conclusively presumed that this was because they failed to satisfy the condition. Where it is the practice for trade unions to supply job applicants, non-members who are refused employment are deemed to have been so refused on account of their non-membership.

It is also unlawful for an agency which finds employment for workers, or supplies employers with workers, to refuse its services to people because they are or are not union members or are unwilling to accept a condition or requirement of the type mentioned in s. 137 of TULRCA 1992. The provisions relating to advertisements also apply to such agencies.

A *complaint* about the infringement of these provisions must normally be presented to an *industrial tribunal* within three months of the date of the conduct complained about. The date of the conduct complained of will be:

1 in the case of an actual refusal, the date of the refusal
2 where there was a deliberate omission to offer employment or deal with an application or enquiry, the end of the period within which it was reasonable to expect the employer to act
3 in the case of conduct causing the applicant to withdraw or cease to pursue an application, the date of that conduct
4 the date when an offer was withdrawn, and
5 in a case where an offer was made but not accepted, the date the offer was made.

If a complaint is upheld the tribunal must make a declaration to that effect and may make such of the following remedies as it considers just and equitable:

● an order obliging the respondent to pay compensation, which may include damages for injury to feelings;
● a recommendation that the respondent takes such action as the tribunal thinks practicable in order to obviate or reduce the effect on the complainant of the conduct to which the claim relates. If such a recommendation is not complied with, any award of compensation can be increased although the total award cannot exceed the amount stipulated in s. 75 of the Employment Protection (Consolidation) Act (EPCA) 1978 (£11,000 at the time of writing.)

It should be noted that a trade union may be joined as a defendant in tribunal proceedings where an employer or agency maintains that it was induced to act in the manner complained of by union pressure. If compensation is awarded the union may be ordered to pay all or part of it. Appeals against tribunal decisions go to the Employment Appeal Tribunal (EAT) if a point of law is involved.

Ex-offenders

Normally the law does not require applicants to disclose facts about themselves which could hinder them in getting jobs, unless their silence amounts to fraud. Under the Rehabilitation of Offenders Act 1974 certain persons are relieved from the obligation to disclose 'spent' convictions to a prospective employer and it is unlawful for an employer to deny employment on the grounds that the applicant had a conviction which was 'spent'. However, this protection is not afforded to those applying for a whole range of jobs: for example, social workers, probation officers, teachers or nurses.

What is a 'spent' conviction?

Sentences of over two and a half years' imprisonment never become 'spent'; otherwise convictions become 'spent' after periods which are related to the sentence imposed. Thus a sentence of imprisonment for a period of between six months and two and a half years is 'spent' after ten years. Imprisonment for less than six months requires a rehabilitation period of seven years and fines and community service orders take five years to become 'spent'. A probation order, conditional discharge or binding over will be 'spent' after a year or when the order expires, whichever is the longer. Absolute discharges are 'spent' if six months has elapsed since sentence. Finally, it should be noted that the courts cannot compel an employer to engage a rehabilitated offender: they can only declare the exclusion of the applicant to be unlawful.

Disabled persons

Under the Disabled Persons (Employment) Acts 1944 and 1958 organizations with more than twenty employees must ensure that at least 3 per cent of their labour force consists of registered disabled people. In addition handicapped persons must be given preference for certain jobs, for example car park or lift attendants. Exceptions are allowed if the employment of a handicapped person might be hazardous and special permission can be obtained if it proves impossible to meet the quota because either the work is unsuitable or no suitable disabled person has applied. It is a criminal offence to breach the provisions of these Acts.

In addition the annual directors' report of companies which employ on average more than 250 people must include a statement which outlines the policy the company has applied during the previous financial year in relation to the employment training, career development and promotion of disabled persons.

Thus the following advice should be given to the managing director of *Minor Holdings plc* (see case illustration on page 59). Although age discrimination is not currently unlawful in the UK, in most circumstances it will be unlawful to hire workers on the basis of their sex, race or union membership. Ex-offenders may not be detectable owing to the fact that convictions may be 'spent' and there is a duty to ensure that at least 3 per cent of the labour force consists of people who are registered as disabled.

TYPES OF EMPLOYMENT CONTRACTS AND THEIR CONTENTS

Case illustration

Lament Communications plc has a policy of not issuing any employment documentation to staff who work from home. This is justified on the basis that such workers are regarded as self-employed and all provide their services for less than sixteen hours a week.

Box 3.2 Lament Communications plc

The legal implications of maintaining such a policy need to be considered.

What are the main types of contract found in the workplace?

Contracts of service and contracts for services

There are significant legal differences drawn between workers who are engaged under contracts of service (employees) and those who are engaged under contracts for services (self-employed or independent contractors). Employees gain the benefit of a number of individual rights under employment protection legislation and are subject to the unwritten general obligations implied in all contracts of employment (see p. 67). When employees, as opposed to self-employed persons, are engaged, employers are required to deduct social security contributions and tax.

Unfortunately, it is sometimes difficult to determine whether someone works under a contract of service or for services. It is the operation of the contract in practice rather than its appearance that is crucial. Thus a person may be described as self-employed but be treated by the law as an employee. If there is a dispute, it will ultimately be for the court or tribunal to decide whether the person was carrying on a business on his or her own account.[1] The fact that workers pay their own social security contributions and tax is not conclusive. Indeed, people who work at home may be classed as employees so long as there is a degree of mutual obligation to continue the relationship with the person for whom they are working. Although individuals engaged under special employment schemes may not be categorized as employees, for certain purposes they are to be treated as such, for example under health and safety regulations.

Indefinite and fixed-term contracts

Employees may be hired for an indefinite period or for a fixed-term (i.e. on a contract which has a defined beginning and a defined end). Provided it is for a specified period, a fixed-term contract exists even though it may be terminable by the giving of notice within that period. From an employer's point of view the main advantage of a fixed-term contract is that it is possible for the employer, by means of an exclusion clause, to remove the right to claim unfair dismissal (if the contract is for a year or more), or a redundancy payment (if the contract is for two years or more).

Temporary and part-time employees

Since Parliament has not provided a definition of temporary status, an employee *described* as 'temporary' who has satisfied any necessary qualifying period of service and worked the requisite number of hours (see below) will have exactly the same statutory rights as other employees.

'Part-time employment' is only indirectly defined by legislation and the statutory provisions are frequently at variance with the boundaries drawn in practice by employers and trade unions. The law stipulates that any person who has a contract of employment for more than sixteen hours per week, or who has been continuously employed for the previous five years under a contract for more than eight hours per week can qualify for the full range of statutory protection. However, in certain circumstances, part-timers may be able to show that they have suffered indirect sex discrimination.[2]

How are contracts of employment formed?

Apart from apprentices, who can only be employed under written deeds, contracts of employment may be oral or in writing. In theory the parties to a contract of employment are free to negotiate the terms and conditions that suit them. However, in practice many employees do not negotiate on an individual basis but are engaged on such terms and conditions as are laid down in currently operative collective agreements. Express terms are those which are expressly agreed as forming part of the contract. An express term normally takes precedence over an implied term. The exception is where the implied term derives from statute, for example minimum notice entitlement (see p. 77).

What information must be supplied to an employee about the terms and conditions of their employment?

Not later than two months after commencing employment an employee must be given a *written statement* which provides the following particulars:

1 the identity of the parties
2 the date on which the employee's period of continuous employment began
3 the scale or rate of remuneration, or the method of calculating remuneration, and the intervals at which remuneration is paid. Additionally, there is a right to receive an itemised pay statement
4 any terms and conditions relating to hours of work and normal hours of work
5 any terms and conditions relating to holidays and holiday pay. It should be noted that there is no general statutory right to any holiday
6 any terms and conditions relating to incapacity for work owing to sickness or injury, including any provision for sick pay
7 any terms and conditions relating to pensions and a statement as to whether a contracting-out certificate is in force
8 the length of notice that the employee is entitled to receive and obliged to give (see p. 77)
9 the title of the job
10 where the employment is temporary, the period for which it is expected to continue, or if it is for a fixed term, the date when it is to end
11 the place of work, or if the employee is required or permitted to work at various places, an indication of that fact and the employer's address
12 any collective agreements which directly affect the terms and conditions of employment, including, where the employer is not a party, the person by whom they were made
13 where the employee is required to work outside the UK for more than a month: (i)   the period of work outside the UK, (ii)   the currency in which payment will be made, (iii)   any additional pay and benefits to be provided by reason of the work being outside the UK, (iv)   any terms and conditions relating to the employee's return to the UK
14 the name or description of the person to whom employees can apply if they are dissatisfied with any disciplinary decision or wish to redress a grievance. Where there are further steps consequent upon any such application, the employee must receive details explaining those steps or be referred to a reasonably accessible document which explains them. These requirements do not apply in relation to discipline if the employer has less than twenty employees.

It should also be noted that for particulars of any of the matters mentioned in 6, 8 and 14 above, the statement may refer the employee to some other reasonably accessible document. Changes cannot be made to a contract of employment without the consent of the employee but, where agreement is reached to alter the terms, the employee must receive a written statement detailing the changes within one month.

It is important to understand that the statement issued does not constitute a contract. It is merely the employer's version of what has been agreed. Nevertheless, if an employee confirms that what has been issued is an accurate summary of the main employment terms the particulars may be treated by the courts as having contractual status. Where there is no written statement, or an incomplete or inaccurate statement is issued, the employee can complain to an industrial tribunal.

What terms are implied into all contracts of employment?

Certain terms are regarded by the law as being inherent in all contracts of employment. In the remainder of this section the major obligations which are imposed automatically on the parties to a contract of employment will be outlined.

The duties of the employer

The duty to pay wages

This is the basic obligation of the employer and is normally dealt with by an express term. However, in certain circumstances the law does not leave the parties entirely free to determine the amount of remuneration payable, for example, if an equality clause operates (see p. 72). The normal rule is that wages must be paid if an employee is available for work. Thus if employees voluntarily absent themselves from work (for example by taking strike action) an employer is entitled to withhold wages for the period of the absence. As regards deductions from wages for any other reason, the Wages Act 1986 provides that a deduction will be unlawful unless it is required by statute, for example, PAYE or social security contributions, or if the worker has agreed to it beforehand.

The duty to provide work

Employers are not usually obliged to provide work and most employees who receive their full contractual remuneration cannot complain if they are left idle. Nevertheless, in exceptional circumstances the failure to provide work may amount to a breach of contract, as for example in the case of a pieceworker whose earnings depend on work being provided.

The duty to co-operate with the employee

One effect of the unfair dismissal provisions (see p. 78) has been that the courts have frequently stated that employers must not destroy the mutual trust and confidence upon which co-operation in the workplace is built. Although each case depends on its particular set of facts, it may be interesting to note that employers have been held to be in breach of contract in the following situations:

- where an applicant for transfer had not been treated fairly
- where there was a failure to investigate a genuine safety grievance or allegations of sexual or racial harassment
- where there was false accusation of theft on the basis of flimsy evidence
- where an employer has persistently attempted to vary an employee's conditions of service.[3]

The duty to take reasonable care of the employee

See Chapter 4 for details of this duty.

The duties of the employee

The duty to co-operate with the employer

For convenience this can be divided into:

- the duty to obey lawful and reasonable orders
- the duty not to impede the employer's business.

The duty to obey lawful and reasonable orders   The obligation to carry out lawful orders has two distinct aspects. First, it means that employees are not required to obey an order if to do so would break the law, for example falsifying accounts. Second, it also means that employees are not obliged to obey orders which fall outside the scope of the contract. This is consistent with the view that, at least in theory, the terms of a contract cannot be unilaterally varied. However, this does not prevent employees from being *fairly* dismissed for refusing to follow instructions which are outside their contractual obligations. (See the section headed 'some other substantial reason' on p. 80.)

The duty not to impede the employer's business   Since the essence of the employment relationship is that the employee is ready and willing to work in exchange for remuneration, it follows that going on strike breaches a fundamental term of the contract. Indeed, it would seem that all industrial action is likely to be unlawful.

The duty of fidelity

Employees must avoid putting themselves in a position whereby their own interests conflict with those of their employer. Thus employees must not accept any reward for their work other than from their employer, for example a secret gift or commission. It is worth noting that there are three particular aspects to this duty: the obligation not to compete with the employer, the duty not to disclose confidential information and the law relating to inventions and copyright. (See also Chapter 7.)

The duty to take reasonable care

See Chapters 1 and 4 for details of this duty.

What can be done if either party breaks the contracts of employment?

The choices available to the innocent party will depend on whether the breach is of a minor or serious nature. An innocent party may choose to continue with the contract as if nothing had happened, they may sue for damages or, in the case of a serious breach, they may treat the contract as at an end. In most cases, however, employers will prefer to take disciplinary rather than legal action.

Traditionally the law has placed great emphasis on the personal nature of the contract of employment and courts have been reluctant to order a defaulting party to continue to perform the contract of employment. Thus, although an injunction (an order restraining a particular act) may sometimes be available, in most cases where there has been a breach of contract damages will be the normal remedy. Those who get damages will be compensated for the direct and likely consequences of the breach. This is a complicated legal formula that tries to take into account the loss to the innocent party that arises as a result of the breach of contract and express it in financial terms. Finally, it should be noted that ordinary breach of contract cases, for example failure to pay wages, are heard by the *civil courts* (in most cases the local county court) and *not by industrial tribunals*.

Thus the implications for *Lament Communications plc* of their policy on employment documentation are as follows. The homeworkers may be able to establish that they are employed by the company and are not in business on their own account. If this is the case they will be entitled to benefit both from the common law implied terms and statutory rights. For example, employees who work eight hours a week or more will be entitled to written particulars of the key terms of their employment.

ANTI-DISCRIMINATION LEGISLATION

Case illustration

The *Gammer Group plc* is proposing to introduce a policy of not promoting employees to management positions until they have five years' continuous service. They also wish to pay their nightshift supervisors more than the dayshift supervisors because of the unsocial hours they work. At present all the female supervisors work on the day shift.

Box 3.3 Gammer Group plc

The legal ramifications of implementing such proposals will be examined.

Sex and race discrimination

These issues will be dealt with together since the relevant statutes are drafted in virtually identical terms. The definitions of sex and race discrimination were considered on p. 60.

What is the difference between direct and indirect discrimination?

Both the SDA 1975 and RRA 1975 draw a distinction between direct and indirect discrimination. *Direct discrimination* occurs when a person is treated less favourably than a person of the opposite sex, a single person, or a person not of the same racial group would be treated. A person can complain of *indirect discrimination* where an employer applies a requirement or condition which would apply equally to a person of the opposite sex, a single person, or a person not of the same racial group, but which is such that the proportion of the applicant's sex, marital status, or racial group, who can comply with it is considerably smaller than the proportion of persons of the opposite sex, single people, or persons not of the same racial group. For example, a height requirement might have a disproportionate impact. The applicant must also show that they suffered a detriment as a result of being unable to comply with the requirement or condition. Employers can avoid liability by demonstrating that the requirement or condition was *objectively justifiable* irrespective of the sex, marital status, or race, of the person to whom it is applied.

A number of points need to be made about the above definitions:

1 both statutes stipulate that, when drawing comparisons, the relevant circumstances of the complainant and his or her comparator must be the same or not materially different

2 the statutory definitions cover cases where the reason for the discrimination was a generalized assumption that people of a particular sex, marital status or race possess or lack certain characteristics, for example the assumption that married men rather than married women are the principal breadwinners.

3 the words 'requirement or condition' refer to something that has to be complied with

4 the words 'can comply' have been interpreted to mean 'can in practice comply' rather than physically or theoretically comply

5 the courts have ruled that a person only suffers detrimental treatment where its effect is such that a reasonable employee could justifiably complain about his or her working conditions or environment.

What would amount to unequal treatment in the course of employment?

It is unlawful for employers to discriminate:

● under the RRA 1975, in the terms of employment afforded (terms which discriminate on the grounds of sex are covered by the Equal Pay Act 1970; see p. 72)

● in the way they afford access to opportunities for promotion, transfer or training, or access to any other benefits, facilities or services, or by refusing or deliberately omitting to afford access to them. However, special arrangements are permitted for the training of persons of a particular sex or racial group if it can be shown that within the previous twelve months only a small minority of that sex or racial group was performing a particular type of work

● by dismissing or subjecting the employee to any other detriment.

It should also be noted that dismissal on the grounds of pregnancy or maternity amounts to sex discrimination (see p. 74).

How is the anti-discrimination legislation enforced?

If the provisions of the SDA 1975 or RRA 1975 are not complied with, both the employing body and named individuals can be sued. Individuals may be liable for instructing or putting pressure on someone to perform an unlawful act and for knowingly aiding another person to do an unlawful act. Employers will be liable for the acts of employees in the course of employment, whether or not they were done with the employer's knowledge or approval, unless it can be proved that the employer took such steps as were reasonably practicable to prevent the employee doing that act. Indirect discrimination is unlawful whether it is intentional or not.

To whom should complaints be made?

Both statutes permit individuals to bring complaints before an industrial tribunal within three months of a discriminatory act occurring, although out-of-time claims can sometimes be heard. The Equal Opportunities Commission (EOC) and the Commission for Racial Equality (CRE) can provide financial support for complainants and, if they think it desirable, they can instigate *formal investigations* of anyone believed to be discriminating unlawfully. While the burden of proof is on the complainant to show unlawful discrimination,[4] once a *prima facie* case of indirect discrimination has been established, the employer will have to satisfy the tribunal that the discriminatory requirement or condition was justifiable. Both statutes provide that customer or union prejudices cannot constitute a defence.

What remedies are available to the complainant?

If no settlement is reached and the complaint is upheld, three possible remedies are available. First, the tribunal can make a *declaration* of the complainant's rights, i.e. make a simple declaration that discrimination has occurred, which might be of sufficient symbolic importance to satisfy an applicant in some cases. Second, the person who has been sued (respondent) can be required to pay *compensation*, which may include an element to cover hurt feelings. Third there may be a *recommendation* that the employer takes action within a specified period designed to reduce the effect of the discrimination that has taken place. It should be observed that where a discriminatory dismissal is alleged to have occurred an unfair dismissal claim may prove more attractive to the employee. Not only does the employer have to show a fair reason for dismissal but the remedies of *reinstatement* or *re-engagement* are available.

Equal pay

When is an employee entitled to equal pay?

An *equality clause* operates when a person is employed on any of the following:

- 'like work'
- 'work rated as equivalent'
- work of 'equal value' to that of a person of the opposite sex in the same employment.

The effect of the equality clause is that any term in a person's contract (whether concerned with pay or not) which is less favourable than in the contract of a person of the opposite sex must be modified so as to be not less favourable.

What is 'like work'?

This concept focuses on the job rather than the person performing it. Once a person has shown that their work is of the same or broadly similar nature as that of a person of the opposite sex, unless the employer can prove that any differences are of practical importance in relation to terms and conditions of employment, for example the performance of supervisory duties, that person is to be regarded as employed on 'like work'. Attention must be paid to the frequency with which any differences occur in practice as well as to their nature and extent. Thus tribunals investigate the actual work done rather than rely on theoretical contractual obligations.

What is 'work rated as equivalent'?

A person's work will only be regarded as rated as equivalent to that of a person of the opposite sex if it has been given equal value under a properly conducted job evaluation scheme. If the work has been rated as equivalent there is no need to show that a similar job is performed.

When can an 'equal value' claim be brought?

Because of the complexities involved in bringing an 'equal value' claim, it is likely that this procedure will only be invoked where it cannot be shown that like work, or work rated as equivalent, is being performed. Indeed, where work has been given different ratings under a job evaluation study, an equal value claim cannot proceed unless a tribunal is satisfied that there are reasonable grounds for concluding that the evaluation study was discriminatory.

What defence is available to the employer?

An employer can defeat a claim for equal pay by proving that the variation between the woman's and the man's contract was 'genuinely due to a material factor which is not the difference of sex'; for example, the variation is due to differences in geographical location. However, the burden of proof will only be discharged if the employer can demonstrate objectively justified grounds for any difference in pay.[5]

How is the equal pay legislation enforced?

Employees can apply to an industrial tribunal and claim arrears of pay. Complainants must identify a comparable person of the opposite sex in the same employment, i.e. a person employed at the same establishment or at another of the employer's establishments where broadly similar terms and conditions are observed. Although comparisons cannot be made with a hypothetical person, a complainant can make comparisons with a previous job incumbent.[6]

Victimization on trade union grounds

Action short of dismissal

Employees have the right not to have action short of dismissal taken against them as individuals by their employer for the purpose of:

- either preventing or deterring them from being, or seeking to become, a member of any independent trade union or penalizing them for doing so
- or preventing or deterring them from taking part in the activities of an independent trade union at any appropriate time, or penalizing them for doing so
- or compelling them to become a member of any trade union or of a particular trade union or of one of a number of particular trade unions.

Several points must be made about the nature of this protection:

1 'action' is defined as including omissions. Thus a failure to promote, as well as more positive acts, like segregation, are covered
2 tribunals have the task of determining what are 'activities of an independent trade union'. The following have been accepted as such: attempting to recruit new members or form a workplace union branch; taking part in union meetings and consulting a union official
3 'appropriate time' is defined as being outside working hours or within working hours in accordance with arrangements agreed with the employer. The employer's consent may be express, for example in a collective agreement, or it may be implied from the conduct of the parties.

Dismissal on trade union grounds is dealt with below on p. 81.

Maternity rights

Since the law is both detailed and complicated this section will merely list the maternity rights that exist. The reader seeking more detailed information is advised to refer to specialist texts on employment law.

1 It is unfair to dismiss an employee if: (a) the reason or principal reason for dismissal is that she is pregnant or any other reason connected with pregnancy; (b) her maternity leave is ended by dismissal and the reason or principal reason for dismissal is that she has given birth or any other

reason connected with her having given birth; (c) her contract was terminated after the maternity leave period and the reason for dismissal is that she had taken maternity leave; (d) the reason or principal reason for dismissal is a requirement or recommendation relating to suspension on health and safety grounds; (e) her maternity leave period is ended by dismissal and the principal reason for it is redundancy, but the duty to offer alternative employment has not been complied with.

2 A woman who is dismissed at any time while she is pregnant, or after childbirth in circumstances in which her maternity leave ends by reason of dismissal, is entitled to written particulars of the reason for dismissal irrespective of her length of service.

3 If an employer has available suitable alternative work for an employee who cannot continue her usual job because of a relevant health and safety provision, she is entitled to be offered that work. Where a woman is suspended on maternity grounds she is entitled to be paid unless she has unreasonably refused an offer of suitable alternative employment.

4 A pregnant woman who, on the advice of a registered medical practitioner, midwife or health visitor, has made an appointment to receive ante-natal care, has the statutory right not to be unreasonably refused time off during working hours to keep the appointment.

5 Women who are absent from work wholly or partly because of pregnancy or confinement are entitled to either statutory maternity pay or maternity allowance depending on their length of service and level of earnings.

6 Female employees have a right to fourteen weeks' maternity leave irrespective of their length of service or working hours. However, women who have been continuously employed for two years have the right to return to work at any time before the end of twenty nine weeks, beginning with the week in which the confinement occurred.

If *Gammer Group plc* attempt to implement the proposals (see case illustration on p. 70), then they are likely to be in breach of the sex discrimination and equal pay legislation. The policy of not promoting employees to management positions until they have had five years' continuous service might indirectly discriminate against women who tend to stop work in order to have children and who would find it more difficult to build up five years' continuous experience. *Gammer Group plc* could avoid liability by showing that the requirement was objectively justifiable. Indeed any form of service requirement (cumulative or otherwise) may have a discriminatory effect. However, even if seniority is used as a criterion for assessing suitability for promotion, it is questionable whether it needs to be continuous rather than cumulative.

Gammer Group plc may also be in breach of the equal pay legislation, as all the supervisors on the night shift are men doing the same work as the supervisors on the day shift, some of whom are women. *Gammer Group plc* will be able to claim that the unsociable hours amount to a genuine material difference. However, they will be in breach of the sex discrimination legislation if they do not provide men and women with equal access to night work.

THE TERMINATION OF EMPLOYMENT

Case illustration

Hazlitt Holdings plc moved to Hendon from a site ten miles away. Rather than make twenty four workers, who lived near the previous workplace, redundant the company provided a bus to transport them to Hendon. Since the move half of these workers have resigned, leaving only twelve workers using the bus. The company has now withdrawn the bus service on economic grounds. Six of the workers previously using the bus have found alternative means of transport but the other six still have difficulty getting to and from work. They have complained to the company's personnel manager, Hatchett, who maintains that the recognized trade union (TGWU) agreed to the withdrawal of the bus as part of a package deal on wages and conditions agreed with the company. The six workers concede that the union entered into such an agreement but claim that they protested vehemently to both the works manager and the union when the deal was announced.

Box 3.4 Hazlitt Holdings plc

After reading all the material which is contained in this section on 'the termination of employment' (i.e. pp. 76–87), advise Hazlitt Holdings plc of any legal liabilities that may have been incurred.

Although the bulk of this section deals with the statutory rights to claim unfair dismissal and redundancy payments, it might be helpful to begin by outlining the basis on which an action for breach of contract can be brought. (See also Chapter 1.)

Dismissal in breach of contract

The first distinction to be made is that between dismissal without notice and dismissal with notice.

Dismissal without notice

Where the employer terminates the contract without giving notice the employee is said to be summarily dismissed. In order to justify a summary dismissal the employee must be in breach of an important express or implied term of the contract, i.e. guilty of gross misconduct. Although certain terms are always regarded as important, for example the duty not to steal or damage the employer's property, the significance of other terms will depend on the nature of the employer's business and the employee's position in it. If employers do not invoke the right to dismiss summarily within a reasonable period of the conduct occurring, it will be assumed that they have waived this right (although they may be able to dismiss fairly with notice, see below). What is a reasonable period will depend on the facts of the particular case.

Dismissal with notice

Usually either party is entitled to terminate a contract of employment by giving notice and once notice has been given it cannot be unilaterally withdrawn. For notice to be effective it must be possible to ascertain the date of termination and not infrequently employees have confused an advance warning of closure with notice of dismissal. The length of notice will be determined by the express or implied terms of the contract. Apart from the situation where the employee is guilty of gross misconduct, the law provides that certain minimum periods of notice must be given. After a month's service an employee is entitled to a week's notice and this applies until the employment has lasted for two years. At this point two weeks' notice is owed and from then on the employee must receive an extra week's notice for each year of service up to a maximum of twelve weeks. An employee with a month's service or more need only give one week's notice to terminate, but there is nothing to prevent the parties agreeing that both should receive more than the statutory minimum.

What are the remedies for wrongful dismissal?

Basically a wrongful dismissal is one without notice, or with inadequate notice in circumstances where proper notice should have been given. The expression also covers dismissals which are in breach of agreed procedures. Thus where there is a contractual disciplinary procedure an employee may be able to obtain an injunction or declaration from the courts to prevent a dismissal or declare a dismissal void if the procedure has not been followed. However, in the vast majority of cases the employee's remedy will be damages for breach of contract. Since damages are not available for hurt feelings or the manner in which the dismissal took place, an employee will normally only recover the amount of wages lost.

Unfair dismissal

Who can claim unfair dismissal?

Whilst the law grants many employees the right not to be unfairly dismissed, and the right to seek reinstatement and compensation if they are unfairly dismissed, there are nevertheless a number of general exclusions from and qualifications upon this right. First, no claim can be made if on or before the effective date of termination the individual had attained the normal retiring age for an employee in that position or, if there is no normal retiring age, was 65 years old. Second, two years' continuous service is required before the right arises. However, neither the age limit nor the service qualification apply if the dismissal is automatically unfair (see p. 81). Third, while Crown employees are covered by the legislation, those who ordinarily work outside Great Britain are excluded.

What is a dismissal?

For both unfair dismissal and redundancy purposes an employee is to be treated as dismissed if:

1 The contract under which the employee is employed is terminated by the employer with or without notice. It should be noted that where an employer has given notice to terminate, an employee who gives counter-notice, indicating that they wish to leave before the employer's notice has expired, is still to be regarded as dismissed. Obviously if people resign of their own volition there is no dismissal at law, although if pressure has been applied the situation will be different, for example where the employee is given the choice of resigning or being dismissed. A mutually agreed termination does not amount to a dismissal.
2 A fixed-term contract expires without being renewed under the same contract (see p. 65 for exclusion clauses in fixed-term contracts).
3 The employee terminates the contract with or without notice in circumstances such that they are entitled to terminate it without notice by reason of the employer's conduct. This is commonly referred to as a *constructive dismissal*. Employees are only entitled to treat themselves as constructively dismissed if the employer is guilty of conduct which is a fundamental breach of contract,[7] for example where employees are demoted or a significant change of job duties is imposed without their consent. If employees continue for a lengthy period after such a breach without leaving, they will be regarded as having elected to affirm the contract and will lose the right to treat themselves as discharged.

Must an employer give a reason for a dismissal?

Once an employee has proved that there has been a dismissal, the tribunal will require the employer to show the reason, or if there was more than one, the principal reason for dismissal and that it falls within one of the following categories:

- it related to the capability or qualifications of the employee for performing work of the kind which they were employed to do
- it related to the conduct of the employee
- the employee was redundant
- the employee could not continue to work in the position held without contravention of a duty or restriction imposed by statute, for example, where a person loses a driving licence
- there was some other substantial reason of a kind such as to justify the dismissal of an employee holding his or her particular position.

In all the above cases the reason for dismissal must have existed and been known to the employer at the time of dismissal. This makes it impossible for an employer to rely on subsequently discovered misconduct.

Must the employer put the reasons for the dismissal in writing?

A person who has been continuously employed for two years and has been dismissed, has the right to be supplied with a written statement giving particulars of the reason for dismissal. The employer must provide the statement within fourteen days of a request being made. If it is alleged that the employer unreasonably failed to provide such a statement, or that the particulars given were inadequate or untrue, a claim may be presented to an industrial tribunal. If the complaint is well founded the tribunal may make a declaration as to what it finds the employer's reasons for dismissing were, and must order that the employee is to receive two weeks' pay from the employer.

What reasons for dismissal are potentially fair?

Capability or qualifications

Capability is to be assessed by reference to 'skill, aptitude, health or any other physical or mental quality' (on incapability arising from pregnancy, see p. 74). Qualifications means 'any degree, diploma or other academic, technical or professional qualification relevant to the position which the employee held'. For our purposes it is convenient to consider capability in terms of competence and ill health.

As regards incompetence, unless it can be shown that a warning would have been 'utterly useless', for example where the inadequacy of the employee's performance is extreme or the actual or potential consequences of a mistake are grave, employees should not be dismissed unless warnings have been issued.[8]

In relation to ill health, it should be emphasized that the decision to dismiss is not a medical one but a matter to be determined by employers in the light of the medical evidence available. The basic question is whether in all the circumstances the employer could have been expected to wait any longer for the employee to recover. Clearly, where there has been long-term absence because of illness a discussion of the position with the employee will be more appropriate than a warning.[9]

Conduct

In this context conduct means behaviour of such a nature, whether done inside or outside the course of employment, which has an impact in some way on the employer/employee relationship. It is not the function of tribunals to decide whether misconduct is gross or criminal but whether the employer has, in the circumstances of the case, acted reasonably in dismissing.

Redundancy

It is well established that employers have a duty to consider the alternatives to compulsory redundancy. If compulsory redundancies cannot be avoided, in the absence of an agreed procedure or customary arrangement, the personal circumstances of employees must be taken into account. While the absence of consultation does not render a dismissal automatically unfair, an employer will be expected to show some special reason for not consulting.

See p. 83 on the circumstances in which an employee is redundant and see p. 81 on automatically unfair dismissals.

Some other substantial reason (SOSR)

This was included in the legislation so as to give tribunals the discretion to accept as a fair reason for dismissal something that would not conveniently fit into any of the other categories. It covers such diverse matters as dismissal for failing to obtain a fidelity bond, refusing to sign an undertaking not to compete and personality clashes between employees. SOSR has frequently provided a convenient peg where employees have been dismissed as a result of a reorganization of the business.

Will dismissal ever be automatically unfair?

A dismissal will be automatically unfair if the reason for it (or if more than one, the principal reason) was that the employee:

1 was or proposed to become a member of an independent trade union; or
2 has taken, or proposed to take part in the activities of an independent trade union at any appropriate time (see p. 74)
3 was not a member of any trade union or of a particular trade union, or had refused or proposed to refuse to become or remain a member; or
4 carried out, or proposed to carry out, activities designated by the employer in connection with preventing or reducing risks to the health and safety of employees; or
5 performed, or proposed to perform, any of their functions as a safety representative or a member of a safety committee; or
6 asserted a statutory right. Employees are protected if they have brought proceedings against the employer to enforce a 'relevant' statutory right or have alleged that the employer has infringed such a right
7 was pregnant or took maternity leave (see p. 74 on maternity rights for other 'inadmissible' reasons).

If the reason a person was selected for redundancy related to any of the above, dismissal will be unfair.

In addition where the transfer of an undertaking (or a reason connected with it) is the reason or principal reason for dismissal, then the dismissal is to be treated as unfair, unless there is an economic, technical or organizational reason entailing changes in the workforce. For these purposes an 'undertaking' includes a trade or business.

Finally, where at the date of dismissal the employee was locked out or taking part in a strike or other industrial action, a tribunal has no jurisdiction to determine whether a dismissal was fair or unfair unless it can be shown that one or more 'relevant' employees of the same employer were not dismissed in the circumstances or that, within three months of the complainant's dismissal, any such employee has been offered re-engagement and the complainant has not. If at the time of dismissal the employee was taking part in unofficial action no complaint of unfair dismissal can be made.

In what circumstances will a dismissal be reasonable?

Where the employer has given a valid reason for dismissal, the determination of the question whether the dismissal was fair or unfair depends on: whether in the circumstances (including the size and administrative resources of the employer's undertaking), the employer acted reasonably or unreasonably in treating it as a sufficient reason for dismissing the employee. That question must be determined in accordance with equity and the substantial merits of the case.

Thus, at this stage, tribunals must take account of the wider circumstances. In addition to the employer's business needs, attention must be paid to the personal attributes of the employee, for example seniority and previous work record. The words 'equity and the substantial merits' also allow tribunals to apply their knowledge of good industrial relations practice and to ensure that there has been procedural fairness. However, it is not the function of tribunals to ask themselves whether they would have done what the employer did in the circumstances; their function is merely to assess the employer's decision to dismiss to see if it falls within a range of responses which a reasonable employer could have taken.[10] Although reference may be made to the ACAS *Code of Practice on Disciplinary Practice and Procedures* (1977), this document does not have the force of law and a failure to comply with it does not make a dismissal automatically unfair.

What are the remedies for unfair dismissal?

Re-employment

When applicants are found to be unfairly dismissed tribunals must explain their powers to order reinstatement or re-engagement and ask employees if they wish such an order to be made. Only if such a wish is expressed can an order be made and if no order is made the tribunal must turn to the question of compensation.

Where re-employment is sought a tribunal must first consider whether reinstatement is appropriate, i.e. should the complainant be treated in all respects as if they had not been dismissed. If reinstatement is not ordered the tribunal must then decide whether to order re-engagement and, if so, on what terms.

Where a person is re-employed following a tribunal order but the terms are not fully complied with, if the matter is referred again to the tribunal the employee can be compensated for the loss caused by the non-compliance. If a complainant is not re-employed in accordance with such an order compensation will be awarded, together with an additional or special award, unless the employer satisfies the tribunal that it was not practicable to comply with the order.

Awards of compensation

Compensation will be calculated in accordance with the following formula.

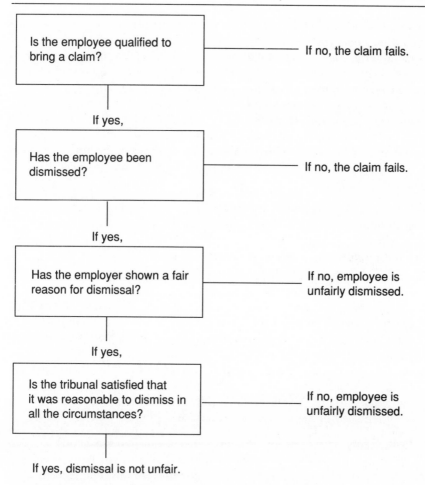

Figure 3.1 Unfair dismissal flow chart

Basic award   Normally this will be calculated in the same way as a redundancy payment and will be reduced by the amount of any redundancy payment received. Where the reason or principal reason for dismissal related to any of the first five reasons listed on p. 81, there is a current minimum award of £2,700. The basic award can be reduced, by such proportion as the tribunal considers just and equitable, on two grounds: namely that the complainant unreasonably refused an offer of reinstatement; and any conduct of the complainant before the dismissal.

Compensatory award   The amount of this award is that which a tribunal 'considers just and equitable in all the circumstances having regard to the loss sustained by the complainant in consequence of the dismissal in so far as that loss is attributable to action taken by the employer'. However, it should be noted that a complainant cannot be reimbursed for the cost of pursuing an unfair dismissal claim.

The compensatory award can be reduced where the employee's action caused or contributed to the dismissal and where the employee failed to mitigate the loss. The maximum compensatory award is currently £11,000.

The legislation aims to reimburse the employee rather than to punish the employer. Thus employees who appear to have lost nothing, for example where it can be said that irrespective of the procedural unfairness that occurred they would have been dismissed anyway, may not qualify for a compensatory award.

Redundancy

In what circumstances is an employee redundant?

Employees are redundant if their dismissals are attributable to:

- the fact that the employer has ceased, or intends to cease, to carry on the business for the purposes for which the employees were employed, or to carry on that business in the place where the employees were so employed
- the fact that the requirements of that business for employees to carry out work of a particular kind, or for employees to carry out work of a particular kind in the place where they were so employed, have ceased or diminished or are expected to cease or diminish.

In this context 'cease' or 'diminish' mean either permanently or temporarily and from whatever cause. Thus employees will be entitled to a payment notwithstanding that it could be seen from the commencement of the contract that they would be dismissed for redundancy. It is also important to note that in this context dismissals are presumed to have been by reason of redundancy unless the contrary is proved.

What is the effect of an offer of alternative employment?

If before the ending of a person's employment an employer makes an offer to renew the contract, or to re-engage under a new contract which is to take effect either on the ending of the old one or within four weeks afterwards, the law operates as follows:

1 if the provisions of the new or renewed contract as to the capacity and place in which the person will be employed, together with the other terms and conditions, do not differ from the corresponding terms of the previous contract; or

2 the terms and conditions differ but the offer constitutes an offer of suitable employment (for example, work at another location); and

3 in either case the employee unreasonably refuses that offer, the employee will not be entitled to a redundancy payment.

The burden is on the employer to prove both the suitability of the offer and the unreasonableness of the employee's refusal.

Where the terms and conditions will differ from those of the previous contract a trial period may be invoked. This will last for four calendar weeks unless a longer period has been agreed for the purpose of retraining. If during the trial period the employee for any reason terminates the contract, or the employer terminates the contract for a reason connected with or arising out of the change (as, for example, when the employer terminates the contract because the employee is incapable of doing the new job), the employee is to be treated for redundancy purposes as having been dismissed on the date on which the previous contract ended.

Who can claim a redundancy payment?

Employees who have two years' continuous service over the age of 18 qualify for a payment. Certain categories are specifically excluded, for example civil servants and National Health Service employees. Also ineligible are employees who ordinarily work outside Great Britain and those who have reached the age of 65 (or a normal retirement age of less than 65). As to exclusion clauses in fixed-term contracts, see p. 65.

Workers will normally only be entitled to make a claim if within six months of their employment terminating they have:

- either given notice to the employer that they want a payment
- or referred a question as to their right to a payment, or its amount, to an industrial tribunal
- or presented a complaint of unfair dismissal to a tribunal.

How is a redundancy payment calculated?

Redundancy payments are calculated according to the following formula, with a maximum of twenty years' service being taken into account. Starting at the end of the employee's period of continuous service and reckoning backwards:

- one and a half weeks' pay is allowed for each year of employment in which the employee was between the ages of 41 and 64. Those who are aged 64 have their entitlement reduced by $\frac{1}{12}$ in respect of each month they remain in employment

- a week's pay for each year of employment in which the employee was between the ages of 22 and 40
- half a week's pay for each year of employment between the ages of 18 and 21. A week's pay is calculated on a gross basis but the reckonable maximum is currently £205 per week.

Can an employee get time-off to look for work when facing redundancy?

A person who has been continuously employed for two years or more, and is under notice of dismissal by reason of redundancy, is entitled to reasonable time-off during working hours to look for new employment or to make arrangements for training. Such an employee should be paid at the normal hourly rate throughout the period of absence.

A complaint that an employer has unreasonably refused time-off, or has failed to pay the whole or part of any amount to which the employee is entitled, must be presented to an industrial tribunal within three months of the day on which it is alleged that the time-off should have been allowed. If the complaint is well founded the tribunal must make a declaration to that effect and order the employer to pay the amount which it finds due to the employee. However, the maximum that can be awarded is two-fifths of a week's pay.

As regards the advice that should be given to *Hazlitt Holdings*, the first thing to be established is whether or not any of the six workers are qualified to claim unfair dismissal. Assuming they are qualified, they will have to show that they were constructively dismissed because they have not been dismissed by the employer. Although the provision of a bus service may have become an express or implied term, its withdrawal is not necessarily a breach of contract. For example, if the six were employed 'on such terms and conditions as are agreed from time to time between the company and the TGWU', it is unlikely that there will be a breach of contract. If the six are not (expressly or implied) obliged to accept the outcome of collective bargaining, it may be possible to argue that the withdrawal of the bus amounted to a breach of contract. However, this is unlikely to be sufficiently serious to amount to a constructive dismissal unless an individual can demonstrate that it is now impossible to perform the contract.

Assuming that there is a dismissal at law, the company will argue that it was for 'some other substantial reason'. It should be noted that the six workers are not redundant since the requirements of the business for employees to do work of a particular kind are unaltered. Finally, a tribunal will have to assess the reasonableness of the dismissal in all the circumstances. Clearly, it is difficult to criticise an employer for failing to warn, consult or offer alternative employment where it is maintained that there was no intention to dismiss.

ACAS AND INDUSTRIAL TRIBUNALS

Advisory, conciliation and arbitration service (ACAS)

ACAS is an independent body with the general duty of promoting the improvement of industrial relations. One of its functions is to provide advice to workers, trade unions and employers on any matter concerned with employment.

In addition, ACAS has the task of conciliating in industrial tribunal cases (other than claims for redundancy payments). When a claim is received by an industrial tribunal a copy of it will be sent to a conciliation officer who has the duty to promote a settlement without the matter having to go to a tribunal hearing. Conciliation officers can intervene if requested to do so by the employee or employer or where they believe they could act with a reasonable prospect of success. Most importantly, the conciliation officer can act before a complaint has been made to the tribunal if there is a dispute which could be the subject of tribunal proceedings. Where a settlement is reached after the involvement of a conciliation officer, or a 'compromise agreement' is reached, the employee is prevented from taking the case to a tribunal hearing.

What are industrial tribunals?

Although breach of contract cases are normally heard in the county court or High Court, contract claims which are outstanding at the end of employment and most employment protection rights are enforced at industrial tribunals. Usually tribunal cases are heard by legally qualified chairpersons and two other persons, known as lay members who are nominated by organizations of workers and employers. Hearings at industrial tribunals are relatively informal. The parties can represent themselves or be represented by a lawyer, trade union official or any other person. While legal aid is not available for tribunal hearings it is possible to obtain advice and assistance in preparing a case under the Legal Aid Scheme.

Complaints, known as originating applications, most normally arrive at an industrial tribunal within three months of the action complained about, for example, the date of the employment terminating in a claim for unfair dismissal. Each party has to bear its own costs unless it can be shown that the other party behaved frivolously, vexatiously, abusively, disruptively or otherwise unreasonably in bringing or conducting the proceedings.

STRATEGIES FOR MANAGERS

Managers should aim to hire the best person available to fill a vacancy. Thus it makes economic and legal sense to use objective criteria in recruiting and selecting and to avoid any process that could infringe anti-discrimination legislation. Managers should ensure that application forms and interviewers only ask questions and insist on qualifications which are relevant to the requirements of the job.

Managers should weigh the legal and practical advantages of using employed rather than self-employed labour. Whereas the law relating to fixed term contracts would appear to make them very attractive at first sight, many employers find that such contracts do not suit their purposes, for example temporary staff may not be so well motivated. In order to avoid allegations of indirect discrimination, part-time workers should be afforded contract rights on a pro-rata basis. Indeed, it seems likely that in the near future such employees will have a more comprehensive set of statutory rights.

Since both individuals and employers are liable for sex or race discrimi-nation in the course of employment, it is not sufficient for managers merely to introduce an equal opportunities policy. It will also be necessary to check that such a policy has been communicated to all staff, understood and implemented. Additionally, employers should ensure that informal prac-tices do not develop which could lead to an act of unlawful discrimination.

Where employees break their contracts of employment, it will normally be more efficient to take disciplinary rather than legal action. If termination proves necessary it is good practice, irrespective of length of service, for managers to give proper notice and written reasons for dismissal. Managers should also check that agreed procedures are adhered to, warnings are issued and adequate consultation takes place.

Managers who are faced with a redundancy situation should endeavour to avoid compulsory dismissals and, where possible, make offers of alter-native employment. The latter is desirable not only on the grounds of economic efficiency but may also be useful in deterring or resisting claims of unfairness. Since statutory redundancy payments are set at such a low level it will often make sense to offer enhanced sums in order to smooth a reorganization.

Finally, managers may find it cost effective to use the services of ACAS in reaching a binding settlement of some employment protection claims.

KEY LEARNING POINTS

- **Managers are free to hire whoever they please so long as: they do not discriminate on the grounds of sex, race or union membership; they engage at least the quota of registered disabled persons and they disregard 'spent' convictions.**
- **Discrimination on the grounds of sex, race or union membership is forbidden throughout the employment process. Thus managers must ensure equality of treatment in respect of terms and conditions of**

employment, access to training and promotion and in relation to discipline. Positive or reverse discrimination is not permitted.

- Workers may be engaged as employees or on a self-employed basis and may be given indefinite or fixed-term contracts. In some circumstances both temporary and part-time employees will acquire statutory rights. Certain terms are implied into all contracts of employment and certain information about the relationship must be supplied in writing.

- Those who are guilty of gross misconduct may be dismissed without notice but otherwise employees are entitled to minimum periods of notice. Those who have two years' continuous service can only be sacked for a fair reason. Employers should always be able to demonstrate that they behaved reasonably in the circumstances they faced.

- Employees who are redundant should be consulted, offered alternative employment if it exists and warned of the consequences of unreasonably refusing it.

- Managers with industrial relations or employment law difficulties might avail themselves of the specialist services offered by ACAS. In certain circumstances, a private settlement may prevent a claim being brought before an industrial tribunal.

EXERCISES

1   How does your enterprise attempt to ensure that no unlawful discrimination occurs during the recruitment process?

2   How are the details of the terms and conditions of their employment communicated to your employees?

3   How does your enterprise monitor the impact of its equal opportunities policy?

4   How does your enterprise monitor the effectiveness of its disciplinary rules and procedures?

5   You have to make three members of your department of twelve staff redundant. How should you select the staff who are going to be made redundant?

NOTES: CASE REFERENCES

1 *Lee Ting Sang* v *Chung Chi-Keung* [1990] 2 AC 374; [1990] 2 WLR 1173.
2 *R* v *Secretary of State for Employment ex parte EOC* [1994] 2 WLR 409; [1994] IRLR 176.
3 *Woods* v *WM Car Services* [1982] IRLR 413; [1982] ICR 693.
4 *King* v *Great Britain–China Centre* [1991] IRLR 513; [1992] ICR 516.
5 *Enderby* v *Frenchay Health Authority* [1994] 1 All ER 495; [1993] IRLR 591.
6 *Macarthys Ltd* v *Smith* [1981] QB 180; [1980] IRLR 209.
7 *Western Excavating Ltd* v *Sharp* [1978] QB 761; [1978] 1 All ER 713.
8 *Polkey* v *Dayton Ltd* [1988] AC 344; [1987] IRLR 503.
9 *Links Ltd* v *Rose* [1991] IRLR 353.
10 *British Leyland* v *Swift* [1981] IRLR 91.

JOURNALS

Industrial Relations Law Bulletin.
Incomes Data Brief.
Industrial Law Journal.

FURTHER READING

Bowers, J. and Honeyball, S. (1993) *Labour Law*, London: Blackstone Press.
Jefferson, M. (1994) *Employment Law*, Cavendish Publishing.
Lewis, D. (1994) *Essentials of Employment Law*, IPM.
Selwyn, N. (1993) *Law of Employment*, London: Butterworths.
Smith, I. and Wood, J. (1993) *Industrial Law*, London: Butterworths

USEFUL ADDRESSES

Department of Employment
Caxton House
Tothill Street
London SW1H 9NA   Tel. no. 0171 273 3000

Advisory, Conciliation and Arbitration Service Head Office
27 Wilton Street
London NW1 1AA   Tel. no. 0171 210 3613
(Regional Offices can be found in Newcastle-upon-Tyne, Leeds, London, Bristol, Birmingham, Manchester, Glasgow and Cardiff)

Central Office of the Industrial Tribunals
Southgate Street
Bury St Edmunds
Suffolk IP33 2AQ   Tel. no. 01284 762300
Fax: 01284 766334

Central Office of Industrial Tribunals
St Andrew's House
141 West Nile Street
Glasgow G1 2RG   Tel. no. 0141 331 1601
Fax: 0141–332 3316

Commission for Racial Equality
Elliot House
10–12 Allington Street
London SW1E 5EH   Tel. no. 0171 828 7022

Health and Safety Executive
Baynards House
1 Chepstow Place
Westbourne Grove
London W2 4TF   Tel. no. 0171 243 6000

Equal Opportunities Commission
Overseas House
Quay Street
Manchester M3 3HN   Tel. no. 0161 833 9244.

Chapter 4

The enterprise and its environment
Occupational health and safety

Brenda Barrett

An enterprise has control over its own premises but its activities may also have an impact upon neighbouring areas. While Chapter 5 will look at the broader environmental issues, this chapter is chiefly concerned with the legal responsibilities and liabilities which an enterprise has in regard to the health and safety of individuals who work on its premises. The two themes of this chapter reflect the twin concerns of the law which are: accident prevention and accident compensation.

Case study

A car assembly plant contained a spray painting booth which had a piped supply of highly flammable thinners. Beneath the booth was a large sump to collect excess paint and thinners. Austin Rover, the car manufacturers, employed a contractor to clean the booth; the work to be done when the manufacturer's own employees were not working. The agreed system of work stipulated that no one should work in the sump when anyone was working in the booth; the contractors should supply their own thinners which should not be tipped into the sump, and only a safe electric lamp should be taken into the sump. All these stipulations were ignored; there was a flash fire in the sump and the employee cleaning it was killed.[1] Austin Rover were prosecuted by the enforcement agency, the Health and Safety Executive. They were initially convicted for breach of a duty imposed on controllers of premises under the Health and Safety at Work Act 1974[2], but successfully appealed against their conviction.

Box 4.1 Mailer v Austin Rover Group plc (1989)

A civil claim for damages might have been brought on behalf of the deceased but there is no record of such an action: the civil claim would be either for negligence or breach of statutory duty.

THE CRIMINAL LAW: ACCIDENT PREVENTION

Introduction

The background

The law aims to create and maintain a working environment in which the potential for accidents and ill-health is kept to a minimum. In Great Britain there has been legislation for securing workplace health and safety, mostly with criminal sanctions, since the beginning of the nineteenth century; by 1970 there were over thirty relevant Acts of Parliament in force. In 1974 the Health and Safety at Work Act (the 1974 Act) was enacted to provide a broad and up-to-date framework for securing both the health, safety and welfare of persons at work and protecting persons other than persons at work against risks to health or safety arising out of, or in connection with, the activities of persons at work. The 1974 Act applies to almost all work situations (there remain certain exclusions such as merchant shipping): it also embraced the earlier statutory provisions, such as the Factories Act 1961 and the Offices, Shops and Railway Premises Act 1963. Most of the pre-1974 legislation has now been repealed.

It is possible that in the *Austin Rover* case certain of the then remaining provisions of the Factories Act 1961 may have been broken, but prosecutions under the earlier laws have not been very usual since 1975: the inspectorate has used the 1974 Act, and regulations made under it, wherever possible.[3]

Systems under the 1974 Act

The Act is known as framework (or enabling) legislation because it set up a system for making and enforcing safety standards at the workplace: it is concerned with protecting health as well as preventing accidents. It established the Health and Safety Commission as the governing body (related to, but independent of, the Department of Employment) and the Health and Safety Executive (employers of the inspectorate). It set out the powers of inspectors: they are entitled to enter any place where they believe persons to be at work and they may issue improvement and prohibition notices and prosecute offenders. They still act independently of the Crown Prosecution Service. Thus in the *Austin Rover* case the prosecution, even on appeal to the House of Lords, was in the name of the inspector who first investigated the fatal accident.

The only health and safety laws in the 1974 Act itself are a number of general duties in ss. 2–9. These are so broad, however, that they provide for almost all work situations and all persons at work. These duties are placed on various persons whose activities might endanger either persons at work or the public. Such duties particularly look to employers to assess situations, identify hazards and then set up and maintain safe systems.

Since 1974 numerous regulations and codes of practice have been made, to replace old laws and also to provide for protection against new hazards in a wide range of workplaces. The new regulations often apply in all workplaces, and they are often accompanied by codes of practice, e.g. the First Aid at Work Regulations 1981. Such regulations impose standards which are obligatory and failure to observe them can lead to prosecution. It is not mandatory to observe codes of practice, but if a person is prosecuted for a health and safety offence the relevant code may be put in evidence as indicating a proper way to discharge the statutory duty.

The manager who has a grasp of current health and safety legislation will be familiar with such of the pre-1974 law as remains in force, the general duties under the 1974 Act, and regulations and codes of practice made under the 1974 Act, though not all these laws may be relevant for any one workplace.

The general duties in the 1974 Act are similar to the EC Framework Directive on health and safety, but the 1974 Act has, since 1 January 1993, been supplemented by the Management of Health and Safety at Work Regulations to implement the Directive and five other sets of new Regulations to implement subsidiary Directives.[4] Much legislation which pre-dated the 1974 Act was repealed on 1 January 1993.

Since the aim of the regulatory system is to prevent accidents, the law may be invoked against a person even though no person has been injured, if, in view of the inspector, there is a hazard which is likely to lead to injury. If there is to be a criminal conviction the inspector will have to show that the law has not been observed; given the breadth of the general duties this will not be difficult if the evidence establishes there was a hazard.

Enforcement of the law

Notices

Almost certainly the inspector would have invoked the 1974 Act had he come on to Austin Rover premises while the contractors were working, but before the accident. In such a circumstance, however, he might well have issued a prohibition notice, ordering that work be stopped until such time as a safe system could be put in place, whether or not he intended to prosecute. Notices are in fact used more frequently than prosecutions when the objective is to correct a situation which is unsatisfactory. Immediate prohibition notices are appropriate in respect of activities which involve a risk of serious personal injury. In less serious cases the notice may be a deferred one, i.e. permitting work to continue for the time needed for the situation to be remedied.

Improvement notices may be served if the inspector is of the opinion that steps should be taken to bring the working environment up to the standard required by the law. For example, an inspector unsuccessfully invoked the employer's general duty in an attempt to require banking premises to install bandit screens. In this case the inspector's order was appealed against because it had such important implications for the banking industry as a whole.[5] Persons who fail to comply with a notice which has been served upon them may be prosecuted. Any person who contravenes a notice may be sentenced to up to two years' imprisonment.

Prosecutions

In most instances the penalty for contravention of the 1974 Act is a fine. Most of the offences, being 'either way' offences, may be tried either in the magistrates' court or in the Crown Court. There is no limit on the fine which may be imposed in the Crown Court; many of the offences carry up to £20,000 fines upon conviction in a magistrates' court. The 1974 Act is broad enough to enable managers to be personally convicted if they are the persons who are responsible for their workplace being unhealthy or unsafe.

The general duties

Duty to employees

Section 2 of the 1974 Act imposes duties on employers for the protection of their employees. While the law report in the *Austin Rover* case does not say so, there is little doubt that the employer of the dead man could have been convicted for failing to honour the employer's general duty 'to ensure so far as is reasonably practicable, the health, safety and welfare at work of all his employees'. Section 2(2) spells out aspects of this general duty stating, for example, that it includes 'the provision and maintenance of plant and systems of work' and, very importantly, 'the provision of such information, instruction, training and supervision as is necessary to ensure, so far as is reasonably practicable, the health and safety at work of his employees'.

Safety policy and risk assessment

Employers are required (unless their organization is so small as to be exempt) to have a safety policy, stating their commitment to safety, and their organization's arrangements for putting the policy into practice; this policy must be brought to the notice of all employees. Since 1 January 1993 employers are also required to carry out a risk assessment, record the findings and set down a response.

Safety representatives

If the employers recognize a trade union and that union has appointed safety representatives, the employers should consult with these representatives about safety arrangements, and in the *Austin Rover* case safety representatives may well have wished to inspect the scene of the accident.

'Right to know'

Whether there are safety representatives or not, the inspector would have been under a duty to give the employees at the *Austin Rover* premises factual information about the premises (in so far as their health, safety and welfare might be affected by them) and of any action he proposed to take.

Employer's duty to third parties

The situation which led to the fatal accident in the *Austin Rover* case involved a contract between two organizations: *Austin Rover* and the deceased's employer. Since 1974 the law has attached great importance to organizations setting up safe systems when arrangements are made for two or more workforces to operate in close proximity. A general duty in s.3(1) of the 1974 Act provides for situations such as this; it is at first sight rather surprising that the inspector did not use it when prosecuting *Austin Rover*. It requires 'every employer to conduct his undertaking in such a way as to ensure, so far as is reasonably practicable, that persons not in his employment who may be affected thereby are not thereby exposed to risks to their health or safety'. Since 1 January 1993 the law expressly requires co-operation between employers sharing a workplace.[6]

Analysis of the *Austin Rover* case

The inspector's argument was that the accident would not have happened if *Austin Rover* had sealed off the supply of thinners so that the visiting workers could not use them. He said that it was not sufficient that Austin Rover had relied on a contractual stipulation while leaving the thinners readily available. He argued that they were in breach of the duty placed upon them as controllers of premises by s.4 of the 1974 Act.

The inspector might possibly have argued that for *Austin Rover* to leave the supply available to 'tempt' the workers was an unsatisfactory way of conducting their organization, and therefore contrary to the general duty in s.3. In one case cleaning contractors, who left faulty electrical equipment at a client's premises, where it was used by, and caused injury to, one of the client's employees, were found guilty of a breach of their duty under s.3, although they were not present at, or working on, the site at the time of the accident.[7]

The facts of the *Austin Rover* case may also be compared with those of a case where *Swan Hunter* were prosecuted following a fatal accident at their shipyard. Employees of sub-sub-contractors of *Swan Hunter* had gone on to a ship to do some welding. The visiting workers were unaware that there was a leaking oxygen cylinder and so welding resulted in a flash fire in which a number of workers died. Both *Swan Hunter* and the welders' employers were convicted of offences under the 1974 Act. *Swan Hunter* appealed against conviction arguing that they had discharged their obligations under s.2 because they had a 'blue book', which they had given to their own employees, explaining how to carry out welding operations safely. In the view of the appeal court they ought, as head contractors, to have given the blue book to the visitors; both their duty to their own employees (s.2) and their duty to the visiting workers (s.3) required this, for without such guidance the visitors' conduct might endanger both themselves and *Swan Hunter's* own workforce.[8]

While *Austin Rover*, like *Swan Hunter*, had brought contractors' employees on to their site, the facts of the *Austin Rover* case differ from the *Swan Hunter* case in that *Austin Rover's* employees were not present at the time when the contract work was carried out, and so it would be difficult to argue that *Austin Rover* were in breach of their duty to their own employees. Had they been at fault in not disconnecting the supply of thinners they might arguably have been liable under s.3(1).

Duty of controllers of premises

The provision of the 1974 Act which was under consideration by their Lordships in the *Austin Rover* case was s.4, which imposes duties upon controllers of premises. Section 4(1) imposes duties on persons in relation to those who

(a) are not their employees; but
(b) use non-domestic premises made available to them as a place of work or as a place where they may use plant and or substances provided for their use there.

Section 4(2) imposes on each person who has, 'to any extent, control of premises to which the section applies'. The duty is 'to take such measures as it is reasonable for a person in his position to take to ensure, so far as is reasonably practicable, . . . ' that the premises are safe for the persons using them.

The Law Lords found that *Austin Rover* had made their premises available for use by the contractor's workmen, the organization was a person who had some control over the premises, and it did have a duty to take measures to ensure that the premises were safe for the visiting workmen. The accident showed that the premises had been unsafe. The onus then lay on the defendant to show that, weighing the risk to health against the means, including cost, of eliminating the risks, it was not reasonably practicable for the defendant to have taken measures to make them safe. In their Lordships' view if the premises were not a reasonably foreseeable cause of danger to persons using them in a manner or in circumstances which might reasonably be expected to occur, it was not reasonable to require any further measures to be taken to guard against unknown and unexpected events which might imperil the users' safety. Their Lordships did not think it was reasonable for *Austin Rover* to take measures to make the spray painting booth and sump safe (as by disconnecting the supply of thinners) against the unanticipated misuse of them by the contractor's employees, therefore they concluded that the magistrates had been wrong to convict *Austin Rover*.

'Reasonably practicable'

This analysis illustrates the significance of the words 'reasonably practicable' which are used on many occasions in the 1974 Act to qualify what would otherwise be strict (some might say absolute) duties. Once the prosecution has established that there was a risk then, under the 1974 Act, the burden shifts to the defendant to prove that it was not reasonably practicable to remove that risk. What is reasonably practicable must depend on the facts of the particular situation, but it is generally agreed that the criterion is that stated by Lord Justice Asquith:

'Reasonably practicable' is a narrower term than 'physically possible', and implies that a computation must be made in which the quantum of risk is placed in one scale and the sacrifice involved in the measures necessary for averting the risk (whether in money, time or trouble) is placed in the other . . .[9]

Determining what it is reasonably practicable to achieve at any workplace is a technical matter which those who are managing that workplace are in the best position to decide, either themselves or by engaging the services of competent consultants.

Employees' duties

It is worth considering whether the workmen involved at the time of the accident were guiltless. The 1974 Act imposes a general duty on every employee while at work:

(a) to take responsible care for the health and safety of himself and of other persons who may be affected by his acts or omissions at work; and

(b) as regards any duty or requirement imposed on his employer or any other person by or under any of the relevant statutory provisions, to co-operate with him so far as is necessary to enable that duty or requirement to be performed or complied with.

It is possible that both the workman who was in the paint booth and the man who was killed while in the sump might have been in breach of this duty. However managers would do well to remember that the law is reluctant to impose responsibilities for achieving safe systems on individual workers. If employees are conducting themselves without proper regard to safety, questions will almost certainly be raised as to why their employer is permitting them to do this. Unsafe conduct by employees acting contrary to instructions from their employer may well be misconduct which should set in motion disciplinary proceedings leading, in the last instance, to dismissal.

THE CIVIL LAW: ACCIDENT COMPENSATION

Introduction

It is not known whether any claim was made for damages for compensation for this fatal accident. Civil claims are often settled out of court, through insurance companies, and even if there is litigation the case is not generally reported unless it involves a point of law.

In order to win a claim for compensation for personal injury the plaintiff must prove either that the defendant has committed the tort of negligence, or else prove that the defendant is liable to compensate the plaintiff for breach of statutory duty. An employer may also be vicariously liable if the actual wrongdoer was their employee acting in the course of employment. If, as here, the victim is dead the claim may be brought by a dependant or by a personal representative. Employers' liability has a long history, but today there is little distinction between it and the general law relating to compensation for personal injuries.

The tort of negligence

In order to succeed in the tort of negligence the plaintiff must prove that the defendant owed the plaintiff a duty of care, that the defendant broke that duty by negligent conduct, and that the defendant's breach of duty caused the damage which the plaintiff claims to have suffered.

Duty

On the facts of the case there is little doubt that both *Austin Rover* and the deceased's own employer were the victim's 'neighbours' and so owed him a duty of care; so also did any other workers engaged on the work with him. 'Neighbours' according to a famous pronouncement by Lord Atkin are:

> persons who are so closely and directly affected by my act that I ought reasonably to have them in contemplation as being so affected when I am directing my mind to the acts or omissions which are called in question.[10]

Breach

The question is whether the conduct of any of these persons has been negligent so as to put them in breach of duty. The traditional criterion of negligent conduct is to be found in the words of another judge, namely Alderson B:

> Negligence is the omission to do something which a reasonable man, guided upon those considerations which ordinarily regulate the conduct of human affairs, would do, or doing something which a prudent and reasonable man would not do.[11]

The decision as to whether or not the defendant's conduct has been negligent depends on the judge's interpretation of the evidence. Where the defendant is a business organization judges expect a very high standard of care, particularly if the activity being undertaken is a dangerous one.[12] There is a great deal of case law illustrating the aspects of the employers' duty to provide a safe system of work for their employees.[13] This duty includes providing the employee with instruction and supervision to ensure that he knows how to work safely and does in fact work in this way.[14]

The breach caused the damage

The victim must also satisfy the judge that the damage for which the claim is made was caused by the conduct of the defendant.

Litigation strategy

The most likely course of action on the facts of the case would be to sue the deceased's employers. This strategy is specially attractive because, if they are in compliance with the law, they will have insurance cover in respect of their liability to employees for accidents arising out of and in the course of employment, as required by the Employers' Liability (Compulsory Insurance) Act 1969. It must be stressed, however, that the burden of proving the employers' liability rests with the plaintiff and the defendant will not be liable if no negligence can be established, or if the court takes the view that the victim has voluntarily assumed the risk of injury.

Significant factors

The view of a court considering the *Austin Rover* case would almost certainly depend on what instruction and training the deceased had been given for the particular task and whether he was a skilled workman who ought to have been trusted to work without supervision.

Contributory negligence

It would appear likely that any award of damages would be reduced because the court regarded the deceased to have been at fault himself to some extent. Where the defence of contributory negligence succeeds the damages are reduced according to the percentage of blame the court attributes to the victim.

Negligent fellow workers

The facts suggest that the victim's fellow workers may have been negligent in working in the booth with him, but suing them would hardly be worth-while as it is unlikely that they would have the money with which to pay compensation. However, if the plaintiff could establish the wrongdoing of these workers, and that it was committed in the course of their employment, then the rules of vicarious liability would require their employer to pay compensation to the victim, even though the employer were personally without fault. The defence of contributory negligence could again be pleaded by the employer.

Civil action for breach of statutory duty

Principles of liability

A plaintiff is sometimes able to succeed in a civil action for damages by establishing that the defendant was in breach of a statutory duty. In the past judges have been prepared to interpret the intention of Parliament in such a way as to allow plaintiffs to rely, in the civil courts, on statutory provisions which impose duties whose primary sanction is criminal. In more recent years Parliament has stated, when creating the duty, whether civil actions will lie in addition to criminal ones.

In order to succeed in such a case, the plaintiff has to establish that the statute imposed the duty on the defendant for the protection of persons like the plaintiff; that the defendant has broken the duty and that the breach has caused the plaintiff's injury. If the statutory duty is a strict one then the defendant will be civilly liable without proof of negligence. Actions for breach of statutory duty usually lie, if at all, in respect to duties owed by employers to their employees.

Liability under the 1974 Act

The Health and Safety at Work Act 1974 states that no civil actions may be brought in relation to the general duties created by the Act. On the other hand it preserved the rights which judges had granted under earlier statutes, such as the Factories Act 1961, and also creates a presumption that civil actions may be brought for damages related to breach of regulations made under the 1974 Act.

Application to this case

It seems unlikely that there is a statutory provision which could be invoked given the facts of this case.

The Fatal Accidents Act 1976

Where the victim has died before the case is brought to court, it may be possible for litigation to proceed through the deceased's personal representative claiming a debt owed to the estate of the deceased, or, in personal injury cases, on behalf of a dependant of the deceased under the Fatal Accidents Act 1976. As death was apparently immediate in this case, the only claim would seem to be under the Fatal Accidents Act 1976. In order to attach liability, it must be shown that the defendant would have been liable to the deceased had he lived, that the claimant was in a recognized relationship with the deceased (primarily the statute aims to assist spouses and children, but persons in other relationships, such as parents, may be entitled) and that the claimant was dependent on the deceased as a 'breadwinner'. If the claim is established, the court will make an award calculated to compensate the dependant(s) for loss of the benefit they would have received from the deceased's income, for what the court estimates to be the likely remainder of the working life of a person of the age, and in the employment circumstances of, the deceased, at the time of the accident. A small bereavement award may also be claimed by the spouse or, in the case of a minor, the parents, of the deceased.

STRATEGIES FOR MANAGERS

The Health and Safety Executive have published a valuable booklet *Five Steps to Successful Health and Safety Management* to provide special help for directors and managers. In it they identify the five steps as:

1 **Set your policy**: a clear written policy specifying who is responsible and the arrangements for identifying hazards, assessing risks and controlling them.
2 **Organize your staff**: develop a health and safety culture. There are 'four Cs' in a positive health and safety culture: competence; control; co-operation; communication.
3 **Plan and set standards**: includes systems for dealing with risks and training and supervision of people.
4 **Measure your performance**: active (before things go wrong) and reactive (after things have gone wrong), monitoring the implementation of standards.
5 **Learn from experience**: audit and review.

The HSE's final word is 'You get the level of health and safety that you demonstrate you want. Health and safety is no accident: it has to be managed'.

KEY LEARNING POINTS

- **An accident at work may lead to both prosecution in the criminal courts, and to a compensation claim which may be pursued in the civil courts if an out of court settlement is not reached.**
- **The relevant criminal law is largely contained in the Health and Safety at Work Act 1974 and regulations made under it to implement EC Directives.**
- **The Act is a framework Act which grants powers to inspectors to enter workplaces.**
- **An inspector may issue an improvement or prohibition notice or even prosecute if a workplace appears to be unhealthy or unsafe, whether or not anyone has been injured.**
- **The Act is so comprehensive that it is hard to envisage any unsafe situation which would not be unlawful.**
- **The responsibility lies with management to assess workplaces, identify the hazards there and remove or control them at least to such extent as is reasonably practicable.**

EXERCISES

1   Does your organization have a safety policy? Are you familiar with its provisions?

2   Has your organization carried out, and responded to the findings of, a risk assessment?

3   When your organization engages contractors to work on site (or the employees of other workers are to work on another site where your own employees are working), are arrangements made, by contract or otherwise, to ensure that the various organizations work together safely?

4   Are the employees of another employer ever given copies of your organization's safety policy, or of arrangements made for dealing with specific hazards?

5   Does your organization recognize safety representatives? Is there a safety committee at your workplace?

6   Does your organization have the insurance cover required by the Employers' Liability (Compulsory Insurance) Act 1969? Does it have other insurance cover, e.g. for vehicles (to ensure the requirements of the Road Traffic Acts are met) or for public liability?

7   Has an HSE inspector ever visited your workplace? If so, has he given information to persons who work there?

NOTES: CASE REFERENCES ETC

1 *Mailer* v *Austin Rover Group plc* [1989] 2 All ER 1087; [1989] 3 WLR 520.
2 Health and Safety at Work Act 1974, s.2.
3 Since 1 January 1993 the Provision and Use of Work Equipment Regulations 1992, SI 1992 No. 2932, reg. 5, would seem to be relevant to the unsuitable 'safety' lamp employed.
4 Manual Handling Operations Regulations 1992, SI 1992 No. 2793; Health and Safety (Display Screen Equipment) Regulations 1992, SI 1992 No. 2792; Provision and Use of Work Equipment Regulations 1992, SI 1992 No. 2932; Personal Protective Equipment at Work Regulations 1992, SI 1992 No. 2966; Workplace (Health, Safety and Welfare) Regulations 1992, SI 1992 No. 3004.
5 *West Bromwich Building Society Ltd* v *Townsend* [1983] ICR 257.
6 Management of Health and Safety at Work Regulations 1992, SI 1992 No. 2051.
7 *R* v *Mara* [1987] ICR 165; [1987] IRLR 154.
8 *R* v *Swan Hunter Shipbuilders Ltd* [1982] 1 All ER 264; [1981] ICR 831.
9 *Edwards* v *National Coal Board* [1949] 1 KB 704; [1949] 1 All ER 743.
10 *Donoghue* v *Stevenson* [1932] AC 562 at p. 580; [1932] All ER Rep 1.
11 *Blyth* v *Birmingham Waterworks Co.* (1856) 11 Ex 781; 156 ER 1047.
12 *Read* v *Lyons* [1947] AC 156; [1946] 2 All ER 471.
13 E.g. *Wilsons and Clyde Coal Co.* v *English* [1938] AC 57; [1937] 3 All ER 628.
14 *Boyle* v *Kodak* [1969] 2 All ER 439; [1969] 1 WLR 661.

JOURNALS

Health and Safety Information Bulletin (Industrial Relations Service).
Health and Safety Commission Newsletter (This is available from the Health and Safety Executive or Dillons Bookstores.)

FURTHER READING

Barrett, B. and Howells, R. (1995) *Health and Safety Law*, London: Pitman.
(1992) *Five Steps to Successful Health and Safety Management*, HSE. (This and other free leaflets are available from the HSE Information Centre.)
Successful Health and Safety Management, HSE (HMSO).
Essentials of Health and Safety at Work, HSE (HMSO).

USEFUL ADDRESSES

HSE Books
Subscriptions Department
PO Box 1999
Sudbury
Suffolk CO10 6FS   Tel. no. 01787 881 165

HSE Information Centre
Broad Lane
Sheffield S3 7HQ
Free leaflet line   Tel. no. 01742 892346

Health and Safety Executive
St Hugh's House
Stanley Precinct
Bootle
Merseyside L20 3QY   Tel. no. 0151 951 4450

Chapter 5

The enterprise and its environment
Planning and pollution controls

Penny Childs and Stephen Homewood

The law is not just concerned with ensuring that an enterprise's activities comply with health and safety requirements which are aimed at protecting the workforce. The law is also concerned with regulating those activities which might be detrimental to the wider community. Such regulation has in the past been mainly enforced through planning controls. However, increased concern about environmental protection has resulted in the introduction of complex statutory controls aimed at reducing pollution. This chapter looks at key aspects of these controls, in particular:

- planning control
- pollution control
- waste management and control
- noise control and similar problems.

Case study: part 1

Setting up or expanding a business

SHPC Ltd wish to expand their plant and processes. The proposal requires a new factory and access to the site, close to existing housing. Building works and transportation will create a great deal of noise. Waste will be produced by the processes and will need to be stored, treated and disposed of. The processes themselves involve the use of a number of substances which will be discharged into the air, water and onto land.

Box 5.1 SHPC Ltd

Many of the legal provisions apply not only to setting up a new process but also to the upgrading of existing processes.

INTRODUCTION

Issues which *SHPC Ltd* would have to consider include:

- Development of the site which may necessitate planning permission and conditions which may be imposed with respect to the noise, waste, etc.
- Expansion of the processes which may be subject to Integrated Pollution Control (IPC) and require authorization from Her Majesty's Inspectorate of Pollution (HMIP) before beginning the process. Alternatively, they may be governed by Air Pollution Control (APC) and require authorization from the relevant local authority.
- Discharge of certain substances into air which may be subject to IPC. Discharge of substances into water may require a consent from the National Rivers Authority (NRA). Discharges of effluent into sewers may require a trade effluent consent from the local sewerage undertakers.
- Production, storage, treatment and disposal of waste which may necessitate obtaining a Waste Management Licence (WML) or a Waste Disposal Licence (WDL) and registration of carriers and/or consignment notices. It also means that *SHPC Ltd* will be subject to the duty of care (s. 34 of the Environmental Protection Act (EPA) 1990) in respect of waste management.
- The noise level may give rise to common law liability and statutory nuisance. It is advisable to seek local authority consent in advance.

PLANNING CONTROL

Planning authorities (county councils or district councils) are required to draw up development plans for their areas. County councils draw up the overall strategy called structure plans; whilst district councils deal with the details through local plans. There is a third kind of plan known as a unified development plan for the Metropolitan areas. In drawing up plans, authorities are required to have regard to the environmental implications of their plans. These plans are important as planning permission must normally be granted in accordance with the development plan.

When is planning permission needed?

Planning permission is needed 'for any development of land'. Development includes building, engineering or other operations in, on, over or under land or making a material change (i.e. a substantial alteration or much more intensive use) to the land or to the use of buildings. However, there are certain exemptions from the need for planning permission:

- those developments covered by the General Development Order 1988 where permission is given automatically, e.g. agriculture, small scale extensions or alterations to industrial premises, public service

- those which count as a change of use within the same class under one of the sixteen classes of the Use Classes Order 1987
- there may be a long-standing existing use of the land which may not require permission
- other exemptions relate to the special (and more liberal) planning regimes in areas such as urban development areas, enterprise zones and (more rarely) simplified planning zones.

On the other hand, developments in certain areas such as national parks, conservation areas and sites of special scientific interest are much less likely to be allowed.

It may thus be unclear as to whether permission is actually needed. In addition to the common practice of consulting the local planning officer, there are two other alternatives:

- an application for outline planning permission, i.e. an application to the local planning authority to see whether they will grant permission in principle
- a new procedure introduced under the Planning and Compensation Act (P and CA) 1991 that allows the applicant to ask the planning authority whether an existing or proposed development requires permission, and if it does not, to issue a certificate of lawfulness which is binding on the authority

A final option, rather than applying for planning permission, is to try to enter into a voluntary planning obligation with the planning authority. This is a legally binding agreement and may be enforced by either party. It may also be able to achieve what both parties wish and avoid the necessity of the planning permission procedure.

Application for planning permission

If it is clear that the company has to apply for planning permission, the procedure is laid down by regulations. The application is made to the local planning authority (district or borough council), together with the fees, a plan and drawings, and notification must be made to the owner (if the owner is not the applicant). Some further publicity to the public is required.

The planning authority has the discretion to decide the application but must exercise that discretion in accordance with the development plan and in accordance with government guidance. This can be found in Department of Environment circulars and in planning policy guidance notes, both of which are publicly available. It is essential to consider such guidance when making an application.

The authority is obliged to consult widely with such bodies as the Waste Regulatory Authority (WRA), the local sewerage undertaker and the NRA, although it is not obliged to consult HMIP (but usually does). It will consider also the particular facts of the application, any local objections and other material issues, such as transport and employment needs, and at this stage it may have to consider an Environmental Impact Assessment (EIA) or whether one is needed (see p. 111).

The decision

The planning authority may take one of four courses of action.

Grant permission without conditions

This decision may only be challenged by judicial review, normally, of course, by those who oppose the development.

Grant permission with conditions

This is the norm and whilst the authority can decide which conditions are appropriate for the development, it must again have regard to government guidance which, amongst other things, requires that the conditions must be relevant, clear, precise and reasonable. Conditions might include, for example, limits as to noise, the aftercare of waste sites, time limits of work, etc. It is here that problems occur in relation to the overlap in control which could arise between the planning conditions and conditions imposed by other regulatory bodies such as the WRA and the NRA. Whilst this issue is not entirely clear, government guidance suggests that planning authorities should not duplicate conditions where controls are better left to the relevant environmental regulatory agency.

The imposition of conditions may be challenged by judicial review, for example on the basis that they are ultra vires (beyond the powers) of the planning authority, but it is far more likely that an applicant would use the statutory right of appeal to the Secretary of State under the Town and Country Planning Act (T and CPA) 1990. This is a complete rehearing of the issues, normally by an inspector on the basis of written documentation, but there may be a public inquiry. There is a further statutory right of appeal from the Secretary of State's decision to the High Court on similar grounds to a judicial review. Any 'aggrieved person' and not just the applicant, may appeal.

Refuse planning permission within eight weeks

Refusal may be challenged on the same basis as conditions.

Not make a decision within the time limit of eight weeks

An appeal may then be made.

Complaints may also be made to the Local Government Ombudsman against the granting or refusal of permission.

Enforcement

Assuming planning permission has been obtained (with or without conditions), the planning authority has a wide range of powers relating to supervision and enforcement of the permission. However, it is interesting to note that, first, there are some specific exemptions from enforcement action, e.g. where there is a certificate of established use or lawfulness (see p. 108), or where it is ten years since the breach and no action has been taken. Second, a development or use of land without permission is not by itself an offence. This is because the system of control is based on a two stage procedure whereby various notices are served by the authority and it is failure to comply with these notices that creates criminal liability.

The methods of enforcement which can be used by the authority include the following.

Enforcement notice

The authority may issue a notice whenever it thinks there is some breach of planning control. Planning authorities are the only ones who may do so, and they have a very wide discretion, subject once again to government guidance. The notice will require the owner (or occupier) of the property to take steps to remedy the alleged breach and to do so within a specified time. Twenty eight days' minimum notice must be given and failure to comply with the notice is an offence. Penalties will be up to £20,000 in the magistrates' courts, and unlimited fines in the Crown Court. In addition, if the required steps are not taken, or not taken in time, the authority can enter the property, do the necessary work itself, and then charge reasonable expenses to the owner or occupier.

The notice is subject to challenge by judicial review. It is also possible for the authority to vary or revoke the notice. More importantly, there is a right of appeal to the Secretary of State, provided it is made before the notice comes into effect. The T and CPA 1990 lays down the grounds of appeal, e.g. that the time limits are too short, or that the matters complained of are not a breach, or that planning permission ought to be granted.

The Minister decides the appeal and may do a number of things including granting permission, dismissing the conditions or adding new ones. It is important to note that during the appeal the notice is suspended and has no effect. This has sometimes led to abuse, with appeals being made to delay enforcement.

Stop notices

As enforcement notices may take a considerable time, an authority may deal with this by serving a stop notice, which has the effect of prohibiting the activity within a shorter time once the notice has come into effect. It is an offence to continue in breach of the notice and there is no appeal as of right. The problem with such notices is that the authority may have to pay compensation if the notice is withdrawn (a disincentive to the authority) and stop notices require an enforcement notice to be in force at the same time. They are, therefore, little used.

Planning contravention notice

This is a new power given under the P and CA 1991 and is a discretionary procedure for authorities to get information about activities on land where they suspect a breach of planning control. Failure to comply within twenty one days is a summary offence.

Breach of condition notice

This is another new discretionary power allowing an authority to take action against a breach of a planning condition. This is done by serving a notice requiring it to be complied with within not less than twenty eight days. There is no appeal and failure to comply is a summary offence.

Injunctions

Whilst local authorities have a general power to get these court orders where necessary to protect or promote the interests of the local community, authorities also have the specific power to seek an injunction against an actual or proposed breach of planning control. These orders are discretionary, but if granted, failure to comply is contempt of court with possibilities of unlimited fines and/or imprisonment. They are thus potentially very useful to an authority.

Environmental impact assessment

United Kingdom regulations passed in 1988 to implement the 1985 Environmental Assessment Directive[1] require certain types of development to be subject to environmental impact assessment and for it to be made available to the authority when considering a planning application.

Such an assessment will be necessary when any one of a list of major developments is planned, e.g. oil refineries, power stations or landfill of special waste. However, the authority must also decide whether one is necessary where it judges that any project is likely to give rise to significant environmental effects. An appeal against a decision to require an environmental impact assessment can be made to the Secretary of State. Guidance is available from Department of Environment circulars. The assessment is a statement drawing together the evidence on the anticipated effects of the proposal and ways of reducing its effects. If it is required, it is usual to submit it at the same time as the application.

POLLUTION CONTROL

The process and its substances

SHPC Ltd's plans to expand their process and discharge substances into the environment will be subject to some kind of regulatory control and may require consent before implementation. Different bodies may have to be approached according to the nature of the process, the substance to be discharged, and medium into which it is discharged. Figure 5.1 is intended to give an outline of the steps to be taken when considering whom to approach for authorization and should be used with the following text. The first step is to decide whether or not the activity is subject to Integrated Pollution Control (IPC). This involves considering whether or not the process is prescribed and whether it involves the discharge of a substance which is prescribed.

Prescribed processes

A prescribed process is one considered sufficiently harmful to the environment to require special permission before it can go ahead. For example, processes undertaken by the chemical and metal industries are likely to be prescribed. The EPA 1990 gives power to the Secretary of State to list, in regulations, all those processes which are prescribed.

Schedule 1 of the current regulations[2] divides industries into six sectors (i.e.: energy; waste disposal; chemical; mineral; metal; and others). Certain processes are identified within each sector (for example, halogen processes in the chemical industry and incinerating processes in the waste disposal industry) and are divided into two groups, namely Part A and Part B.

If the process falls within Part A, it is normally subject to IPC under the EPA 1990. It will not be subject to IPC if a prescribed substance (see p. 114) will not be released or will cause no harm, but it may still be subject to controls other than IPC (see p. 115). If it falls within Part B it may not be subject to IPC (this depends on the substances used; see p. 114) but may be

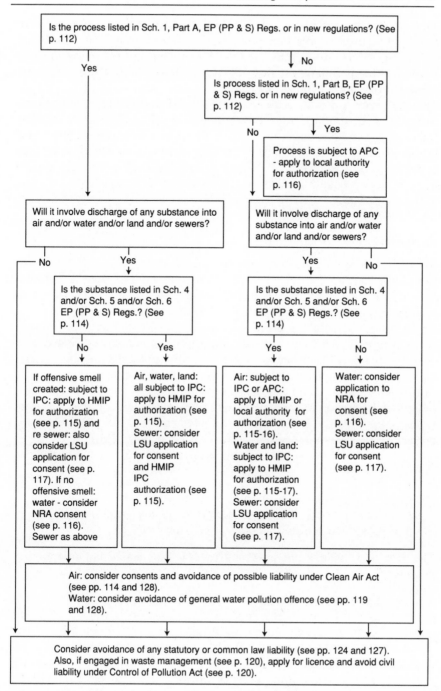

Figure 5.1 Processes and discharges: implications

subject to other regulatory controls, in particular local authority Air Pollution Control (APC) (see p. 116). If it falls within both Part A and Part B it is subject to IPC. IPC covers 5,000 or so plants which are likely to cause greater pollution and are therefore subject to the most stringent controls covering all forms of releases.

If the process is subject to IPC, *SHPC Ltd* must obtain authorization from HMIP before beginning the process. Failure to do so may result in criminal prosecution under s. 23(1) of the EPA 1990 (see p. 119). New processes, substantial variations of existing processes and large combustion plants have been subject to IPC since 1 April 1991. Other processes will become subject to authorization in phased stages between 1 April 1991 and 31 January 1996.

Prescribed substances

Both prescribed and non-prescribed processes may involve the use of substances that have been prescribed. Thus, *SHPC Ltd* need to consider whether or not the substances to be discharged are prescribed. A list of prescribed substances is given in Schedules 4, 5 and 6 of the 1991 Regulations.[3] Schedule 4 prescribes certain substances released into air (for example, sulphur and nitrogen oxides and compounds). Schedule 5 covers releases of substances into water (for example, mercury, polychlorinated biphenyl (PCBs) and dichlorodiphenyltrichloroethane (DDT) isomers). Schedule 6 covers substances released to land (for example, organic solvents, oxidising agents and pesticides). If a substance is prescribed, the activity is subject to IPC (whether or not the process is prescribed) and again an authorization is needed from HMIP.

In considering these issues, it is therefore possible to reach a number of positions:

1 a prescribed process (Part A) plus prescribed substance(s)
2 a prescribed process (Part B) plus prescribed substance(s)
3 a non-prescribed process plus prescribed substance(s)

These three situations are governed by IPC and HMIP authorization is necessary.

4 a prescribed process (Part B), no prescribed substance(s). This is not covered by IPC but is governed by Air Pollution Control (APC) and authorization must be obtained from the relevant local authority. If the substances involved may be discharged into water, it may also be necessary to obtain a consent from the National Rivers Authority (NRA) and a Waste Management Licence. If trade effluent will be discharged to sewers, it is also necessary to obtain a consent from the local sewerage undertaker.

5 a prescribed process under Part A which releases no prescribed substances (or such trivial amounts as not likely to cause any harm) will not be governed by IPC. However, consents may well be needed from the NRA and from the local sewerage undertaker, and a Waste Management Licence may be necessary.

6 a non-prescribed process and no prescribed substance(s). Consents may still be required from the NRA, local sewerage undertakers and the Waste Regulatory Authority.

Irrespective of these categories, if the process emits grit, dust or fumes from furnaces, under the Clean Air Act 1993 the local authority should be notified, since an authorization may be needed before carrying out the process. Additionally applications should be made for chimney height approval under the Clean Air Act 1993. It is an offence to operate without such an authorization or approval.

In the case of *SHPC Ltd*, let us assume that there is a list A prescribed process, involving a prescribed substance and a list B prescribed process, involving no prescribed substances. In both instances the substances will be discharged into air, water and onto land. What applications for authorizations and consents must be made by *SHPC Ltd*?

Applications for authorizations/consents

Integrated Pollution Control (IPC): application to Her Majesty's Inspectorate of Pollution (HMIP)

SHPC Ltd must make an application to the regional office of HMIP covering the location of the process. In applying *SHPC Ltd* must amongst other things, give details of: the location and description of the process; its components, purpose, category and the nature of any releases (and the medium into which discharges will occur); and assess its local, regional and global environmental implications. Technical data on releases is vital and *SHPC Ltd* must also give details of techniques to be employed to prevent/minimize releases (this means providing information about BATNEEC; see p. 117). Reference to the qualifications of staff, training and management is required and it is probably necessary to refer to British Standards Institution procedures or Total Quality Management systems. It is also necessary to advertise the application for authorization. Moreover, since details of all IPC processes are kept by HMIP and the relevant local authority in public registers, *SHPC Ltd* could apply for exclusion from the register wherever it feels that the information in question is commercially confidential or a matter of national security. However, such an application is unlikely to be granted.

Where IPC applies, no additional applications need to be made to the local authority (air pollution) or NRA (water pollution). However, discharges of trade effluent still require a local sewerage undertaker (LSU) consent in addition to HMIP authorization, and a waste management licence may be needed in respect of disposal, treatment or keeping of waste (see p. 122).

Air Pollution Control (APC): applications to local authority

For any prescribed process listed in Part B (or a substance prescribed in Sch. 4) that is not subject to IPC, application must be made to the relevant local authority covering the location of the process. The application covers authorization related to air pollution only. For other forms of pollution, other consents may be necessary. Applications in respect of new processes should be made during the design period. The information required is similar to that in HMIP applications: details are available in regulations. Again, the most important issues are to provide information about pollution abatement techniques (with evidence of BATNEEC (see p. 117)) and about arrangements for monitoring air emissions and for assessing the impact on the atmosphere. Provisions relating to advertisement, public registers and confidentiality are similar to those for IPC.

Water discharges: applications to National Rivers Authority (NRA)

Any of *SHPC Ltd*'s processes or substances which are not subject to IPC but which may give rise to discharges to the aquatic environment, may require NRA consent. These are needed for any discharge of trade effluent or sewerage effluent into controlled waters. It is also advisable to obtain a consent for any discharge of poisonous, noxious or polluting matter or any solid waste into controlled waters, since such a consent may be a defence to the general water pollution offence. Controlled waters are defined in s. 104 of the Water Resources Act 1991 and include inland and underground waters and in certain circumstances territorial and coastal waters. Discharges of trade or sewer effluent by pipe into the sea beyond controlled waters, and certain other selective discharges into water, also require consents. Consents are required for each separate discharge and the information to be supplied should include such matters as the nature of the discharge, quality and rate of flow.

The procedures involving NRA consents are more public than those for IPC and APC, with more extensive advertising and with more information available in the public register. As with IPC and APC, it is possible to apply for an exemption from the register where inclusion would prejudice a trade secret or be contrary to the public interest.

Discharges to sewers: applications to local sewerage undertaker

Whether or not the process is subject to IPC, an application for a trade effluent consent will be necessary whenever any effluent (other than surface water) from trade premises is to be discharged into a sewer. A trade effluent notice must be served on the relevant local sewerage undertaker, who, after probably imposing certain conditions, may grant a consent (see p. 118).

Grant of authorizations/consents and conditions

Her Majesty's Inspectorate of Pollution Integrated Pollution Control authorizations

When granting an authorization, HMIP may impose specific conditions including things such as monitoring, pollution abatement, analysis and quality assurance plans. Quite apart from specific conditions, it is implied, by law, that the authorization is subject to using Best Available Techniques Not Entailing Excessive Cost (BATNEEC) to control pollution. Even existing processes will have to meet BATNEEC within four years of grant of authority and all authorizations are reviewed four years after grant. BATNEEC is not defined because it will depend on the different circumstances of each application. However, guidance is available from HMIP which has a large discretion in interpreting the conditions.

SHPC Ltd will have to show that the system is the most effective available in controlling pollution in the light of all techniques in existence (even if these techniques are not being used). This includes not just technology but also training of staff, design of the plant etc.

The best available techniques need to be balanced against the cost involved. What is excessive is considered in the light of the nature of the industry and the desired level of environmental protection. Where the situation is one of a prescribed process and prescribed substance(s), BATNEEC must be used to prevent the release of the substance or, if that is not practicable, to reduce the release to a minimum and render it harmless. Where the situation is one of a prescribed process but non-prescribed substances, the requirement is simply to use BATNEEC to render the release harmless. Existing processes which have acquired NRA or trade effluent consents may now be subject to IPC and BATNEEC may create more stringent conditions than those previously laid down. The rise in standards must be considered because existing processes have to be upgraded as soon as possible (generally within four years of the date of the previous grant of consent and in any event before the year 2001).

Finally, where the discharge may affect more than one environmental medium, HMIP will also take into account the Best Practical Environmental Option (BPEO). This means that the applicant must show that, given a number of techniques available at similar cost, the one which achieves the best overall environmental result will be adopted.

Local authority Air Pollution Control authorizations

These authorizations contain specific and other conditions and the residual BATNEEC condition. BATNEEC must be used to minimize the pollution and render it harmless. Particular emission standards may be imposed and account is taken of emission limit values and air quality limit values. Guidance notes are available from the Department of Environment.

National Rivers Authority consents

NRA consents are highly individualized and the NRA can impose conditions as it sees fit. For example, conditions relating to the nature, composition and volume of discharges may be attached to such consents and numerical limits imposed. National water quality objectives and standards are taken into account, along with relevant EU standards and directives. The NRA recovers the costs of monitoring discharges and water quality from the discharger.

Local sewerage undertaker consents

These undertakers have complete discretion about grant and conditions. However, if the sewers can cope with the discharge, the applicant will normally get consent, subject to conditions specifying such things as the place and time of discharge and payment of charges.

Refusal to grant

Grant of HMIP or local authority APC applications may be refused if required information is not supplied, or the fees are not paid. Grant will be refused if the regulator feels that the applicant cannot comply with the conditions. NRA and LSU consents can be refused at the discretion of the regulator. There is a right to appeal to the Secretary of State against either IPC, APC and NRA refusals to grant, or the imposition of unreasonable conditions. Appeals from LSU decisions are made to the Director General of Water Services.

After grant

There is an annual charge for all authorizations and consents. Contravention of authorizations and consents is a criminal offence (see p. 119). If a process subject to IPC or APC runs a serious risk of imminent pollution, HMIP or the local authority can issue a prohibition notice (even if the authorization is not contravened), or can impose new conditions. If conditions are breached or a breach is imminent, an enforcement notice may be issued. Both types of notice give details of the steps to be taken and the time limit for remedying the problem. In either case it is a criminal offence not to comply.

All the regulators have a wide range of powers of entry, inspection, sampling and monitoring. They also have the power to revoke an authorization or consent and they can vary it to bring it up to date. An applicant can also apply for variation where plants are upgraded or processes change. A charge is required for substantial variation and re-advertisement is necessary. HMIP and local authority consent is also required for any transfer of authorization to another operator (for example on sale of the business). Failure to notify of transfer is an offence (see below). Transfers of NRA consents do not require NRA permission.

Possible penalties

In relation to IPC and APC, it is a criminal offence to:

- operate prescribed processes without an authorization
- contravene conditions of an authorization
- fail to inform of a transfer of authorization
- fail to comply with a prohibition/enforcement notice
- fail to comply with a requirement from an inspector or to obstruct an inspector intentionally
- fail to provide relevant information
- give false or misleading information deliberately or recklessly
- make a false entry intentionally.

Under the Water Resources Act 1991, the offences are similar to those listed above (excluding the third and fourth listed offences). The three main offences are:

- causing or knowingly permitting the discharge of trade or sewer effluent into controlled waters. This offence requires no proof of pollution, simply a discharge. The offence of causing the discharge is one of strict liability
- causing or knowingly permitting any poisonous, noxious or polluting matter or any solid waste to enter controlled waters. This offence may also not require proof of pollution and covers both deliberate and accidental (non-routine) escapes. The offence of causing the matter to enter is one of strict liability and all that needs to be shown is a causal link between the entry and the discharge.[4]

It is a defence to both offences that the discharge or entry is in compliance with a NRA consent, HMIP authorization, waste management or disposal licence, a statute or statutory order.

● breaching the conditions of a consent.

It is a defence to all three offences that the discharge was in an emergency to avoid danger to life or health and all reasonably practicable steps were taken to minimize the pollution and inform the NRA.

It is also an offence to discharge trade effluent without a consent or to breach the conditions of a consent.

Minor offences are subject to a maximum penalty of £1,000. Other offences attract maximum penalties from £2,000 to £20,000. All the offences are triable either way and therefore, if tried in the Crown Court, are subject to unlimited fines and/or imprisonment.

Generally, the company may be prosecuted for such offences, but unless it is a strict liability offence, a corporation may only be liable where a director or similar company officer had the necessary criminal intention.

Under the Environmental Protection Act (EPA) 1990, where the offence is committed by a body corporate with the consent, connivance or neglect of any director, manager or similar officer, that officer may be prosecuted and found liable as well as the company. Where the activity is due to the act or default of some other person, that person may also be prosecuted as well as the company. Moreover, if the offence is committed by an independent contractor, both that contractor and the operator of the process can be prosecuted (even where the operator was not at fault).

In addition to criminal liability, a court may order the company to take relevant remedial action and the full cost of clean-up operations may be recovered from the company.

WASTE MANAGEMENT AND CONTROL

The storage, treatment and disposal of *SHPC Ltd*'s waste raises a number of issues.

What is 'waste'?

One man's waste is another man's raw material. The judicial approach has been to look to the nature of the material when it is discarded even though it may be re-used.[5] There are three different kinds of waste: controlled waste, special waste and hazardous waste.

Controlled waste is 'household, industrial and commercial waste or any such waste, including any substance which is scrap or is effluent or unwanted surplus from a process' (s. 75 of the EPA 1990).

Special waste is 'waste which may be so dangerous or difficult to treat, keep or dispose of that special provision is required for dealing with it' (s. 62 of the EPA 1990). See also the Control of Pollution (Special Waste) Regulations 1980[6] for further details.

Both controlled and special waste were regulated under the Control of Pollution Act (COPA) 1974, but from 1 May 1994 they are governed by Part II of the EPA 1990.

Hazardous waste is dealt with by different legislation and is defined in 1992 Regulations.[7] This kind of waste will be related to certain characteristics such as whether it is explosive, toxic or carcinogenic. All hazardous waste must be identified and controlled at the storage, transport and disposal stages. The storage of such waste will normally need a consent from the local hazardous substances authority (borough or district councils), the Health and Safety Executive will need to be informed and health and safety legislation will need to be complied with.

In the case of controlled waste, it was necessary up until 1 May 1994 to obtain a waste disposal licence to cover the depositing of the waste on land. Such licences were obtained from the relevant county or district council waste disposal authority (WDA). The licence also covered using plant or equipment for the disposing of waste. It was an offence to deposit or dispose of, or knowingly permit the deposit or disposal of such waste on land without a licence. A similar licence was required for special waste. Waste disposal licences were not granted (in the absence of an existing use certificate) unless planning permission had been granted. Applications for planning permission were made to the local district planning authority.

When granting a waste disposal licence, the WDA could impose any conditions considered appropriate, including types of waste covered, duration of licence and steps needed for compliance with planning permission. Planning permission could also contain similar or more extensive conditions and therefore was obtained at the same time.

There were only two grounds on which the WDA might refuse a licence. These were to prevent water pollution (the WDA consulted with the NRA) and to prevent a danger to public health. There was a right of appeal to the Secretary of State.

The WDA could and still can issue a compliance order where the licence was or is not being observed. Failing to comply might have led or may lead to revocation of the licence. The conditions of a waste disposal licence could and can also be varied or the licence transferred or revoked at a later stage. There was and still remains a right of appeal, the right of appeal now being found in s. 43 of the EPA 1990 and in the Waste Management Licensing Regulations 1994.[8]

Should controlled waste be transported from the premises, the Control of Pollution (Amendment) Act 1989 provides that the carrier must normally be registered. Different regulations (currently under review) govern transporting special waste and provide that consignment notices must be submitted to waste disposal authorities before transportation takes place. Failing to have the relevant registration or consignment notice is an offence.

New system

From 1 May 1994, with the publication of the new waste management Regulations[9] a new system has been introduced governing controlled waste management in all its aspects, including storage, disposal, treatment, transportation, etc. One licence (a waste management licence) covers all these activities and can be obtained from a waste regulatory authority (WRA). There are four criminal offences of which managers should be aware. It is an offence:

- either to deposit, or treat, or keep, or make a disposal of controlled waste without a licence (s. 33 of the EPA 1990)
- to breach any condition of a waste management licence
- knowingly to permit or cause the occurrence of any of the above activities
- to treat, keep or dispose of controlled waste in a manner likely to cause pollution or harm to human health even though a licence has been obtained.

There are a number of defences available, including taking all reasonable precaution and exercising due diligence, or taking action in an emergency to avoid harm. The maximum summary penalty for such an offence is currently £20,000 or six months' imprisonment. On indictment the fine is unlimited and the maximum imprisonment period is two years.

It will therefore be important for *SHPC Ltd* to consider whether they need to apply for such a licence. Civil liability may also arise either under s. 73 of the EPA 1990 or at common law (see p. 124) if *SHPC Ltd* is in breach of the EPA 1990 and causes damage.

Obtaining a licence

SHPC Ltd, like any applicant, must demonstrate that they are a fit and proper person (technically, financially and without previous relevant convictions) and that planning permission is in force. A WRA may reject an application if it is necessary to prevent pollution, or harm to human health, or serious disruption of amenities in the locality. Conditions may be imposed on the grant in relation to activities and precautions. A WRA will ensure compliance with the licence and may revoke and prosecute in cases of breach. There is a right of appeal to the Secretary of State.

It is important to note that IPC authorization cannot cover the final disposal or deposit of controlled waste in or on to land, and therefore a waste management licence will be needed in addition to any IPC author-ization. However, treatment and keeping of controlled waste may be adequately covered by an IPC authorization in which case a waste management licence is not also required.

Transfer of a licence

If the company wishes to cease to operate a waste management licence, it may attempt a transfer. In cases of transfer, both parties apply to the WRA. If the WRA do not consider the transferee a fit and proper person, no transfer is allowed. If so, the company's only option is to surrender the licence (or find a suitable transferee). The WRA will only allow surrender of a licence if the premises do not present a risk of pollution or harm to human health. Thus it may be necessary to engage in clean-up activities before being allowed to surrender the licence.

New duty of care

Regulations made in 1991[10] provide a registration system for carriers of waste and s. 34 of the EPA 1990 introduces a new duty of care in relation to waste management. This will apply to any holder, importer, producer, carrier, keeper, treater or disposer of controlled waste. Such a person is under a threefold duty to take all reasonable steps to:

- prevent contravention of s. 33 (see p. 122) by any other person
- prevent the escape of waste from their control or that of any other person
- ensure that any transferee is an authorized person (for example, a waste collection authority) and that sufficient written detail is given to enable the transferee to avoid liability under s. 33 (see p. 122).

Guidance on discharge of the duty can be found in a code of practice.[11] Any breach of this duty is a criminal offence and persons damaged by the activity may then also sue in civil law. As before, this gives rise to corporate liability but individual managers may also be liable (see p. 120). A conviction may adversely affect any future applications for a licence.

NOISE AND SIMILAR OPERATIONAL PROBLEMS

The noise (and any vibration) from the building works may give rise to actions in common law or statutory nuisance. These are dealt with at p. 124. However, it is worth noting that under s. 61 of the Control of Pollution Act 1974, the company can apply to the local authority, in advance, for a consent governing the times, duration etc. of the building work. Assuming a consent was granted and the conditions were complied with, it would prevent a local authority notice being served.

Case study: part 2

A mishap

SHPC Ltd's process is up and running. It is very noisy and in order to meet production demands, the process has been run at night for the last week. The process creates waste, fumes and smoke. The waste is stored prior to removal and one evening it escapes into a nearby stream where it contaminates the water and nearby farm land. Local residents are unable to sleep because of the noise and unable to use their gardens because of the fumes, smoke and smell of the waste.

Box 5.2 SHPC Ltd continued

INTRODUCTION

SHPC Ltd now face a number of potential liabilities, both criminal and civil at common law or under statute. Liabilities may arise despite *SHPC Ltd* having previously obtained the relevant authorizations and consents. Any breach of such authorizations would give rise to liability as already indicated. Further potential liability includes:

- civil liability in tort
- criminal liability for failure to comply with a statutory nuisance abatement notice
- civil liability under the Control of Pollution Act 1974 for damage done by waste
- criminal liability under the Clean Air Act 1993
- criminal liability for water contamination.

Civil liability

SHPC Ltd may be sued by anybody who has suffered personal injury or damage to their property caused by, for example, the waste, noise or smell emanating from *SHPC Ltd*'s premises. The company's liability may also extend to any economic loss caused by the activity. The plaintiff will normally have the burden of proving their case on a balance of probabilities.

One or more of the following torts is likely to form the basis of a successful claim:

- private nuisance
- public nuisance

- trespass
- *Rylands* v *Fletcher*
- negligence.

Private nuisance

At common law individuals may sue in the tort of private nuisance. Anyone who has title to land affected and who suffers unreasonable interference with their use and enjoyment of land or rights over it may sue. Occupiers of the farm land and any local occupants affected by the noise and smell may therefore sue, as may the owners of the land adjoining the stream. The plaintiffs have to show that the company's conduct caused reasonably foreseeable damage to their land or loss of enjoyment of it. There may be tricky problems of proof involved since causation and foreseeability are not always easy to establish. Assuming, however, that the plaintiffs can show that the company contributed to the pollution, it will be no defence to plead that the company was not the sole cause. Defendants can be held liable even though a number of them have contributed to the pollution.

Plaintiffs and their land must not be abnormally sensitive to the nuisance, but assuming that the noise and smell would have affected a reasonable person and that the damage to the fields would have affected other property, an action could proceed. The final issue is whether the interference with the plaintiff's use of land is unreasonable. The tort of nuisance deals with balancing the company's activity against the plaintiff's rights to reasonable enjoyment of their property. In deciding this issue, the courts will take a number of factors into account.

Locality   In cases of loss of amenity (for example, the smell and noise), where the plant is located becomes important. What would be a reasonable interference in one area (e.g. residential) may not be unreasonable in another (e.g. industrial). In cases of physical damage (to the fields and the water pollution), the locality is not taken into account.[12]

Time   What is reasonable at one time of day may be unreasonable at another time. So, for example, whilst it may be reasonable to undertake the processing during the day, it may well be that to do so at night is an unreasonable interference and the noise is a nuisance.[13]

Duration   Nuisance requires proof of some continuity of affairs and the longer something goes on, the more likely it is that it will be accounted unreasonable. The night processing may be unreasonable even though it has only been going on for a week, although the more temporary or isolated the activity, the less likely it is that it is a nuisance. The single isolated escape of the waste will not in itself be a nuisance, although the state of affairs on *SHPC*'s land that gave rise to that escape may be.

Method If the plaintiffs show that the company adopted an unreasonable method for carrying out the process, that is prima facie evidence of nuisance. Proceeding within the terms of an authorization and using BPEO may establish a reasonable method.

Danger The more dangerous the activity or the consequences, the more likely it is that the courts will impose liability.

There are very few defences to an action[14] and so it is unlikely that *SHPC Ltd* could plead that the plant/activity is socially useful/beneficial. Nor is it a defence that the people affected moved to the area where the process already existed. In addition to disputing that the interference was unreasonable, the only possible defences are prescription, statutory authority, or act of nature or a third party. Prescription would require proof that the activity had been carried on continuously for twenty years and had been actionable for that time and that the plaintiff had done nothing about it. Assuming that the process is a new one, this defence would not be available. Statutory authority would require proof that the nuisance was caused whilst acting in pursuance of a statutory obligation or power conferred by Parliament. Whether or not this provides a defence would depend on the construction and interpretation of the statute. If the noise, toxic fumes and waste escape were caused by a third party, or an act of nature, then *SHPC Ltd* would only be liable if they knew or ought to have known of the activity and did nothing about it.[15] A third party is someone other than an employee (for whom *SHPC Ltd* would be vicariously liable) or a contractor employed to carry out the work (for whom *SHPC Ltd* would still be personally liable).

If unsuccessful in an action, *SHPC Ltd* face the prospect of damages being awarded to compensate the plaintiffs for their loss. This includes things like clean-up costs, damages for any reduction in the value of the land and loss of profits. Injunctions are also available, although they will normally be suspended to give the company time to correct matters. In some cases, injunctions may be granted to prohibit a particular aspect of the activity (e.g. in the case of the noise, an injunction may be granted to prevent the processing at night but allowing it to continue during the day).

Public nuisance

An activity may amount to both a private and a public nuisance. A public nuisance is one that 'materially affects the comfort and convenience of life of a class of Her Majesty's subjects'. It is a crime as well as a tort. Wherever the nuisance is indiscriminate in its effect (as here), it may amount to public nuisance. Actions for injunctions in respect of public nuisances are usually brought by the relevant local authority, or may be brought by the Attorney-General suing on behalf of the class in a 'relator action'. However, any member of the class suffering 'special damage' (i.e. that 'over and above' the rest of the class) may also sue individually. The remedies are the same as in private nuisance and the defences are similar.

Trespass

Any direct interference with the land of another may be a trespass. Deliberate or negligent discharges may therefore be trespasses, as long as there is a direct causal link between the act (of discharge) and the entry onto the plaintiff's land. If it is inevitable that the matter discharged will enter the plaintiff's land, a trespass may have occurred.

Rylands v *Fletcher*[16]

This is a form of strict liability, so proving that it was not *SHPC Ltd*'s fault that a discharge occurred is no defence. The tort is committed where the defendant brings onto land, for his own purposes, something likely to do mischief if it escapes. The defendant is then liable for any reasonably foreseeable consequences of such an escape. It is, however, necessary for plaintiffs to show that the usage of the company site is non-natural and so anything common to ordinary industrial usage is likely to fall outside the scope of the tort. Courts frequently find ordinary industrial usage is natural use, particularly where planning permission provides prima facie evidence that the site was a suitable one.[17] It may also be a defence to show that the activity of the company is carried out under statutory authority, or is for common benefit, or that the escape arose due to an Act of God.

Negligence

An action in negligence would be subject to the same requirements as those indicated in Chapter 4 at p. 99. In trying to establish lack of fault on *SHPC Ltd's* part, it would be relevant to consider the state of technology at the time of the incident and the general approved practice in the industry.

Apart from these common law actions, there is also the possibility of a statutory nuisance.

Statutory nuisance

Part III and s. 79(1) of the EPA 1990 deal with statutory nuisance.[18] Amongst other things, in certain circumstances, it covers dust, smell, smoke, fumes, accumulations, animals and noise which are prejudicial to public health or a nuisance.

In deciding whether there is or is likely to be a statutory nuisance, the local environmental health officer will take a number of factors into account, including the locality, time, duration and utility of the activity. In cases of an existing or anticipated statutory nuisance, the relevant local authority may issue an abatement notice. Failure to comply with the notice may either lead to a court order or to the local authority remedying the nuisance without going to court. The notice may specify abatement steps, or prohibit the activity, restrict it or put time limits on it.

Moreover, any person aggrieved (i.e. someone whose land or health is affected) by an existing statutory nuisance may apply to the magistrates' court for an abatement order.

It is a criminal offence to fail to comply with an abatement notice. The maximum penalty is £2,000 (or £20,000 in respect of industrial/trade or business premises) with an increased penalty of £200 for every day the nuisance continues thereafter. However, there are defences available. These include having used Best Practical Means (BPM) to abate or counteract the nuisance (but this defence does not apply to cases of fumes and gases). In considering BPM, factors such as the locality, circumstances, technical knowledge, cost, design and maintenance are taken into account. There is a right of appeal from the magistrates' court (during which time an abatement notice may be suspended). The right of appeal also covers unreasonable requirements set in the notice, and defective notices.

Other liabilities

In addition to the liabilities listed above, and the liabilities that may arise from not obtaining or breaching authorizations and consents (see p. 119), it is worth noting the following.

There may be civil liability under the Control of Pollution Act 1974 for damage done by poisonous, noxious or polluting waste.

There may be criminal liability under the Clean Air Act 1993, for the discharge of any 'dark smoke' from chimneys or industrial/trade premises respectively. Dark smoke is assessed by reference to a visual chart and liability is strict. There are very limited defences (such as act of a trespasser).

There may be criminal liability for contamination of water under the general water pollution offence in s. 86 of the Water Resources Act 1991. This would cover the escape of the waste even if it is accidental because liability is strict, and it is unlikely that any discharge consent or waste management licence would cover this form of pollution.

There may also be criminal liability for breach of s. 33 of the EPA 1990 in treating or keeping controlled waste in a manner likely to cause pollution to the environment. It is equally possible that there may be criminal liability under s. 34, which concerns the duty of care not to allow the escape of controlled waste.

STRATEGIES FOR MANAGERS

Enterprises must keep aware of the rapid changes in national and EC law, policy and practice. The necessary information should be made available to relevant managers. This should include legal and other issues such as the European Community Action programmes and Eco audits. There is an increasing need to consider, develop, research, or purchase new systems and technology. Enterprises must become more proactive about identifying, preventing and collating information about possible pollution of the environment by their activities.

Regular training should also be given to management and employees as well as where appropriate to customers and suppliers.

The enterprise needs to be familiar with the range of agencies involved in the enforcement of planning and environmental law and the scope of their powers. The enterprise should identify and maintain a close working relationship with the agencies relevant to its activities so that advice can be obtained and any difficulties resolved at an early stage.

An accurate system should be in place for recording the details of incidents which could give rise to legal liability, such as accidental discharges, or night time deliveries. Insurance cover has a vital role, especially for liability arising out of contaminated land, waste disposal and water pollution. The enterprise should also assess the need for and value of Environmental Auditing.

The public has access to registers kept by the enforcement agencies. These registers have details of corporate activities which may assist individuals or groups in bringing a case against an enterprise. Litigation and legal liability should be avoided by an enterprise for a variety of reasons including cost, damage to the reputation and image of the company, which might make it more difficult to obtain licences and permissions in the future.

Every enterprise should adopt the British Standard (BS 7750) on environmental management systems, which lays down an overall approach for management strategy.

KEY LEARNING POINTS

- **If an enterprise wants to build or expand the activities undertaken on its property, it should normally obtain planning permission to do** so. The planning authority has a wide range of powers to ensure compliance with planning laws.

- In certain circumstances an enterprise will have to provide an environmental impact assessment.
- If an enterprise uses a process which discharges prescribed substances then it must obtain an IPC authorization from HMIP.
- If an enterprise uses a Part B prescribed process, but no prescribed substance is involved, then it must obtain APC authorization.
- If an enterprise discharges trade or sewerage effluent, poisonous, noxious or polluting matter or solid waste into controlled waters, then it must obtain a NRA consent.
- If an enterprise discharges trade effluent it must obtain a consent from the local sewerage undertaker.
- If an enterprise deals with hazardous waste then it should obtain a consent from its local HSA.
- If an enterprise transports, or deposits or disposes of controlled or special waste on land, then it should obtain a licence from its local waste authority.
- An enterprise must comply with its obligations under s. 33 of the EPA 1990.
- An enterprise should obtain a local authority consent for building work noise.
- An enterprise should ensure that its activities do not amount to a breach of its civil law obligations to its neighbours, or to a breach of the criminal law.

EXERCISES

1   Try to find out the planning status of the premises where you are employed and the range of activities which are permitted to be undertaken there.

2   Does IPC apply to your enterprise's activities?

3   Is a consent or a licence required for any of your enterprise's activities? If the answer is yes, does the enterprise have such a consent or licence and what are its terms? How does it or should it affect working practices in the enterprise?

4   Are any of the activities undertaken by your enterprise potentially or actually a 'nuisance'? If they are, what do you think should be the response of the enterprise?

5   How should your enterprise implement BS 7750?

NOTES: CASE REFERENCES ETC

1 Directive 85/337/EEC.
2 Environmental Protection (Prescribed Processes and Substances) Regulations 1991, SI 1991 No. 472 (as amended).
3 As footnote 2 above.
4 *Alphacell* v *Woodward* [1972] AC 824; [1972] 2 All ER 475. For recent cases, see e.g. *National Rivers Authority* v *Yorkshire Water, The Times*, 24 November 1993; *National Rivers Authority* v *Wright Engineering, The Independent*, 19 November 1993.
5 Note that the government has proposed that the definition of 'waste' in EU Directives should be adopted, and would mean materials which are discarded in the sense of 'falling out of the commercial cycle or out of the chain of utility'.
6 SI 1980 No. 1709.
7 Planning (Hazardous Substances) Regulations 1992, SI 1992 No. 656.
8 SI 1994 No. 1056.
9 Waste Management Licensing Regulations 1994, SI 1994 No. 1056.
10 Controlled Waste (Registration of Carriers and Seizure of Vehicles) Regulations 1991, SI 1991 No. 1624.
11 *Waste Management: Duty of Care*, made by the Secretary of State in 1991 under s. 34(7) of the EPA 1990.
12 *St. Helen's Smelting Co.* v *Tipping* (1865) 11 HL Cas 642.
13 See e.g. *Halsey* v *Esso Petroleum Co.* [1961] 1 WLR 683; [1961] 2 All ER 145.
14 See e.g. *Cambridge Water Co.* v *Eastern Counties Leather plc* [1994] 1 All ER 53; [1994] 2 WLR 53, on the strict nature of the liability of the creator of a nuisance.
15 *Ibid*. This case confirms that the liability of a continuer of a nuisance is based on negligence.
16 *Rylands* v *Fletcher* (1868) LR 3 HL 330; (1868) LR 1 Ex 265, is the case from which this tort is derived.
17 See footnote 14 above. This House of Lords decision is also a recent example of a case concerning the scope of the rule in *Rylands* v *Fletcher*. It contains a useful discussion on the meaning of 'non-natural' use but appears to limit the scope of the tort quite considerably.
18 See also the Noise and Statutory Nuisance Act 1993.

JOURNALS

Journal of Planning and Environment Law.
Journal of Environmental Law.
Environmental Data Services (ENDS) Reports.
Environmental Law and Management (formerly the *Land Management and Environmental Law Report*).

FURTHER READING

Ball, S. and Bell, S. (1994) *Environmental Law*, London: Blackstone Press.
Hughes, D. (1992) *Environmental Law*, London: Butterworths.
Johnson, S. and Corcelle, G. (1989) *The Environmental Policy of the European Communities*, London: Graham and Trotman.

Moore, V. (1994) *A Practical Approach to Planning Law*, London: Blackstone Press.

Salter, J. (1992) *Corporate Environmental Responsibility: Law and Practice*, London: Butterworths.

USEFUL ADDRESSES

Department of the Environment
2 Marsham Street
London SW1   Tel no. 0171 276 0900

Department of Trade and Industry Environment Division
Buckingham Palace Road
London SW1   Tel no. 0171 215 5000

Her Majesty's Stationery Office
(Various local offices)

National Society for Clean Air and Environmental Protection
136 North Street
Brighton BN1 1R   Tel no. 01273 326313

National Rivers Authority
30 Albert Embankment
London SE1 7TL   Tel no. 0171 820 0101

Her Majesty's Inspectorate of Pollution
Romney House
43 Marsham Street
London SW1   Tel no. 0171 276 8061

Health and Safety Executive
Baynard's House
1 Chepstow Place
London W2 4TF   Tel no. 0171 243 6000

British Standards Institution
Linford Wood
Milton Keynes MK14 6LE   Tel no. 01908 221166

Local authority: e.g. environmental health; planning; waste collection; waste disposal; hazardous substances.

Greenpeace
Canonbury Villas
London N1 2HB   Tel no. 0171 354 5100

Friends of the Earth
26–28 Underwood Street
London N1 7JQ   Tel no. 0171 490 1555

Council for the Protection of Rural England
Warwick House
25 Buckingham Palace Road
London SW1W 0PP   Tel no. 0171 976 6433.

Chapter 6

The enterprise and its product

Anne Ruff and Malcolm Leder

The product is central to an enterprise's existence. If the product goes wrong, or does not live up to the claims made for it by the enterprise, then this can have legal as well as commercial consequences. Managers should try to ensure that their enterprise avoids such repercussions. This chapter identifies the major legal pitfalls for the unwary, concentrating upon:

- advertising and sales promotion
- selling
- remedies and sanctions against the seller, the manufacturer, the producer and the supplier
- unacceptable trading practices.

Case study

B. Dixon-Bate Ltd were manufacturers of a dual-purpose towing hitch known as the Dixon-Bate DEDLOC towing jaw. The towing hitch was dual purpose as it could be coupled to either a cup or a ring attachment. In their leaflets advertising and accompanying the hitch the manufacturers stated that it was foolproof and required no maintenance.

Lexmead (Basingstoke) Ltd were retailers who ran a garage. They sold one of these hitches to Donald Lewis, one of their customers, who wanted a towing hitch to couple his Land Rover to a cup attachment on his trailer. *Lexmead* relied mainly on the manufacturer's reputation but also on their leaflets when they sold Mr Lewis the hitch which they attached to his Land Rover. *Lexmead* had obtained the hitch from one of their suppliers, but their records did not show which one.

Donald Lewis used the trailer attached to the Land Rover on his farm and in a building business. A brass spindle and handle became detached from the towing hitch and only dirt was holding the towing pin in position when Hugh Larkin, an employee, was driving the Land Rover coupled to the trailer along a road in Farnborough. The trailer suddenly became detached from the Land Rover and careered across the road into the path of a car. In the resulting accident the driver of the

car, George Lambert and his son, Kirby were killed. The driver's wife, Iris and her daughter, Tracey were injured.[1]
The following claims were made in the court case:

1 Iris and Tracey Lambert sued Donald Lewis, Hugh Larkin, *Lexmead* and *B. Dixon-Bate Ltd* for negligence (law of tort) and under the Fatal Accidents Acts.
2 Donald Lewis claimed an indemnity from *Lexmead* on the basis that *Lexmead* were in breach of an implied term in the contract of sale (see p. 141).
3 *Lexmead* claimed an indemnity from *B. Dixon-Bate Ltd* on the basis that *B. Dixon-Bate Ltd* were liable for their negligent statement (see p. 136) in their sales material, for breach of warranty (see p. 136) and for the tort of negligence (see p. 149).

Box 6.1 Lambert v *Lewis* (1982)

INTRODUCTION

Any enterprise which supplies defective or dangerous goods or services will incur legal liability. Liability may be criminal as well as civil, it may arise out of the law of contract or the law of tort, and it may arise out of English or EC legislation. Effective managers need to organize their business so as to minimize or, if possible, avoid legal liability arising from the manufacture or distribution or sale of defective or dangerous products.

This chapter covers both goods and services. In the case study *B. Dixon-Bate Ltd's* products, the towing hitches, are 'goods'. Many enterprises also provide 'services' as well as 'goods'. *Lexmead* sold the towing hitch but also provided a service by fixing it to the Land Rover. Such a service is part of the company's business and can also be regarded as a product. Some enterprises, such as repairers of electrical appliances, solicitors, and management consultants, mainly provide services.

First of all this chapter looks at some of the legal aspects of marketing. The law is particularly concerned with ensuring that false and misleading statements are not used in advertising and promotional material, and this is examined on pp. 135–9. In addition the law attempts to regulate unfair practices which adversely affect consumers, and this is looked at generally on pp. 155–6. (Unfair trading practices which adversely affect the enterprise are also considered in Chapter 8.) The law relating to protecting the brand image of a product, and so on, is explained in Chapter 7.

After considering legal controls on advertising and promotional material, there is an explanation of the rights and obligations arising out of the contract for the sale or supply of the product. This is followed by a detailed discussion of the various types of civil and criminal liability which can arise where the product supplied is defective or not supplied as agreed.

Finally, the chapter considers what strategies managers could adopt to ensure that their enterprise operates within the law and, where appropriate, use the law for the benefit of the enterprise.

ADVERTISING AND SALES PROMOTION

Enterprises must successfully promote and sell their products or services if they are to stay in business. This is done in a variety of ways including advertising, sales brochures, packaging and displays as well as by sales personnel. If anything written or said about the product is false or mis-leading, then the enterprise is potentially liable under civil or criminal law. Marketing managers, therefore, need to be aware of the legal constraints on such information and the legal liability which can arise if the law is broken. In addition managers should be familiar with the system of self-regulation adopted by the advertising industry.

When does civil liability arise?

The law is not usually concerned with statements that are clearly just the seller's or manufacturer's sales hype. These are described as 'traders' puffs', for example, the description of a face lotion as 'anti-ageing' or a 'bio-technical innovation'. In *Lambert* v *Lewis* the retailers, *Lexmead*, unsuccessfully claimed that the manufacturers' description of the towing hitch as foolproof and requiring no maintenance was not a 'mere puff'.

Nevertheless the law has imposed some restrictions on the kind of statements which can be legally made in, for example, advertisements or sales talk.

Liability can arise where false statements are made to the other party to the contract, for example by the seller to the buyer. Such misrepresenta-tions are statements of fact made by one party to a contract which has induced the other party to enter into the contract. For example, this could have been the case if *Lexmead* had told Donald Lewis when he first looked at the towing hitch that it could pull trailers carrying a maximum weight of two tons when in fact the maximum recommended weight was one and a half tons, and subsequently Donald Lewis purchased the towing hitch in reliance on this statement.

Advertisements, for example, should not falsely misrepresent factual details. This would include statements of opinion where the advertiser has special knowledge on which to base the statement. The statement must be one of the main reasons why the customer has purchased the goods or services.[2] The remedies available to the customer depend upon the state of mind of the advertiser. If the advertiser knew that the statement was untrue, or negligently failed to check its accuracy, then the customer is entitled to recover the price paid and any additional losses resulting from the deceit. Alternatively, if the advertiser can show that there were reasonable grounds for believing it to be true, then the customer would in effect only be entitled to recover the price paid on making a prompt complaint.

Liability can also arise in limited circumstances where A makes a statement to B which B relies upon and enters into a contract with C. For example, *Lexmead* claimed without success that the statements in the publicity leaflets distributed by the manufacturers had induced them to purchase the towing hitch from their supplier. If the manufacturers had made the statements directly to *Lexmead*, who had then relied upon the assurances when buying the towing hitch, the manufacturers might have been liable to Lexmead for any financial loss which they suffered.

Descriptions of goods or services can also be an express or implied term of the contract of sale or supply. The customer is then entitled to claim the appropriate remedies for breach of contract. (See at p. 147 for remedies.)

When does criminal liability arise?

Criminal liability will arise from:

- false trade descriptions attached to goods, or property, or their price
- false or misleading statements about services, or their price.

There are three pieces of legislation designed to protect the consumer.

- the Trade Descriptions Act 1968
- the Consumer Protection Act 1987
- the Property Misdescriptions Act 1991.

They do not control purely private transactions. They do not apply to statements made by private sellers. Misleading price indications are dealt with in Part III of the Consumer Protection Act 1987. 'Property' in the 1991 Act means building and land, which are not dealt with in this chapter.

'False' usually means false as to a material degree, or likely to be misleading to a material degree; for example, describing a sweatshirt as being the 'Marc O'Polo' brand so that the consumer might confuse it with the 'Marco Polo' range.[3] Arguably it was a false trade description by *B. Dixon-Bate Ltd* to describe the towing hitch as foolproof and requiring no maintenance.

The goods supplied must form an integral and not merely incidental part of the defendant's trade or business.

A false trade description covers any statement, whether written or oral, which refers to the goods. 'Description' includes any marking of the goods or their packaging or any advertising. Requests made by the customer where it is reasonable to infer that the goods should correspond with that request would also fall within the definition. For example, if a customer says to a car dealer, 'I want to buy a new car' and is sold a car which is not new, that would amount to a false trade description. It is worth noting that a burnt out and refurbished Range Rover was not 'new' whereas a Ford car which sustained minor damage prior to delivery to the dealer, was still 'new' as it had been perfectly repaired.

Liability for false trade descriptions is strict, subject to certain defences. However, it is possible to avoid liability by the use of an appropriate and conspicuous disclaimer. Car dealers in particular have used disclaimers to neutralize false odometer readings.

Under the Consumer Protection Act 1987, Part III, it is an offence, in the course of business:

- to give to any consumers a misleading indication as to the price of any goods, services, accommodation or facilities
- to fail to take reasonable steps to correct an indication which has subsequently become misleading.

There is a Code of Practice which gives practical guidance on the requirements of these provisions.

The Trade Descriptions Act 1968 makes it an offence for any person in the course of trade or business intentionally or recklessly to make a false statement concerning, for example, the nature or provision of any services, accommodation or facilities provided in the course of any trade or business.

It is likely that this provision will apply to misdescriptions made in the course of providing professional services, e.g. statements as to qualifications or experience. In the case of a corporate defendant (see Chapter 2), this would mean that the intention or recklessness is that of one of the directors (or other responsible individuals) of the company rather than an employee.

Defences

There is a 'due diligence' defence available, where a criminal charge is brought, under the Trade Descriptions Act 1968 or the Consumer Protection Act 1987. This requires the defendant to prove:

- that they were mistaken, or
- that they relied upon information provided by a third party, or
- that the offence arose out of circumstances outside their control, and
- that all reasonable precautions had been taken and all due diligence exercised to avoid such an offence being committed.

If an employee of a company, for example, a store manager, commits an offence, then the company will not be liable so long as the company can show that it had taken all reasonable precautions and exercised due diligence in setting up an effective system of control to avoid offences under the Acts. Employers are not vicariously liable for the criminal acts or omissions of their employees in this context.

If the defendant claims to have exercised due diligence by reasonably relying on information supplied by a third party, the defendant must show that they took reasonable steps to verify the information. For example, if a company purchases goods for retail sale in its shops, and the supplier falsely guarantees that the goods comply with safety regulations, the company, as well as the supplier, will be liable unless it can show that it verified the guarantee by for example, sample testing on a valid statistical basis.

Self-regulation

The Advertising Standards Authority (ASA) supervises a self-regulatory system of control of advertising, which is supported by advertisers, agencies and the media. The ASA's powers relate to the content of advertising in the non-broadcast media, such as newspapers and magazines. Advertisements on television, radio and cable services are subject to similar, but statutorily-based, codes administered by the Independent Television Commission (ITC) and the Independent Radio Authority (IRA). The ASA also supervises the British Codes of Advertising and Sales Promotion Practice. The codes are based on the general principle that advertisements and sales promotions should be legal, decent, honest and truthful.

Complaints can be made by members of the public or by anyone with a commercial interest. In 1991 the ASA received over 800 objections to a poster advertising *Benetton*, the clothing company, which featured a blood-smeared, new born baby with the umbilical cord still attached. Eventually, the advertisers agreed to withdraw the poster.

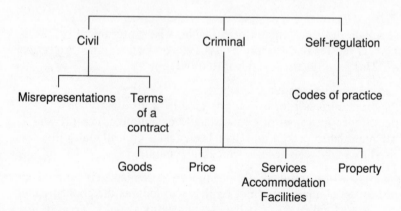

Figure 6.1 Summary of liability for false or misleading statements

If the ASA is unsuccessful in attempting to prevent a misleading advertisement appearing, then the Director General of Fair Trading can use his discretionary powers to obtain an injunction against the advertiser. In practice these powers are rarely needed.

THE SALE

The sale of goods or services gives rise to civil rights and obligations and in certain circumstances to criminal liability. The main civil liability of the buyer and seller or supplier derives from the contract which is the legal basis of the sale. It is important to remember that either party to a contract can limit or exclude their legal liability under the contract by including in the contract an exclusion clause. Finally in relation to a contract for the sale of goods it is important to note the effect on the customer's legal rights of acceptance by the customer of the goods.

In addition to a claim in contract there can often be a claim based on the tort of negligence, or on the Consumer Protection Act 1987. However, it is often more difficult to establish a claim in negligence than in contract.

Rights and obligations under the contract

The first thing that needs to be stressed is that normally only the parties to a contract are bound by its terms. In *Lambert* v *Lewis* contracts of sale existed between the manufacturer, *B. Dixon-Bate Ltd* and the unknown supplier, between the unknown supplier and *Lexmead* the retailing garage, and between *Lexmead* and Donald Lewis, the owner of the Land Rover and trailer. There was no contract of sale between the manufacturer and the garage. A contractual claim could only have arisen if *Lexmead* could have shown that there was a collateral or subsidiary contract between them and the manufacturers. Under current law the manufacturer, as the producer of the towing hitch, would also be subject to the strict liability provisions of the Consumer Protection Act 1987 and the General Product Safety Regulations 1994 (see p. 152).[4]

Three points need to be noted.

1 If the sale is to a consumer who is purchasing goods or services on credit, then the agreement is also subject to the provisions of the Consumer Credit Act 1974.
2 The following sales techniques are subject to additional legal regulation:

   - inertia selling
   - doorstep sales
   - mail-order sales
   - pyramid selling

3 The risk of loss or damage to goods can pass to the buyer when the contract of sale is made. Therefore, the buyer needs to insure against loss or damage to the goods from the time of the contract.

The function of the contract

The contract to sell the goods or provide the services has two functions:

- contract planning
- dispute resolution.

The terms of the contract can reflect the priorities of an enterprise and are one method of implementing its management strategy. They define the enterprise's obligations. These could include: details as to the nature of the goods or services; the date(s) when delivery is due or when the work should be done; the date(s) by which payment should be made; a price variation clause, e.g. to allow for variation in the cost of raw materials. They can also provide for dispute resolution. In addition the contract can be used to limit liability for breach of the contract to a fixed sum of money irrespective of the actual loss suffered by the other party, or even to exclude liability for the breach altogether. This would place the risk of loss arising from the enterprise's breach on the party suffering the loss, who would be well advised to insure against such loss. This would remove the need to insure from the enterprise and so reduce unit costs. Commercial considerations will affect the decision as to whether or not this would be desirable. Alternatively disputes can be settled according to the general rules of contract law.

An enterprise will frequently use standard form contracts which can be drafted to reflect the enterprise's priorities. In some situations the enterprise may negotiate the terms of the contract with the other party, or even have to accept the standard form agreement used by that party. It is also important to note whether the other party is a 'consumer', because consumers have additional statutory protection, for example, in relation to exclusion clauses and consumer credit transactions.

Contract terms

There are two kinds of contractual terms:

- express terms
- implied terms.

Express terms   These are those terms actually agreed by the parties. They are likely to include a description of the goods and/or services, details as to price and delivery dates, and might include a limitation or exclusion clause (see p. 143).

In *Lambert* v *Lewis* there were no express terms in the contract between *Lexmead* and Donald Lewis as to the quality of the towing hitch, nor as to its fitness for the purpose of towing trailers.

Implied terms   These can be implied by statute, by the courts or by custom. This means that the parties may not be aware of these implied terms at the time when they enter the contract. Nevertheless, they will be bound by them.

The most important group of implied terms for managers in the context of their product are those implied by statute under the Sale of Goods Act 1979, ss. 12–15, and the Supply of Goods and Services Act 1982.

Under the 1979 Act (as amended by the Sale and Supply of Goods Act 1994) five terms are implied into contracts for the sale of goods:

The seller has the right to sell the goods   If *Lexmead* sold Donald Lewis a towing hitch which they did not own, then he could recover the purchase price and any money spent, for example, on altering the towing hitch.

The goods shall correspond with their description   If *Lexmead* had described the towing hitch as multi-purpose, then Donald Lewis, on later discovering that this was not the case, could recover the difference in value between the towing hitch as described and the towing hitch he actually bought.

The goods supplied are of satisfactory quality   The goods must 'meet the standard that a reasonable person would regard as satisfactory, taking account of any description of the goods, the price (if relevant) and all the other relevant circumstances'. Aspects of the quality of goods to be considered include fitness for all the purposes for which goods of that kind are commonly supplied; appearance and finish; freedom from minor defects; safety; and durability. This implied term does not apply to specified defects; or (where the buyer examines the goods) to defects which that examination ought to reveal.[5]

The term 'satisfactory quality' thus replaces the former requirement of 'merchantable quality' for contracts made on or after 3 January 1995. The new law emphasises the concept of acceptability to the reasonable buyer instead of usability as previously. Moreover, cosmetic or minor defects now have to be taken into account.

The goods are reasonably fit for the particular purpose for which they are being bought   Donald Lewis purchased the towing-hitch for towing a trailer with a Land Rover around his farm and on the road to carry rubble in connection with his building business. This was not the dual-purpose for which the towing hitch was specifically designed, but *Lexmead* could still be liable for breach of this implied term if this was the purpose for which the hitch was expressly or impliedly being bought.

Where the sale is by sample the bulk of the goods must correspond with the sample and the goods must be free from any latent defect making their quality unsatisfactory

Implied terms in Lambert v Lewis

In *Lambert* v *Lewis* the owner of the Land Rover and trailer, Donald Lewis, who had purchased the hitch from *Lexmead* the retail garage, claimed that *Lexmead* were in breach of the implied terms as to quality and fitness for purpose in the contract of sale. Both of these implied terms were clearly applicable to the contract. The towing hitch should be reasonably fit for the purpose of towing trailers fitted with either a cup-type or a ring-type means of attachment and it should be capable of being used upon a public road without danger to other road-users. However, once Donald Lewis knew that the handle of the locking mechanism on the towing hitch was damaged and so not in the same state as it was delivered, then he should either have got it mended or found out whether it was safe to continue to use it in that condition. His failure to do either of these things meant that *Lexmead* were no longer liable for any breach of the implied terms.

If Donald Lewis had not been negligent then *Lexmead* would have been liable for breach of the implied terms. Once breach of an implied term is proved a trader such as *Lexmead* has no defence even if they can prove that all reasonable care had been taken. Thus retailers are liable to the customer and cannot pass blame onto the manufacturer. However, retailers will be able to sue their suppliers if they are in breach of an implied (or express) term of their contract. In *Lexmead's* case this was not possible because they did not know whom to sue, as their defective method of store-keeping meant that they could not tell from which wholesaler they had purchased the towing hitch.

As can be seen from *Lambert* v *Lewis*, difficulties arise when the product purchased subsequently becomes defective, that is, no longer of satisfactory quality or fit for the purpose for which purchased. Obviously if that happens shortly after the sale there is an implication that the goods were sub-standard at the time of the purchase. The Sale of Goods Act 1979, as amended by the Sale and Supply of Goods Act 1994, now expressly recognises the concept of durability as an aspect of the quality of goods.

What amounts to reasonable durability depends on the nature of the goods. In *Lambert* v *Lewis* the towing hitch had been purchased in January or February 1971, and the accident had taken place on 10 September 1972.

If the towing hitch had remained more or less in its original state then the court (applying the common law) considered that *Lexmead's* obligations under the implied terms would apparently still have existed in September 1972.

If goods do become defective buyers can encounter difficulties in obtaining spare parts and servicing facilities. Although many businesses do provide them there is no legal duty requiring them to do so unless they have expressly promised them. However, the Office of Fair Trading encourages trade associations to draft voluntary codes of practice which can specify the provision of such facilities.

The implied terms in the 1979 Act are also applicable to goods bought under hire purchase agreements (Supply of Goods (Implied Terms) Act 1973, ss. 8–11 (as amended)), to contracts for the transfer of goods, for example, contracts for the supply of work and materials and contracts of exchange or barter, and to contracts for the hire of goods (Supply of Goods and Services Act 1982, Part 1, as amended).

The 1982 Act, Part 2 also provides that the following three terms are to be implied into contracts for the supply of services in the course of a business:

- the supplier will carry out the service with 'reasonable care and skill'. It is not enough to do your incompetent best
- the supplier will carry out the service within a reasonable time unless otherwise specified
- a reasonable charge is payable for the service unless otherwise specified.

Examples of such contracts are vehicle servicing agreements, contracts for office cleaning services, or for the services of an accountant. Management consultancy is also likely to fall within this definition.

Exclusion clauses

The express terms of a contract may include an exclusion or limitation clause. An exclusion clause may exclude or restrict liability for breach of any term of the contract, or for failure to perform the contract at all. A limitation clause in effect accepts liability but places a financial limit on the liability. Exclusion clauses are a method of allocating risk and can affect, for example, the overheads of a business such as insurance.

If exclusion clauses are to exclude liability for breach of contract effectively, they must be incorporated as a term of the contract. This occurs when the party who is bound by the clause either:

- signs the contract, or
- has been given reasonable notice of the clause, or
- has been trading regularly on this basis over a long period of time.

If the exclusion clause is effectively incorporated then the court will examine its wording and will interpret the clause narrowly against the party trying to enforce the clause.

Statutory regulation of exclusion clauses

Many exclusion and limitation clauses are subject to the Unfair Contract Terms Act 1977. Contracts made on or after 1 January 1995 will also be subject to UK regulations implementing the EC Directive on Unfair Terms in Consumer Contracts (1993).[6] The Act applies where one party's liability has arisen in the course of business. Therefore it does not apply where both parties are acting in a private capacity. The Act makes certain clauses invalid and others subject to a reasonableness test.

The 1977 Act regulates clauses dealing with:

- negligence
- manufacturers' guarantees
- indemnity clauses
- breach of express terms
- breach of implied terms.

Negligence in the context of figure 6.2 applies to liability arising for breach of:

- an express or implied term in a contract to take reasonable care
- the tort of negligence
- the Occupiers' Liability Acts 1957 and 1984.

A consumer contract (see Table 6.1) is where one of the parties deals as a consumer, i.e., they do not make the contract in the course of their business, nor are they a buyer at an auction or by competitive tender.

Criminal liability (see Table 6.1) will also arise if a seller or a supplier attempts to exclude liability for breach of a term implied by the Sale of Goods Act 1979, or the corresponding provisions relating to goods supplied under a hire-purchase agreement (see p. 143), and the buyer is buying consumer goods. The seller or supplier will also be criminally liable if they give buyers information about their rights against third parties such as the wholesaler and manufacturer, without ensuring that there is a clear and conspicuous statement to the effect that the statutory rights of the consumer are not affected. Where goods are supplied under a contract for hire or for work and materials, then the supplier will not be criminally liable in these circumstances.

What is reasonable under the Act is determined by reference to circumstances at the time the contract was made and specific guidelines.[7]

Table 6.1 Summary of the effect of the Unfair Contract Terms Act 1977 on exclusion clauses

Invalid (i.e. cannot exclude liability)	*Valid if reasonable* (i.e. can exclude liability if reasonable)	*Not subject to the Act*
Liability for death or personal injury resulting from negligence	Damage to property or financial loss resulting from negligence	
In a guarantee, for example, the liability of a manufacturer or distributor in negligence for defective consumer goods in consumer contracts*	An indemnity clause in a consumer contract	
	Breach of an express term where it is a consumer contract or on standard written terms	Breach of an express term in a private agreement
		Breach of an express term in a commercial agreement individually negotiated
Breach of statutory implied term as to title		
Breach of other statutory implied terms in consumer contracts*	Breach of other statutory implied terms in non-consumer contracts	

* Criminal liability can also arise.

Exclusion clauses and Lambert v Lewis

If *Lexmead* had attempted to exclude their liability for breach of the two implied terms in the contract made with Donald Lewis for the sale of the towing hitch, then it is unlikely that the exclusion clause would be valid. Donald Lewis would arguably be dealing as a consumer when he buys the hitch since he is not in the business of buying and selling vehicles and their parts, and so *Lexmead* would also be committing a criminal offence. Even if he is not dealing as a consumer then the exclusion clause must be reasonable for it to be valid.

EC Directive on unfair contract terms

The new UK regulations[8] implementing the EC Unfair Terms in Consumer Contracts Directive (see p. 114) make any contract term, not just exclusion clauses, invalid in certain circumstances. However, the regulations only apply to terms in a contract for the supply of goods and services, which have not been individually negotiated. Such a term is to be regarded as unfair and not binding on the consumer if, contrary to the requirement of good faith, it causes significant imbalance in the parties' rights and obligations arising under the contract, to the detriment of the consumer. These provisions will exist alongside and occasionally overlap those of the Unfair Contract Terms Act 1977. However, the impact of the new provisions is limited in that a court cannot consider whether the basic bargain, that is the main subject matter of the contract and the price paid, is unfair, provided that these core provisions are in plain intelligible language.

Acceptance of goods

When a customer accepts the goods purchased this means that the customer has lost the right to reject the faulty goods and can only claim damages. Under the Sale of Goods Act 1979, as amended by the Sale and Supply of Goods Act 1994, acceptance in the legal sense is deemed to occur when:

1 The buyer informs the seller that the goods have been accepted.
2 The goods have been delivered and the buyer does any act in relation to them inconsistent with the seller's ownership.
3 The buyer, after the lapse of a reasonable time, keeps the goods without informing the seller that the goods are rejected.

But no deemed acceptance can occur until the buyer has had a reasonable opportunity of examining the goods to ascertain whether they are in conformity with the contract. The buyer who acts as consumer cannot be bound by any waiver of this rule (e.g. by signing an 'acceptance note'). Nor does acceptance occur *merely* because the buyer agrees to repairs or makes a sub-sale or gift. Non-consumer buyers cannot reject goods where the breach is so 'slight' that this would be unreasonable. Finally, there is a new right of partial rejection where only some of the goods are in conformity with the contract.

When Donald Lewis purchased the towing hitch he was not obliged to examine it, but he should have done so at the first reasonable opportunity.

REMEDIES AND SANCTIONS

What happens when something goes wrong? What liability is incurred when, for example, the goods supplied are defective or even harmful, or the service provided is below standard, or the goods are delivered late, or the wrong quantity of goods is delivered, or payment is made late or not at all? What remedies and sanctions are available to the individual or enterprise suffering the wrong?

One or more of the following will normally provide the basis for a claim:

- breach of contract
- manufacturer's guarantee
- the tort of negligence
- the Consumer Protection Act 1987.

The main remedy is financial compensation in the form of damages. Liability under the 1987 Act can include criminal as well as civil liability. In addition it is worth looking at the codes of practice of relevant trade associations which, although not legally enforceable, indicate what is regarded as current good practice.

Breach of contract

Both parties to a contract are required to perform exactly their side of the agreement. If one party does not then the other is not required to perform its obligations. For example, if *Lexmead* had defectively attached the towing hitch to Donald Lewis's Land Rover then he could refuse to pay for the labour and parts unless the defects were very minor. However, if Donald Lewis had paid for the work in advance he would not be able to recover the money paid because he had received some benefit from the contract. Donald Lewis would be required to pay a reasonable price for the work done, but would be able to recover damages for any additional costs incurred in remedial work.

There are generally two remedies available for breach of contract:

- right to treat the contract as at an end
- damages.

Right to treat the contract as at an end

Damages are the more common remedy, but in certain circumstances if one party is in breach of a term of the contract then the other innocent party has the choice of immediately treating the contract as discharged, i.e., at an end, without going to court. Alternatively the innocent party can affirm the contract, i.e., keep it in existence. If Donald Lewis had discovered at the first reasonable opportunity after purchase (see p. 146) that the towing hitch was not fit for its purpose, then he could have treated the contract of sale as terminated. He could also have recovered damages. Alternatively he might have preferred to keep the towing hitch and just claim the cost of repairs from *Lexmead*.

The innocent party only has the choice of treating the contract as discharged immediately, or affirming the contract, when the term broken is a condition[9] or where the effect of the breach is extremely serious.[10] A condition is a term of major importance central to the performance of the contract. Other terms are usually classified as warranties, the breach of which cannot discharge the contract, but does give rise to a claim in damages. The implied terms under the Sale of Goods Act 1979 (see p. 141) are classified under the statute as conditions, which means that a buyer such as Donald Lewis who acts promptly can reject defective goods and claim a refund.

Right to claim damages

The innocent party can in any case of breach of contract claim damages to compensate for economic and other loss which is likely to result from the particular breach.[11] The aim of damages for breach of contract is to put the innocent party in the position he would have been if the contract had been performed. Damages can, therefore, include loss of profit arising out of, for example, a subsequent resale of goods. For example, if *Lexmead* had supplied a towing hitch to Donald Lewis which was not fit for its purpose, then *Lexmead* could have obtained an indemnity from the stockist or distributor who supplied it to them, because it was also an implied term of that contract of sale that the towing hitch should be fit for its purpose. The distributor could then claim from their supplier and so on until the chain reached the manufacturer. Because *Lexmead* were unable to identify their supplier they could not have claimed an indemnity from them. If they had needed to do so they would have been able to claim not just the wholesale cost paid by them for the towing hitch but also any loss of profit incurred.

Damages can also be recovered for wasted expenses, and in certain cases for physical inconvenience and mental distress. However, the damages must not be too remote, that is they must be reasonably likely to result from the particular breach.

Where goods are the subject matter of the contract the measure of damages, that is the amount of damages recoverable from the party who has broken the contract, is usually calculated by reference to the difference in value test. This is the difference in value between the goods which should have been bought or sold under the contract and the cost of buying or selling them in the market place at the time of the breach. Therefore, if *Lexmead* had been in breach for non-delivery of the towing hitch they would have been liable to pay the difference in value between the towing hitch they should have supplied and the cost of buying a replacement.

A second way of calculating damages is by reference to the cost of cure. This is more usually used where building work is the subject matter of the contract, but could also have been appropriate for Donald Lewis. It refers to the cost of putting defects right or completing the work as agreed. Provided that it did not exceed the cost of replacement, *Lexmead* could have been asked to pay for repairs to the towing hitch.

An innocent party who is entitled to damages should attempt to minimize the loss suffered. If *Lexmead* had been liable to pay damages to Donald Lewis, he would have been under an obligation to mitigate his loss. For example he could have obtained a replacement towing hitch or Land Rover so that he could work rather than allow his losses to accumulate. He would be able to recover such expenditure, so long as it was reasonable.

Manufacturer's guarantee

Liability for breach of contract, including breach of statutory implied terms, will only provide a party to a contract with a remedy. This is the effect of the doctrine of privity of contract (see p. 18). A consumer will only have the right to sue the seller for breach of contract if the consumer was also the buyer. In *Lambert* v *Lewis* this meant that neither *Lexmead*, the retailer, nor Donald Lewis, the customer, could sue the manufacturer, *B. Dixon-Bate Ltd* for breach of contract.

Usually a consumer will only have a remedy against the manufacturer under the manufacturer's guarantee (if any), or the tort of negligence. A manufacturer's guarantee is sometimes called a manufacturer's warranty. The only rights which a consumer has against the manufacturer are those specified under the guarantee. In *Lambert* v *Lewis* no claim was made under a manufacturer's guarantee, but Iris and Tracey Lambert, as well as the retailers, did claim that the manufacturers were negligent (see p. 149).

The manufacturers cannot in the guarantee exclude or restrict their liability to a consumer under the tort of negligence. A manufacturer who issues a guarantee which sets out their obligations will be guilty of a criminal offence if the guarantee does not also clearly and conspicuously state that the statutory rights of the seller against the consumer are not affected.

The tort of negligence

Liability in contract may not exist for one or more of the following reasons:

1 The person suffering loss and damage was not a party to the contract. In *Lambert* v *Lewis* the main claim of negligence was raised by the plaintiffs, Iris and Tracey Lambert who did not have a contractual relationship with the manufacturer of the towing hitch.
2 There is no breach of an express or implied term of the contract.
3 A valid exclusion clause excludes liability for breach of contract, but not for negligence.

In order to establish liability for negligence (see also Chapters 1, 4 and 5), the person who has suffered injury, loss, or damage (e.g. Iris and Tracey Lambert) must prove:[12]

1 that the person whose actions caused the injury, loss or damage (e.g. the manufacturer, *B. Dixon-Bate Ltd* and the Land Rover owner, Donald Lewis), owed the injured person a duty of care; and
2 that there had been a breach of that duty of care; and
3 that as a result the plaintiff (e.g. Iris and Tracey Lambert) suffered reasonably foreseeable damage.

The duty of care is owed to anyone who is a 'neighbour', that is someone who is very likely to be affected by the negligent act. Where a negligent act or omission causes a defective product to be manufactured, the duty will only arise where the defect in the product causes damage to property or personal injury. Liability under the tort of negligence will not arise merely because the product itself is defective. The only remedy for defective products is under the law of contract. If, for example, Donald Lewis had discovered the defects in the towing hitch then his only remedy would be as a buyer against the seller *Lexmead*. He would have no remedy against the manufacturers even if the defect was caused by the manufacturers' negligence. Once the accident occurred damage was done to both property, the Lambert's car and Donald Lewis's trailer, and to persons, the Lamberts themselves. Then the manufacturers may be liable in negligence.

'Negligence' is more than mere carelessness. The standard of care expected is that of the reasonable person with the defendant's knowledge and skill where relevant, e.g. the standard of care of a reasonable manufacturer. In *Lambert* v *Lewis* the Lamberts had to prove that, on a balance of probabilities, it was a reasonable inference that the harm they suffered was caused by the manufacturers' and the Land Rover owner's failure to take reasonable care. The Lamberts did not have to show at what stage in the design and manufacturing process the fault arose. Once they established this inference then the manufacturers and the owner had to show respectively that they took reasonable care in the manufacturing process and in the maintenance of the trailer. It is not enough for the manufacturers just to show that there is a safe system of work and proper supervision if it is apparent that one of the manufacturers' employees must have been negligent. The manufacturer is then vicariously liable for the employee's negligence.[13] Even if Donald Lewis, the owner, had not been found to be personally negligent he could have been liable for the negligence of his employee, Hugh Larkin. In fact Hugh Larkin was found not to have been negligent.

In *Lambert* v *Lewis* the manufacturers were found liable in negligence because the towing hitch was unsafe for the use for which it was designed and which it was likely to receive. Expert evidence was given as to the effect of the defect on the operation of the coupling, and the history of the failure of the coupling in at least ten incidents was disclosed. If the defect should have been apparent to Donald Lewis, then this possibility of intermediate examination can protect the manufacturer from liability for negligence, although the retailer may well be liable. In certain circumstances it is possible for the manufacturer and/or the retailer and/or the purchaser to be jointly liable.

In *Lambert* v *Lewis* the owner of the Land Rover, Donald Lewis, as well as the manufacturers, *B. Dixon-Bate Ltd*, was found to have been negligent. He was negligent because he ought to have noticed that the handle which operated the locking mechanism had been missing for anything from three to six months at the time the accident happened, and he ought to have examined the coupling or had it examined by an expert to see if it was safe to use.

Finally, having established that the manufacturer and the Land Rover owner owed them a duty of care and that they were in breach of this duty, the Lamberts had to show that the damage that they suffered, in this case the death and injury, was a reasonably foreseeable consequence of the manufacturers' and the owner's negligence.

It was not necessary for the Lamberts to show that the particular loss and injury they suffered was reasonably foreseeable, merely that it was reasonably foreseeable that some loss or injury would result from manufacturing a defectively designed towing hitch, and from using a poorly maintained towing hitch on a public road. The court held that the loss and injury was a foreseeable consequence of the manufacturer's and the garage's negligence.

It should be remembered that the aim of damages in the tort of negligence is to put the injured party in the position they would have been in but for the injury, loss or damage suffered. In effect, this means that such damages, unlike those for breach of contract, will not be awarded for loss of profit. This is because normally it is not possible to recover pure economic loss in a claim in negligence. A claim for economic loss, or loss of profits, would arise where the product is purchased for re-sale. In this situation it would be advisable to sue for breach of contract.

The Lamberts were awarded damages of £45,000. The manufacturers, *B. Dixon-Bate Ltd*, were found to have been negligent and were liable to pay 75 per cent of this sum. Donald Lewis was also found to have been negligent and liable for the other 25 per cent.

Product liability and product safety

This concept was introduced into English law by the Consumer Protection Act 1987, which imposed a new form of civil liability on producers of defective goods, and criminal liability on the suppliers of consumer goods.

Civil liability – producers, importers and suppliers

The Consumer Protection Act 1987, Part 1 provides that a producer will be liable for any loss or damage caused by a defective product. The producer will be liable even if not negligent. This is known as strict liability. This Act was passed partly in response to an EC Directive on Liability for Defective Products (1985).[15] The legislation was not in force at the time of the events arising in *Lambert* v *Lewis*. If it had been, the main difference would have been that the Lamberts would not have been required to prove that the manufacturers were negligent.

A 'producer' includes manufacturers, producers of raw materials and industrial processors. It also includes EC importers and 'own branders'. Suppliers who cannot identify either the producer or importer or their own supplier (for instance because of poor record-keeping) will likewise incur liability.

The 1994 regulations will also apply to distributors who are required, for example, to monitor the safety of goods placed on the market.

A 'product' covers all goods and electricity and includes components. Part I of the Act is not restricted to consumer products.

'Defect' means that the product is not as safe as the public is entitled to expect. Various factors will be taken into account in determining whether a product is safe. These include how the product has been marketed, the use to which it could be reasonably expected that the product could be put, and the date it was supplied by the producer. In addition the 1994 regulations require the product's characteristics, its presentation, and the categories of consumers, such as children, at serious risk when using the products to be taken into account.

The 1994 regulations also require producers to place only safe products on the market and to inform themselves of risks which might arise, as well as being able, if necessary, to take appropriate action such as withdrawing the product from the market. This means that products must be marked in some way so that they can be identified in the future, and there must be sample testing and a procedure for investigating complaints about the products.

'Damage' is limited to death or personal injury, and to loss or damage to property for private use, occupation or consumption. In other words there is no liability under this head for damage to property used in the course of business, nor for damage to the defective product itself.

The damage caused to consumer property must amount to at least £275. However, although permitted by the EC Directive, the United Kingdom has not imposed a financial ceiling for liability. The claimant will not have to prove that the producer was negligent, but will have to prove that the product was defective, and that the defect caused the damage. The producer of goods cannot avoid or restrict liability under this Act by use of an exclusion clause.

The Act also includes defences available to the producer. For example, the producer will have a defence if he can show that:

- the product was not sold in the course of business, or that
- the defect did not exist when the goods were supplied, or that
- there was contributory negligence by the claimant, or
- because of the state of scientific and technical knowledge at the time the particular product was supplied, producers generally would not have been expected to discover the defect.

This last defence is of great practical importance. Arguably, in effect, it changes the producer's liability in many cases from strict to fault liability. The European Commission is not satisfied that the 1987 Act satisfies the EC Directive on this point.

The Act also provides a defence for a manufacturer of a component if he can show that the defect was wholly attributable to a design fault in the final product.

The claimant must start proceedings against the producer within three years of discovering the damage, the defect and the identity of the producer. In any case no claim can be brought more than ten years after the product was supplied.

Criminal liability – suppliers, producers and distributors

Part II of the Consumer Protection Act 1987 created a general safety requirement, whereby the supplier of unsafe consumer goods (certain goods excepted) incurs criminal liability. Liability is strict, subject to the usual 'due diligence' type of defence (see below). Compliance with other safety legislation is also a defence. Retailers have a special defence if they neither knew nor had reasonable grounds for believing that the goods failed to comply with the general safety requirement.

Co-existing with Part II of the Consumer Protection Act is the new general safety requirement introduced by the General Product Safety Regulations 1994, pursuant to a European Directive of 1992.[15] The 1994 Regulations make it a strict liability criminal offence for producers to place on the market in the course of a commercial activity any unsafe product intended for or likely to be used by consumers (which could include a towing hitch!). This general safety requirement does not apply where the product is covered by other EC safety legislation. The general safety requirement in the Consumer Protection Act is disapplied insofar as it overlaps with the new provisions. Thus in future prosecutions will usually be brought under the new (and expanded) general safety requirement in the 1994 Regulations.

The 1994 Regulations (unlike the 1987 Act) extend to second-hand goods (though not antiques) and also repaired or reconditioned goods unless the goods have been clearly indicated as supplied for repair or reconditioning before use.

'Producer' for the purposes of the 1994 Regulations include EC manufacturers, own label suppliers, and reconditioners; and, when the manufacturer is not established in the European Union, the manufacturer's representative or (if none) the EC importer. Likewise treated as producers are 'other professionals in the supply chain, insofar as their activities may affect the safety of a product placed on the market'.

A product is regarded as safe if it does not present any risk or only the minimum acceptable risks compatible with the product's use, consistent with a high level of protection for health and safety. Clear instructions for use and appropriate warning labels will be necessary. Consumers must be provided with relevant information to enable them to assess for themselves any inherent risks. Producers should adopt suitable precautionary measures such as appropriate batch marking (to facilitate product recall), sample testing, and investigation and notification of complaints. All these considerations would be relevant if the facts in *Lambert* v. *Lewis* were to arise today.

An important new duty is imposed on distributors, defined as 'any professional in the supply chain whose activity does not affect the safety properties of a product'. Distributors must act with due care to help ensure compliance with the general safety requirement and, within the limits of their activities, must participate in monitoring the safety of products, alerting others to risks and cooperating in action taken to avoid them.

Enforcement of the Regulations lies primarily with local authority trading standards departments, acting under the enforcement powers (including power to seize goods) conferred by the Consumer Protection Act. It is a defence for defendants to show that they 'took all reasonable steps and exercised all due diligence to avoid committing the offence'. Reliance on information supplied by another is not enough unless reasonable in all the circumstances, particularly as regards the steps taken by the defendant to verify the information.

Criminal liability can also arise from safety regulations made under the 1987 Act. There are some thirty sets of regulations in force, which apply to particular types of goods. Examples are regulations applying to cosmetics, electrical goods, pencils, toys, and upholstered furniture. Contravention of the regulations is a strict liability offence.

Breach of a safety regulation will entitle an injured party to bring a claim in tort for breach of statutory duty (see p. 20). However, in practice, it is more likely that a claim would be made under Part 1 of the 1987 Act (see p. 152).

Under the 1987 Act, various notices can be issued by the Secretary of State against the supplier of specific unsafe goods. These notices can:

- prohibit the supply of such goods, or
- require the supplier to publish a warning notice about them, or
- require the supplier to provide the Secretary of State with information about them or to produce documents.

In respect of the above-mentioned criminal offences, an individual or a company and its directors can be prosecuted in the magistrates' court. If found guilty, the maximum penalty is £5,000 and/or six months' imprisonment. In addition the court can order the forfeiture and destruction of the goods, and require the defendant to compensate the enforcement authority for the expenses it occurred in seizing and detaining, or forfeiting goods.

Codes of practice

Trade associations often publish codes of practice. Some are published for their publicity value rather than for the protection they in fact give consumers. However, many trade associations do produce such codes in consultation with the Office of Fair Trading and these codes set out what is regarded as current good practice. Managers should be familiar with the contents of the code relevant to their enterprise. Copies of the code are usually obtainable from the particular trade association. There are codes dealing with, for example, double glazing, electrical appliances, domestic laundry and cleaning services, footwear, footwear repairs, funerals, furniture, holiday caravans, the motor industry, package holidays, photography and postal services.

Such codes of practice are usually voluntary and are not legally enforceable, unless a business has indicated to the public that it observes a code's provisions.

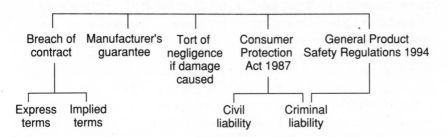

Figure 6.2 Summary of liability for defective products

UNACCEPTABLE TRADING PRACTICES

The position of Director General of Fair Trading was established by the Fair Trading Act 1973. The Act is concerned with ensuring fair competition by regulating monopolies and mergers (see Chapter 8), and with consumer protection. The Director General is given various powers and duties under the Act. These include keeping under review and collecting information as to commercial activities in the United Kingdom which might adversely affect the economic or other interests of consumers. In addition the Director General must encourage trade associations to prepare and monitor codes of practice (see p. 155). There are some thirty codes of practice. Most of the codes include the option of low cost conciliation or arbitration. The Office of Fair Trading (OFT) publishes a considerable number of informative and clear leaflets advising consumers as to their rights. However, the OFT does not formally advise consumers on their individual cases.

The Director General of Fair Trading also has the power to obtain a written assurance from a business which persistently engages in unfair trade practices. These practices must amount to a course of conduct which is detrimental and unfair to consumers and involve breaches of the civil or criminal law. The business must agree to discontinue that course of conduct. Failure to give or abide by the assurance empowers the Director General to take proceedings against the business in the Restrictive Practices Court or the county court, which can require compliance with the assurance. Failure to comply with the court order would make the business liable to a fine or imprisonment for contempt of court.

STRATEGIES FOR MANAGERS

The market for the goods or services should be identified by the supplier whether a manufacturer, a wholesaler, or a retailer. The advertising and other marketing materials should be aimed mainly at the target group, which could be businesses or consumers or a combination of both. Suppliers should ensure that a system exists within their business for checking that the factual content of these materials is not false or misleading.

Suppliers of goods and the provider of services will also have to identify the particular market because this may affect the need for guarantees and the terms which should be included in the particular contracts of sale or supply. Managers should use the contract to plan for possible eventualities, rather than leaving things to chance. Allocation of risk if desired can be achieved through the use of exclusion or limitation clauses and indemnity clauses where valid, as well as by force majeure and hardship clauses. Methods for resolving disputes without resorting to litigation, such as a liquidated damages clause or provision for reference to arbitration, can be included within the contract. Informal resolution must be preferable if the aim is to continue the commercial relationship.

The retailer or seller of goods will bear initial responsibility for defective goods, as will the supplier of services. However, the manufacturer of goods will also be liable to pay compensation for defective goods which cause damage and will be liable in contract for defective goods (where there is a contractual relationship).

Suppliers of unsafe consumer goods will also be criminally liable. The management strategy should stress the importance of manufacturing a safe product. The management system should aim to avoid or at least minimize the risk of defects, for economic as well as legal reasons. However, the management strategy should also recognize that defective goods will be produced and ensure that there exists a system to identify how the product might fail and with what consequences. The residual liability can be shared with the supplier of components or the retailer, or insured against.

The manufacturer first needs to ensure that the design and specification of their goods, and the production process (see Chapter 4) at the very least comply with the requirements of the law and relevant British Standards, for example, BS 5750 Quality Systems, which lays down a national standard for managing the quality of manufacturing procedures. Quality control systems are common in most organizations. The quality of the goods can be affected by, for example, a problem in the production process, the method or length of storage, the packing process, or the means of delivery to the customer. The system should identify the potential location and type of quality defect, and should include procedures to be complied with where, for practical reasons, the design has to be altered.

Second, the manufacturer needs to ensure that there is a procedure for examining and assessing the impact of new technology on the design and production of the goods. Changes to a product or service may be the result of suggestions from staff, customers or users. The organization and the individual staff must be able to cope with change. If the technology used becomes outdated this could create legal liability.

Third, the manufacturer should check that the supplier of components also has a quality assurance system. Wholesalers and retailers must also check that consumer goods supplied to them comply with current safety regulations.

If defective goods are produced and sold, then it is preferable to recall the affected goods, or issue a warning rather than wait for purchasers to bring claims. Recall of goods requires accurate records so that affected goods can be easily identified by, for example, serial numbers. *Lexmead* were unable to identify their supplier. In different circumstances this could have meant that they would have had to bear any loss they suffered and would not have been indemnified by their supplier. Therefore retailers should also be able to trace their suppliers and ideally their buyers by keeping accurate records. Other detailed documentation such as test reports and quality control records can also be crucial in litigation.

Last but not least, staff need to be made aware through, for example, policy documents and staff training programmes of the correct procedures and the possible legal consequences of failing to follow them.

KEY LEARNING POINTS

- **Civil and criminal liability can arise where false statements are made to persuade a person to buy goods, services or property.**
- **The contract of sale sets out the main legal obligations of the parties to a contract. The tort of negligence and the Consumer Protection Act 1987 may impose additional liability on the parties to the contract.**
- **Anyone who is harmed, or whose property is damaged by a defective product may have a remedy against the manufacturer, or the producer or the supplier either under the manufacturer's guarantee, or the tort of negligence or the Consumer Protection Act 1987.**
- **The Consumer Protection Act 1987 imposes civil liability on suppliers of unsafe goods; the General Product Safety Regulations 1994, as well as the 1987 Act, imposes criminal liability.**
- **The Office of Fair Trading is concerned with ensuring fair competition. Self-regulation through codes of practice is encouraged. These codes establish what is regarded as current good trading practice.**

EXERCISES

1   Draft an advertisement of not more than fifty words for one of your enterprise's products. The advertisement should be legal, decent, honest and truthful!

2   Do you know whether the enterprise you work for uses standard form contracts? If it does, look at the terms of any such contract. Try to work out who is liable for what. If it does not use standard form contracts, why doesn't it? Try to draft one.

3   Look at an example of a contract used by your enterprise, or alternatively look at the contract contained in a package holiday brochure. Try to work out the effect of any exclusion clause in the contract.

4   Does your enterprise have a procedure for dealing with complaints about the goods or services it provides? Is its aim to produce an informal

resolution of any dispute? Does it provide for conciliation or arbitration or for a more formal resolution involving lawyers?

5   Does a code of practice apply to the type of goods or services provided by your enterprise? If yes, does your enterprise comply with its provisions? If no, would it be desirable to have a code of practice and what should it address?

NOTES: CASE REFERENCES ETC

1 *Lambert* v *Lewis* [1982] AC 225; [1981] 1 All ER 1185.
2 See, e.g., *Howard Marine & Dredging Co. Ltd* v *A Ogden & Sons (Excavations) Ltd* [1978] QB 574; [1978] 2 All ER 1134.
3 *Horner* v *Kingsley Clothing Co. Ltd*, *The Times*, 6 July 1989; *sub nom. Durham Trading Standards* v *Kingsley Clothing Co. Ltd* (1990) 154 JP 124; [1989] Crim LR 911.
4 SI 1994 No. 2328.
5 S.14(2), (2A), (2B) and (2C) of the Sale of Goods Act 1979 as substituted by S.1 of the Sale and Supply of Goods Act 1994.
6 Directive 93/13/EEC.
7 See, e.g., *George Mitchell (Chesterhall) Ltd* v *Finney Lock Seeds Ltd* [1983] 2 AC 803; [1983] 2 All ER 737. (For Lord Denning's last judgment in the Court of Appeal, see [1983] 1 All ER 108.)
8 These Regulations were delayed by discussions on the right to bring representative actions.
9 See, e.g., *L Schuler AG* v *Wickman Machine Tool Sales Ltd* [1974] AC 235; [1973] 2 All ER 39, where a term described in the contract as a 'condition' was held not to be a condition in the legal sense.
10 See, e.g., *Cehave* v *Bremer*, *The Hansa Nord* [1976] QB 44; [1975] 3 All ER 739, where a buyer unsuccessfully relied on this ground as the basis for refusing to take delivery of 12,000 tons of citrus pulp pellets because part of the shipment had been damaged by overheating.
11 *H. Parsons (Livestock) Ltd* v *Uttley Ingham & Co. Ltd* [1978] QB 791; [1978] 1 All ER 525.
12 *Donoghue* v *Stevenson* [1932] AC 562; 1932 All ER Rep 1.
13 See, e.g., *Lister* v *Romford Ice & Cold Storage Co. Ltd* [1957] AC 555; [1957] 1 All ER 125.
14 Council Directive 85/374/EEC.
15 Council Directive 92/59/EEC on general product safety.

JOURNALS

Consumer Law Journal.
Journal of Managerial Law.
Trading Law.

FURTHER READING

Bagehot, R. (1993) *Sales Promotion and Advertising*, London: Sweet & Maxwell.
Harvey, B. and Parry, D. (1992) *Law of Consumer Protection and Fair Trading*, London: Butterworths.
Leder, M. and Shears, P. (1991) *Consumer Law*, London: Pitman Publishing.
Stapleton, J. (1994) *Product Liability*, London: Butterworths.
Wedlake Bell (eds.) (1994) *Marketing Law That Matters*, London: Pitman Publishing.
Wright, C.J. (1989) *Product Liability, the Law and its Implications*, London: Blackstone Press.

USEFUL ADDRESSES

Advertising Standards Authority
Brook House,
2–16 Torrington Place
London WC1E 7HN   Tel no. 0171 580 5555

Department of Trade and Industry
10–18 Victoria Street
London SW1H 0NN   Tel no. 0171 215 5000

Office of Fair Trading
Field House
Bream's Buildings
London EC4A 1HA   Tel no. 0171 242 2858.

Chapter 7

The enterprise and its intellectual property

John Weldon

The economic value of an enterprise often depends not just upon its tangible assets and its annual profits, but also upon the ideas behind the products, the services, or the packaging. Original ideas are valuable and the law can be used by an enterprise to preserve these ideas for the enterprise's sole use and to prevent unauthorized use. The law calls these ideas 'intellectual property'. This chapter explains:

- the key features of the different types of intellectual property
- how an enterprise can acquire intellectual property
- how an enterprise can protect its intellectual property.

Case study

Acme Enterprise is developing technology to produce high quality magnetic tape for music cassettes and needs to know whether it will get a worthwhile return on its investment. Consequently it needs to know how to develop and protect its intellectual property.

Box 7.1 Acme Enterprise

INTRODUCTION

Issues which *Acme Enterprise* will have to consider include:

- does it understand what intellectual property is and the commercial importance of its legal protection?
- how can it acquire intellectual property and protect it during development?
- how can it secure the maximum legal protection for all aspects of its products?
- how can it exploit its intellectual property?

What is 'intellectual property'?

Intellectual property can be defined as those products of the mind to which the law grants the author legal protection and hence the enhanced ability to exploit. Intellectual property covers a wide range of subject matter including:

- a patent, which is the exclusive right to use a scientific invention such as a drug or a chemical process
- copyright, which is the right to prevent copying of works such as books, music or broadcasts
- a registered design, which is the exclusive right to use the aesthetic appearance of a manufactured product such as furniture
- a design right, which is the right to prevent copying of a functional aspect of the shape or configuration of an article such as a mechanical tool
- design copyright, which is the right to prevent the use of artistic design documents for the purpose of manufacturing articles, for example, jewellery designs.
- a registered trade or service mark, which is the exclusive right to use a name or symbol in connection with a product or service, for example, the 'Adidas' symbol.
- goodwill and reputation, which are the market's perception of the value and quality of a business and its products and which can be protected against interference and damage
- confidential information, which is commercially sensitive information such as business methods or pricing details and which can be protected against unauthorized disclosure or use.

Commercial importance of intellectual property

In the international context there is a direct correlation between investment in research and development and competitive success. Compared with their competitors, Japan and Germany generally have higher levels of long term investment and awareness of the importance of innovation and the design process.

In the domestic context it is not surprising that the two largest manufacturing industries, chemicals and aerospace, also have the highest levels of investment in research and development. Such industries are highly competitive internationally. They contribute significantly to the nation's revenue and balance of trade, employ large numbers of workers and make considerable profits for their shareholders.

The impact on the consumer of the legal protection of intellectual property is enormous. Where products are protected by intellectual property, whether it be by patenting, reputation or trade marks, the manufacturer is able to charge a premium. Brand names in the fashion industry are an obvious example of this phenomenon.

Acme Enterprise needs to understand the concept, range and commercial impact of intellectual property.

ACQUISITION OF INTELLECTUAL PROPERTY

There are a number of ways to acquire intellectual property including:

- innovation
- information gathering
- assignment
- licensing
- franchising
- joint venture.

Innovation

Innovation is the natural way of acquiring intellectual property in the sense that new ideas are the raw material of intellectual property.

Innovation may come from a blinding flash of genius or the grinding work of an entrepreneur, but more realistically an enterprise needs to have effective employment, investment and research and development policies if it is going to develop technology itself.

Information gathering

The enterprise needs employees who are not only fully up to date in their own fields, but who are also aware of, and capable of exploiting tangential technologies.

Effective market research is an important part of the information gathering process. One obvious technique is reverse engineering, i.e., taking apart others' products. A more sophisticated version of this is the careful analysis of the manufacturing and marketing methods used by others.

A rather more mechanical way of acquiring information is simply by searching the Patent Office for patents, registered designs and trade marks in the fields in which one is interested. Private patent publishing firms provide services whereby they will provide abstracts or full copies of patents, domestic and foreign, in any particular field requested. Some international firms of patent attorneys maintain world-wide watches on intellectual property usages and developments and will carry out customized searches and ongoing status reports.

Assignment

An assignment is a contract for the outright transfer of the entire interest in some piece of intellectual property. This method is unusual because the owner is unlikely to choose to give up control of, and potential royalties from their ideas. Assignment is most likely to take place where the owner does not have the skills or finance to develop those ideas.

Licensing

A licence is a contract whereby the owner of intellectual property grants the licensee the right to use the technology, design, name or information on certain terms.

Licences can take a wide variety of forms and it is vital that the contract is clear in its commercial and legal aspects. These include degree of control, warranties, share of profits and liabilities, permitted usage, undertakings as to maintenance of confidentiality and the conditions upon which the intellectual property is to revert to the licensor. By a bare licence the licensor transfers specific intellectual property rights in return for a lump sum and/or royalties. A field licence can be used to transfer rights within a given field of technology, with or without rights to related commercial information, or sometimes with after-acquired knowledge within the given field.

Franchising

A specific type of licensing arrangement is a franchise whereby the owner of a successful branded service will grant a franchise to a franchisee to provide that service for a period of time in a given geographical area. A franchise commonly takes the form of an agreement where the franchisee buys not just the right to use the name and advertising but also the right to adopt the method and style of business of the franchisor. Common examples include chain retailers, e.g. *TieRack*, and restaurants, e.g. *McDonalds*.

A successful franchising arrangement depends upon three important factors. First, the franchisor must have a strong market presence and reputation, i.e., there must be intellectual property worth buying. Second, the intellectual property in the franchise must be protected from copying by competitors. Third, the franchisees must stick rigorously to the standards set in the franchise otherwise the value of the intellectual property will be diminished for the franchisee, franchisor and other franchisees.

Joint venture

Another means of acquiring intellectual property is by moving into co-operative enterprise with another party. This can take a wide variety of forms. It could be the marriage of skills of different innovators into a partnership or jointly owned company. It could be the matching of one party with an idea with another with the money to exploit it.

The investor will usually require some stake in the innovator's intellectual property. This could take the form of an assignment of legal rights in the intellectual property, or a charge on the assets of the company, or a shareholding in the company itself. The joint venture could take the form of the purchase or merger of companies, or an arrangement between companies to set up a jointly owned subsidiary to develop a particular area of technology or product.

Acme Enterprise will have to consider whether it is cost-effective or possible or even necessary to innovate itself, or whether it would be better to acquire technology from outside or in conjunction with partners.

It needs the means to identify the technology available elsewhere, either by its own staff or by using external agencies. It will have to determine what information is useful and adaptable, what is freely available, what information needs clearance to be used, and what method of clearance is the most appropriate.

It may be the case that *Acme Enterprise* will need to have intellectual property such as manufacturing processes or synthetic materials assigned, licensed or franchised to it if they are vital to *Acme's* own developments and cannot be designed around.

Acme Enterprise would have to consider whether it could afford not to enter into a joint venture in order to develop expensive technology.

Acme Enterprise will need to be aware that licence and franchise agreements are subject to EC competition law (see Chapter 8). Generally exclusive licence agreements which restrain trade will be unlawful unless they fall within the categories of block exemptions granted by the European Commission in relation to intellectual property. Large joint ventures and mergers are subject to national and EC competition laws which aim to prevent monopolies and abuse of dominant position in the market.

PATENTS

A patent is the exclusive right to use and exploit an invention for twenty years provided that the invention:

- is new
- involves an inventive step going beyond the state of the art
- is capable of industrial application
- does not fall into the classes of non-patentable material.

Examples of patentable matters include mechanical systems, chemical compounds and micro-biological techniques. In return for the legal protection conferred by a patent, the owner discloses to the world the technology incorporated in the patent application.

The legal protection of inventions in the UK is governed by the Patents Act 1977. There are two international treaty systems whereby one can apply for a bundle of national patents including a British patent. These are the European Patent Convention 1973, which covers thirteen European countries, and the Patent Co-operation Treaty 1970 which covers over forty countries world-wide. An application and grant through either of these systems confers the same rights as a domestic application. Whilst the procedures differ, the basic grounds for validity are, with minor differences, the same as in respect of a domestic application.

The European Community Patent Convention 1985, amended by the Community Patent Agreement 1989, provides that the grant of a patent in any EC country would have effect as a single patent enforceable in the whole Community. This convention has not yet been ratified.

Novelty

The invention must be new in the sense that it is something never before disclosed by publication or use, nor incorporated in an earlier patent application.[1]

It is crucial, therefore, that an innovator ensures that he does not disclose any information before making a patent application. A disclosure anywhere in the world can be fatal. A disclosure in confidence does not constitute making the information public.

Speed in making an application can also be of the essence, especially in fields such as the pharmaceutical industry where it is not uncommon for competitors independently to develop similar ideas, e.g., as in the current race to find an AIDS cure. The first to file an application will win against the first inventor.

Incremental developments can be novel, for instance, a new use of a known compound can be patented provided the claim restricts itself to the functional technical feature which produces the new effect.

Inventive step

There must be an inventive step, i.e., it must involve a step going beyond the state of the art which would not have been obvious to a person skilled in the art. This requirement is not a test of ingenuity or luck of the applicant, but a comparison of the state of the art and the claim to see if the subject of the claim would have been developed in the normal course of using the state of the art or whether it represents technical progress.[2]

A person skilled in the art is someone who is acquainted with the relevant techniques, technical literature and prior patent specifications, but is not necessarily a leading light in the field nor a researcher who has a particular developmental result in mind.

Combining two well known machines would not be an inventive step. The methodology of the development will be important evidence in determining inventiveness. Comparative research to solve a re-defined problem producing a surprising solution would constitute an inventive step.

Industrial application

The invention must be capable of industrial application. An invention is to be taken to be capable of industrial application if it can be made, or used in any kind of industry including agriculture.

A method of treatment of the human or animal body by surgery, therapy or diagnosis is not to be taken to be capable of industrial application. However, a product used in a method of treatment is capable of industrial application. Thus pharmaceuticals are most definitely patentable. Indeed they are an excellent example of the importance of intellectual property. Even the very largest of drug companies are dependent for a large proportion of their profits on a handful of drugs over which they have a monopoly right by virtue of patent protection.

The purpose of the requirement of industrial application is to distinguish patents from other forms of legal protection and to exclude useless inventions.

Patentable subject matter

The claim must be for patentable subject matter. The following are not patentable:

- discoveries
- scientific theories
- mathematical methods
- methods of doing business
- methods of performing mental acts
- immoral inventions
- plants or animals
- presentation of information.

Computer programs and aesthetic creations such as literary works are also excluded but these can be protected by copyright.

A patent application is precluded only in so far as it is for the discovery, method of doing business or mathematical method 'as such'. Thus a patent could be obtained for some practical application based upon a discovery provided that there is some inventive step.[3]

An example of the problem of what is patentable is in the field of bio-technology. Micro-biological processes and their products may be patentable. Patents cannot be obtained for plants or animals or biological processes for the manufacture thereof. However, Harvard University's 'Onco-Mouse' (a method of producing mice that would be born with cancer so that they could be used for medical experimentation) has recently been patented. The case raised technical issues relating to what constitutes biological processes as well as questions of the morality and desirability of genetic engineering.

Procedure

The procedures for applying for a patent are costly and lengthy.

Before filing a patent application it is necessary to ask whether patent protection is really necessary and where it should be sought, taking into account prospective markets, the likelihood of competition, the cost and time involved, the value and expected commercial life of the invention and alternative methods of protection.

A patent agent should draft and submit the application to the Patent Office. The filing date is of great importance: it indicates the applicant's priority against competing applications. The applicant can develop the technology and file for patents in other jurisdictions during the first twelve months and they will have the same priority date in other countries as in the UK.

After about twelve months the application will be re-filed and an official search by the Patent Office is requested to determine whether the technology has been anticipated, after which, normally six months later, the application will be published. The application cannot be altered from this time.

After publication, third parties can object to the grant of a patent and the Patent Office will carry out full examination. If the patent is finally granted it will usually be about four years after initial filing.

Remedies

'Actual infringement' is the re-production of a machine or process as defined in the patent. 'Contributory infringement' is assistance or encouragement in actual infringement, such as sale or importation. A patent owner cannot sue for infringement whilst the patent is being applied for but can subsequently obtain damages for breach during that time.

Various defences lie against an action for infringement of patent. These include that the act was done privately and for non-commercial purposes, or that the act was done in good faith before the priority date of the patent application.

The remedies for infringement include damages, injunction, declaration and delivery or destruction of infringing articles. The damages payable should reflect the damage to the patent owner. This is often calculated by a reckoning of the royalties payable had the patent been licensed.

A patent can be subject to the grant of a compulsory licence after three years from grant. Anyone may apply for a compulsory licence on a variety of grounds. These include that the invention is not being used in the UK, or that demand for it is not being met on reasonable grounds, or is being met substantially by importation.

It should also be noted that patent registration must be periodically renewed and third parties can apply for its revocation.

Acme Enterprise will need to consider whether it has technology capable of patenting. If it has, it must ensure that the technology is kept secret until formal application. It needs to make a commercial analysis of whether patent protection is necessary, and where it should be sought. Given the complexity and length of the patent application procedure, *Acme* cannot realistically avoid using outside professional advice.

COPYRIGHT

Copyright is the right to prevent copying for life, plus fifty years, of the author's concrete expression of:

- original literary, artistic, dramatic or musical works
- non-original publications such as films, sound recordings, technical drawings, broadcasts and typesets.

The legal protection of copyright in the UK is governed by the Copyright, Designs and Patents Act 1988.

Copyright does not apply just to the arts; it has important industrial and commercial applications in that it applies to written works irrespective of subject-matter, interest or aesthetic appeal. The legal protection conferred is to prevent copying: there is no protection against someone who independently comes up with the same idea.

Literary works include mundane but commercially valuable matters such as product instructions, training manuals, standard forms, translations, compilations and written databases.[4] Literary works now also include computer programs.

Artistic works are defined as including graphic works such as diagrams, painting, photographs, plans, works of architecture and works of artistic craftsmanship. Graphic works are important elements in establishing corporate and product identity. Works of artistic craftsmanship include matters such as jewellery, furniture and clothing.

The essential purpose of copyright is to protect the expression of ideas, not the ideas themselves. The expression must be novel in the sense of not being a copy and there must be some labour, skill or capital in creating the expression. Individual titles do not attract copyright. Business or product names are not protected by copyright either but they may be protected as trade marks or names.

Copyright subsists in a work until the end of the fiftieth year from the end of the year in which the author died. The owner of copyright has the right to prevent reproduction of the work. An author who has assigned his commercial interest in the copyright retains certain moral rights which include being identified as the author, not having the work wrongly attributed to another and being able to object to the prejudicial modification of the work.

Procedure

Copyright arises automatically with the expression of the idea and no formal procedure is required for its protection. Sometimes it is useful to maintain proof of the date of production of copyright material where there is a possibility of dispute as to originality.

Remedies

Infringement can be by direct copying, adaptation, broadcasting or performing, and putting into circulation. Infringement must involve use of a substantial part of the work though it can be problematic as to what constitutes a substantial part. Fair dealing does not constitute infringement: the main example of fair dealing is copying for private study or research.

The remedies available for breach of copyright are normally damages or injunction to prevent a repetition of breach. In many cases it is important that copies of copyright material are recovered in order to prevent their use. The remedy of the Anton Piller order is available to seize unlawfully obtained copies. An example of its importance is in the fashion industry where it is vital to recover stolen fashion designs before they are used.

Acme Enterprise should ensure that the graphic design of its products and other publications is sufficiently distinctive so that it will be easy to prove if a competitor is copying the products and other publications. It is very important that *Acme* is vigilant in ensuring that company documents are not copied by competitors. Sensitive documents are protected by copyright but only sufficient secrecy and confidentiality will prevent others gaining the ideas behind the documents. *Acme Enterprise* should be conscious of the full range of types of copyright so that they can be fully exploited.

INDUSTRIAL DESIGN

There are three ways to protect industrial design. Registered designs generally relate to aesthetic appearance. Unregistered design rights relate to the shape internally or externally of products. Design copyright relates to design documents. These three are largely covered by the Copyright, Designs and Patents Act 1988 and the Registered Design Act 1949 (as amended).

They are of great importance in that they give specific legal protection to the added value which good design can give to a product.

Registered designs

A registered design is the exclusive right for up to twenty five years over the outward appearance of a manufactured product.

The design must relate to the shape, configuration, pattern or ornament in the product. The design must be 'of' the article rather than carried by the article. It must be applied to the article by an industrial process. The design must be new, not having been previously published or registered in the UK. It must be aesthetically distinguishable from other designs and the article to which the design applies must be one to which appearance is relevant to the purchaser or user. It must not be determined by the function of the product.[5]

A new design for a hi-fi with a shape radically different from the usual box shape could be registered, provided the new design was not driven by a particular mechanical function. Body parts of a car could not be protected by this method as they are regarded as being determined by the mechanical and aerodynamic design of the car.

Procedure

The proprietor of a design can apply to the Designs Registry of the Patent Office. A series of illustrations or photographs must accompany the application along with a statement which sets out the features which are claimed to be novel. The test of novelty relates to absence of anticipation rather than inventive skill or labour. The application should show the full range of articles to which the design is to apply.

The examination by the Designs Registry takes up to a year. Registration is for an initial term of five years and can be renewed for four further terms of five years each.

Remedies

Registration protects the proprietor against manufacture, facilitation of manufacture, importation and sale of articles to which the design has been applied. The protection afforded the proprietor is similar to the monopoly right of a patent and thus applies against innocent users and not just copiers. The remedies are also the same as for patent breach.

Design rights

A design right is a right to prevent copying of an original design of any aspect of the shape or configuration of the whole or part of an article. This generally relates to the functional internal or external design of an article rather than its aesthetic appeal.

The design must be original in the sense that it must not be commonplace in the design field in question. Protection does not extend to the method of construction or to surface decoration of the article. It does not apply either to a shape or configuration which is designed to enable it to be connected to another article, or where the design is dependent upon the appearance of another article to which it is intended to be connected.

Subject to these limitations the scope of the design right is very wide. It can apply to the shape of virtually any kind of manufactured article including hi-fi components or kitchen utensils.

The design right mechanism has been developed to provide a specific form of protection for semiconductor topographies, i.e. silicon chips. This protection is governed by the Design Right (Semiconductor Topographies) Regulations 1989.[6]

Procedure

The protection arises automatically and does not require any formal procedure for its grant. The right lasts up to fifteen years from first recording of the design but only ten years from the date of marketing.

Remedies

The design right confers the exclusive right to reproduce the article for commercial purposes by making articles to that design. The owner can sue for infringement of design right in order to obtain damages or injunctions. Unauthorized reproduction by copying the design to produce articles, distribution, importation and possession can all constitute infringement.

In the last five years of its duration anyone is entitled as of right to a licence to use the design in any way which would otherwise constitute infringement. The terms of such licence will be settled by the Comptroller General of Patents in the absence of agreement between the parties.

Design copyright

Design copyright protects design documents from being copied to make three dimensional objects. The prime requirement is that the design must be artistic.

It can relate to any aspect of the shape or configuration whether internal or external but not the surface decoration. Once an artistic design has been used in articles manufactured by an industrial process the copyright life is limited to twenty-five years.

To make a piece of jewellery from another's drawn design would be an infringement as the design is of an artistic work. On the other hand, to make a machine from someone else's design would not be an infringement though the latter may constitute infringement of design right.

Procedure

There is no procedure for acquiring design copyright protection, as copyright arises automatically upon recording of a novel design.

Remedies

The copying of a design in written form would in itself be a breach of copyright, so the normal copyright remedies apply. In addition, to manufacture articles based on the copied artistic design would be an infringement and the remedies available in relation to wrongful manufacture of patented products can apply.

Acme Enterprise would have to consider whether the aesthetic appearance of its products can be designed in such a way as to be registrable and whether the shapes of its products and components can be protected as design rights. *Acme* would have to be forward thinking in the design process to force others to design around its designs. However, it may fall foul of the requirement that the design cannot depend on another article to which it is connected.

Acme Enterprise needs to be aware of the possibilities of design copyright but it should also be aware that design copyright is unlikely to apply to its technology.

TRADE AND SERVICE MARKS AND NAMES

Registered trade and service marks give the exclusive right to use names and symbols in relation to goods and services indefinitely, subject to renewal.

The mark can be words, including names, symbols, patterns and including coloration. The mark must be distinctive in that it must be one which is adapted to distinguish the owner's goods from those of any other trader. It must not be deceptive by purporting to describe the goods or imply characteristics in them. There must be no conflict with existing registered or unregistered trade marks.[7]

Marks, such as *Coca Cola*, are of great importance in protecting the underlying intellectual property of the enterprise in the sense of its goodwill and reputation.

Trade names which refer to the entire business as opposed to its products, will be registered along with the corporate registration of the enterprise. The business name registered would have to satisfy the requirements that it is not imitative or deceptive.

The law relating to trade marks is covered by the Trade Marks Act 1938, the Trade Marks (Amendments) Act 1984, the EC Trade Marks Directive 1988,[8] and the Trade Marks Act 1994 (as to which see Chapter 9 at p. 212).

Procedure

In order to secure protection it is necessary to apply to the Trade Marks Registry of the Patent Office to enter a registration in the register. Until 1993 there were two parts to the register, Part A and Part B, but Part A was removed when the EC Trade Marks Directive 1988[8] came into effect. Part A trade marks dealt with the category of marks adapted to distinguish the goods. Shapes of products and containers are now also registrable as trade marks.

Trade marks which can now be registered are those which were in the Part B category which imposed an easier test for registration than Part A. It is only necessary to establish that the trade mark is capable of distinguishing the goods, that is, it may do so in the future.

There is a classification according to types of goods. This is very important as failure to have registration in the right classification will prevent action against users of the mark on goods not in that classification.

Registration confers indefinite protection subject to renewal every seven years.

Remedies

The owner of a registered mark is entitled to sue for infringement anyone who, without authorization, uses the mark or one confusingly similar to it, in the course of trade in relation to goods for which the mark is registered. The remedies include the usual ones of injunction, damages or an account for profits and extend to the destruction of the offending goods.

The tort of passing off can be used to protect against competitors who mimic unregistered trademarks or the unregistrable style of container, or who use confusingly similar names or marks in an attempt to take advantage of another's reputation.[9]

The tort of injurious falsehood is also available to counteract malicious false statements, such as specifically denigrating the plaintiff's goods, or falsely stating that the plaintiff is not the true owner of the goods.

Acme Enterprise should make use of designers and trade mark agents who together can produce a distinctive trade mark and name which can enhance market recognition and reputation.

GOODWILL AND REPUTATION

Goodwill and reputation can be seen as forms of intellectual property, in that they constitute an identifiable value in the enterprise based upon its skill and labour and the perception of its qualities. Where they are manifested in names and symbols identifying the enterprise they can be protected by registration of trade and service marks and names.

The importance of goodwill and reputation can be divided into three areas. First, trade and service marks can be enormous financial assets in themselves for the purposes of licensing and franchising. Second, goodwill and reputation can be valuable in a more general sense in terms of market recognition and sales. Third, goodwill and reputation can be calculated in money terms for the purposes of accounting, share value of the enterprise and the sale value of the whole enterprise.

Procedure

This type of intellectual property is protected by good management in the production and marketing of quality products and services.

Remedies

The remedies for infringement of trade mark, passing off and injurious falsehood may be available. There are other torts which may be actionable where they have damaged an enterprise, e.g., conspiracy or interference with an existing contract.

The foundation of *Acme Enterprise's* goodwill and reputation will be the quality of its products. To exploit these fully *Acme* needs to have a marketing strategy which makes best use of its qualities, so that sales feed reputation and that reputation in turn feeds further sales. It needs to have a strong corporate identity which adds to market recognition. It also needs to be vigilant to ensure that its reputation is not imitated or interfered with.

CONFIDENTIAL INFORMATION

Confidential information, such as trade secrets and know-how, may be protected formally if they fall within the categories of patent, copyright, trademark, etc. However, the information may not be capable of formal protection or it may be of such commercial sensitivity, e.g., pricing, client databases, methods of doing business, that the enterprise wishes to avoid any possible disclosure to competitors. The tort of breach of confidence exists to provide a remedy for unauthorized use of confidential information.[10]

The three requirements for proving the tort of breach of confidence are:

- the information must be confidential
- the information must have been imparted in circumstances importing an obligation of confidence
- there must be an unauthorized use of that information to the detriment of its owner.

Information must be confidential

For information to be regarded as confidential, the owner must reasonably believe it to be confidential and that release of the information would be injurious to him or advantageous to others. Marking information private and confidential will not make it confidential in a legal sense. Whether information has the quality of confidentiality is tested objectively.

The information must be identifiable with some precision, it must be of commercial value though it need not be especially complex or technical. There is an essential requirement that skill and effort has been used to produce the information. The confidentiality of the information will be judged in the light of usage and practices of the particular trade or industry concerned. Once information has been released into the public domain the law of confidence provides no protection.

Obligation of confidence/procedure

The main way to protect confidential information is by the contract of employment (see Chapter 3). An employee has implied duties of confidence, of good faith and to act in his employer's best interests. Ex-employees are also under an implied duty not to disclose confidential information. These duties can be expressly reaffirmed in the contract of employment.

Restrictions on the type or location of employment of an ex-employee can be used but may be held to be invalid for being in restraint of trade. An employer cannot restrain an employee from taking with him his innate skills or knowledge acquired elsewhere (see Chapter 8).

An obligation of confidence can arise where information is divulged in the course of negotiations with third parties. The obligation can be expressly stated or it can be inferred from the sensitivity of the dealings.

Where information has been acquired for the purpose of fulfilling a contract, its use by the contractor or even subcontractors in later profitable dealings with a third party will be a breach of confidence.

Obligations of confidence also arise in a range of formal relationships such as between doctor and patient, or solicitor and client. An obligation of confidence can be imposed on someone who steals or gains unauthorized access to confidential information.

Unauthorized use

Unauthorized use takes place where confidential information acquired in the context of an obligation of confidence is used in such a way as to cause damage to the owner or unjust enrichment to the user.

Remedies

The remedy for unauthorized use is to sue in the tort of breach of confidence for damages. One can apply for an order for the possessor to deliver up the material, or for an Anton Piller order whereby one can, with a court order, seize material obtained in breach of confidence. If the material has been commercially exploited the person in breach may have to account for profits. In extreme cases a court may order the destruction of products manufactured in breach of confidence.

Under the Computer Misuse Act 1990 there are criminal offences relating to computer theft and hacking.

Data protection

Criminal liability for misuse of confidential information can also arise under the Data Protection Act 1984. Any organization which keeps personal data on computer must be registered with the Data Protection Registrar otherwise it can be criminally liable. The entry on the register broadly describes the kind of personal data held, the purposes for which it is used, sources of the data and people to whom it may be disclosed. Certain types of data are exempt such as data used only for calculating wages and pensions.

An enterprise which is registered must follow the data protection principles, which state that the data must be obtained fairly and lawfully, that it is to be used or disclosed only for the purposes described in the entry, that it must be accurate and properly protected and that it is to be relevant and not excessive in relation to the purpose for which it is held. Failure to observe the principles can lead to de-registration, or an enforcement notice requiring compliance which it is a criminal offence to ignore.

Individuals have the right to see data held relating to them, they have the right to have it corrected or removed if it is inaccurate and may obtain compensation if loss has arisen from the inaccuracy. They also have the right to compensation if damage occurs from the loss or unauthorized destruction or disclosure of data.

Acme Enterprise will need to pursue a careful policy of ensuring confidentiality in its dealings with employees and third parties, as well as taking practical security measures against theft.

STRATEGIES FOR MANAGERS

The starting point of an enterprise's intellectual property strategy is the need to be aware of the commercial importance of intellectual property and the full range of rights which attract legal protection. All enterprises need to appreciate the competitive advantage and added value that well exploited intellectual property can give.

An enterprise should have a coherent strategy for acquiring intellectual property. The enterprise needs a general awareness of the different possibilities. It should also determine which activities, e.g., market research or technical research can be better done in-house or by external agencies.

A long term investment strategy in research and development is generally to be found as a characteristic of more successful enterprises. An appropriate management structure is needed to foster the inventive effort. An isolated research and development group is unlikely to be as sucessful as one which is integrated and is aware of the input from market research, production and marketing groups.

Contracts of employment should specify that the employer is to own any patents or copyright in the work of employees. They should also reaffirm the need for confidentiality by employees and ex-employees. An enterprise needs to ensure that those responsible for the making and monitoring of contracts with third parties adequately protect the enterprise's intellectual property. An enterprise should also have an ongoing procedure for maintaining its intellectual property and defending it against attack or breach.

In addition to its marketing strategy, an enterprise should ensure that the full range of rights available are exploited. Good technology can be improved by good design to produce market differentiating products. Good design can be enhanced by well protected copyright and trade marks which in turn can build up goodwill and reputation. An enterprise also needs to consider methods of exploitation other than direct sale, such as transferring its own intellectual property by licensing etc. to others.

KEY LEARNING POINTS

Table 7.1 Key learning points

	Subject matter	Procedure	Duration
Patent	Novel technology involving an inventive step which is industrially applicable	Application to Patent Office	20 years
Copyright	Original literary and artistic works and publications	Arises from expression of the idea	Life of the author plus 50 years
Registered design	Outward design of an article	Application to Designs Registry of the Patent Office	Up to 25 years
Design right	Functional design of an article	Arises from the recording of the design	Up to 15 years
Design copyright	Artistic design documents	Arises from the recording of the design	25 years from the use of the design in a manufactured article
Trade and service marks and names	Names or symbols relating to goods or services	Application to trade marks division of the Patent Office	Indefinite subject to renewal
Goodwill and reputation	Perceived value of an enterprise and its products	Quality management and products	Indefinite subject to maintenance
Confidential information	Trade secrets or other sensitive information	Arises by contract or from the confidentiality of a relationship	Until released into the public domain

EXERCISES

1 See if you can find one example from each of the categories of intellectual property over which your enterprise has legal rights.

2 Is your enterprise aware of copyright restrictions on using material produced by other individuals or organizations, when producing its own information and publicity or advertising material?

3   While eating breakfast see whether any of the cereals or their packets are protected by copyright, or by a registered trade mark. Could the cereal recipe be protected? If so, how?

4   Does your contract of employment restrict where or for whom you can work if you leave your current employer? Is the restriction valid?

5   Does your enterprise keep personal data on computer? Is the enterprise registered with the Data Protection Registrar? How could you find out whether other enterprises hold information on you or your enterprise?

6   How does your enterprise manage its intellectual property? Is it managed in-house or does it employ consultants?

NOTES: CASE REFERENCES ETC

1 *General Tire & Rubber Co.* v *Firestone Tyre & Rubber Co.* [1975] 1WLR 819; [1972] RPC 457.
2 *Windsurfing International Inc.* v *Tabur Marine (Great Britain)* [1985] RPC 59.
3 *Merrill Lynch's Application* [1989] RPC 561.
4 *University of London Press Ltd* v *University Tutorial Press Ltd* [1916] 2 Ch 601; 86 LJ Ch 107.
5 *Interlego AG* v *Tyco Industries Inc.* [1988] RPC 343; [1988] 3 All ER 949.
6 S1 1989 No. 1009.
7 *Smith, Kline & French Laboratories Ltd* v *Sterling-Winthrop Group Ltd* [1976] RPC 511; [1975] 2 All ER 578.
8 Directive 89/104/EEC.
9 *Erven Warnink Vennootschap* v *J Townend & Sons (Hull) Ltd* [1979] AC 731; [1979] 2 All ER 927.
10 *Coco* v *AN Clark (Engineers) Ltd* [1969] RPC 41; [1968] FSR 415.

JOURNALS

European Intellectual Property Review.
Journal of the Chartered Institute of Patent Agents.
Intellectual Property in Business.
Managing Intellectual Property.

FURTHER READING

Bainbridge, D. (1994) *Intellectual Property*, London: Pitman.
Black, T. (1989) *Intellectual Property in Industry*, London: Butterworths.
Cornish, W. (1989) *Intellectual Property: Patents, Copyright, Trade Marks and Allied Rights*, London: Sweet & Maxwell.
Kompass Directory (published annually) Reed United Data.
Pearson, H. and Miller, C. (1990) *Commercial Exploitation of Intellectual Property*, London: Blackstone Press.

USEFUL ADDRESSES

The Patent Office
25 Southampton Buildings
Chancery Lane
London WC2A 1AY   Tel no. 0171 438 4700

The Design Council
28 Haymarket
London SW1Y 4SU   Tel no. 0171 839 8000

Chartered Institute of Patent Agents
Staple Inn Buildings
High Holborn
London WC1V 7PZ   Tel no. 0171 405 9450

Institute of Trade Mark Agents
Canterbury House
2–6 Sydenham Road
Croydon
Surrey CR0 9XE   Tel no. 0181 686 2050

Reed Information Services Ltd
Windsor Court
East Grinstead House
East Grinstead
West Sussex RH19 1XD   Tel no. 01342 326972.

Chapter 8

The enterprise and competition

Penelope Kent

The economic policy of both the United Kingdom and the European Union favours free competition between the manufacturers and suppliers of goods and services. This is reflected in both UK and Community provisions, although exemptions can be granted under both sets of provisions. Certain anti-competitive practices will only be subject to UK law, whereas others will be subject to both UK and Community (EC) law or just EC law. It should be remembered that where there is a conflict between EC and UK law the former prevails. This chapter discusses in the context of an English case and an EC case the principles and application of:

- United Kingdom competition law
- EC competition law
- free movement and the EC single market.

Case study 1

The Net Book Agreements are a series of agreements between publishers and booksellers, both wholesale and retail, under the control of the Publishers Association, to which most publishers in the United Kingdom belong. The agreements lay down standard conditions for the sale of books at fixed prices. Books covered by the agreements (known as 'net books') may not be sold to the public in the UK and Ireland (Eire) at less than the net publishing price.

The validity of the Net Book Agreements was unsuccessfully challenged under UK legislation in 1962[1] before the UK became a member of the EC, and successfully challenged under EC law in 1988.[2]

Box 8.1 The *Net Book Agreements* (1962) *and* (1988)

INTRODUCTION

United Kingdom competition law is mainly concerned with agreements between two enterprises carrying on business in the UK which, for example, restrict the availability of their goods to certain retail outlets, or which try to fix a minimum price at which goods should be sold. Such an agreement will be invalid even if it does not have any effect on competition. In addition the Director General of Fair Trading can investigate anti-competitive practices, and the Monopolies and Mergers Commission can investigate monopolies and mergers. The relevant UK legislation is:

- the Fair Trading Act 1973
- the Restrictive Trade Practices Act 1976
- the Resale Prices Act 1976
- the Competition Act 1980
- the Deregulation and Contracting Out Act 1994.

EC competition law is wider ranging than UK law, and is chiefly concerned with agreements or practices which affect trade between rather than within member states. It too regulates anti-competitive agreements. However, EC law is concerned with the effect of the agreement rather than its form, unlike UK law. EC law is also concerned with preventing enterprises who have a dominant position in the EC market from abusing their dominance by, for example, refusing to supply certain customers for no objectively valid reason. These rules are underpinned by one of the fundamental principles of the EC which is that there should be free movement of goods. This is looked at in the third part of this chapter.

The relevant EC law is:

- Articles 85, 86, 30–36 of the EC Treaty
- regulations, notices and directives.

THE REGULATION OF COMPETITION

To a manager the word 'competition' is likely to imply the free working of the market in areas such as the supply of goods and labour, with the attendant need to determine prices and quality at rates which are economically advantageous in relation to rival enterprises. As 'perfect' competition rarely, if ever, exists in the real world, some regulation of the market prevents powerful enterprises from taking advantage of their economic strength to the detriment of consumers. Without intervention enterprises would be free to enter into price-fixing arrangements or takeovers which might eliminate competition. Large, powerful enterprises could create barriers to entry, preventing new undertakings from entering the market.

Competition law regulates the operation of market power by prohibiting such restrictive practices, with control exercised at both national and EC level.

Competition under UK law

Current UK competition law is based on an examination of the form of the agreement with reference to set criteria. By contrast, as the *Net Books Agreement* case[3] shows, EC law looks to the effects rather than the form of the agreement. Proposals for reform of UK law, if adopted, will lead to an approach modelled on that of the EC.

Restrictive Trade Practices Act (RTPA) 1976

This is the most significant legislation under the existing scheme. This statute applies to agreements between two parties carrying on business in the UK in the supply of goods and services, provided there are restrictions on two parties, such as a specification as to which customers a supplier will serve or an agreement to fix prices. There are various exemptions for agreements such as exclusive supply agreements, export agreements and intellectual property licences. It is important for managers to note that only one category of exemption may be invoked. Complex agreements with a number of restrictions falling within exemptable categories should be registered with the Office of Fair Trading (OFT).

An agreement which is not exempt must be notified to the OFT which will decide whether it is necessary to refer the agreement to the Restrictive Practices Court. This court has the power to order the parties not to enter into any further registrable agreement without first registering with the Office of Fair Trading. Failure to observe this requirement may result in penalties against the undertakings or individuals.

Restrictions may be justified before the Restrictive Practices Court through the eight 'gateways' set out in the RTPA 1976 but such justification is rare. It is more usual for modifications to be agreed with the Office of Fair Trading.

In 1962, the Restrictive Practices Court upheld the validity of the Net Book Agreements on the grounds that price fixing helped to maintain the number of booksellers and of books published, particularly books of literary or academic merit, and to hold down book prices. The conditions in the agreements were held to be indispensable to the sale of books nationally and internationally.[4]

Information agreements, particularly where advance information on prices is exchanged, may also contravene the RTPA 1976. Managers need to be careful of exchanging information, even on an informal basis, which might constitute an 'agreement' under the RTPA 1976. The Act covers agreements or 'arrangements' (not defined), whether or not they are intended to be legally enforceable.

The Resale Prices Act 1976

The Resale Prices Act 1976 prohibits resale price maintenance (RPM or price fixing). As the restriction is placed on one party only it is not covered by the RTPA 1976 (which requires a restriction on two parties). RPM is illegal whether it is carried out collectively between the suppliers of particular goods to fix the resale price of goods, or individually, where a fixed resale price is agreed with a specified purchaser.

Goods may not be withheld from a supplier who has sold goods below the resale price, except where there is reasonable cause to believe that the dealer has been using the same or similar goods as a 'loss leader' in the previous twelve months (that is, to attract buyers to purchase the goods or other products, by offering goods for a limited period below the market price).

The Competition Act 1980

The Competition Act 1980 permits the Director General of Fair Trading (DGFT) to investigate a particular course of conduct to decide whether it amounts to an anti-competitive practice. Small businesses are not usually investigated under the Competition Act 1980. Investigations have been carried out into excessive pricing and refusals to supply. Unlike the RTPA 1976 the Competition Act 1980 does not impose a duty to modify an agreement to comply with the statute.

Investigations involve two phases:

1 preliminary investigation by the DGFT to decide whether there is an anti-competitive practice; if such a practice is found an undertaking may be ordered to refrain from the anti-competitive conduct
2 referral to the Monopolies and Mergers Commission which may in turn require an undertaking from the parties or may make an order prohibiting the practice or providing remedies.

In 1988 the Monopolies and Mergers Commission expressed doubts about the wisdom of retaining the Net Book Agreements. Certain leading booksellers have campaigned for their abolition.

The Fair Trading Act 1973

Mergers with an EC dimension are now covered by EC law rather than by national law (see p. 191). However, mergers in the UK below the thresholds set by the EC Merger Regulation[5] are regulated by UK law. The Fair Trading Act (FTA) 1973 establishes a system for UK merger control through investigation by the Monopolies and Mergers Commission

(MMC). There are two schemes, one for newspapers and the other for non-newspaper mergers.

Newspaper mergers

Under the FTA 1973, newspapers with a large circulation must obtain the consent of the Secretary of State before merger with another newspaper.

Non-newspaper mergers

The FTA 1973 regulates 'merger situations', where two or more enterprises, at least one of which operates in the UK (or is controlled by an enterprise registered in the UK) have ceased to be two distinct enterprises, provided one of two tests is satisfied:

- the value of the assets taken over exceeds £70 million; or
- one party increases its market share of goods or services supplied in the UK (or a substantial part of the UK) by at least 25 per cent.

Managers should appreciate that very small acquisitions may be caught where the market in question is highly specialized or where the value of assets is high, irrespective of market share.

The parties to a merger may notify the merger to the OFT, although they are not obliged to do so. Informal guidance may also be sought from the OFT, but this is not legally binding. The OFT has twenty working days to decide whether to make a reference to the MMC. Notification avoids the risk of a compulsory reference and investigation, provided the merger takes place within the next six months. Otherwise a reference and investigation may lead to an order, including an order prohibiting a particular business acquisition or requiring the disposal of assets.

Many investigations have been carried out under the FTA 1973. In 1989 the MMC examined the tied house system in brewing, finding out that more than 90 per cent of brewers operated in such a way as to restrict competition, for example, by making preferential loans where there was an exclusive purchasing agreement.

Reform of UK law

The Government published a White Paper in 1989[6] proposing repeal of the RTPA 1976 and related legislation, to be replaced by a general prohibition on restrictive agreements based on the EC model in Article 85 of the Treaty of Rome. The prohibition is likely to involve a ban on agreements or concerted practices which have the effect of restricting or distorting competition in the UK, or in a part of the UK. The list of examples proposed is similar to that in Article 85.

These reforms have not yet been implemented. However, the Deregulation and Contracting Out Act was passed in November 1994. The Act gives the DGFT the power to propose that the Secretary of State accepts undertakings instead of monopoly references to the MMC under the FTA 1973. The Secretary of State must arrange to publish undertakings unless publication is against the public interest. The Secretary of State may classify certain agreements other than price-fixing agreements as non-notifiable. The Act also provides for undertakings to be given to the MMC before investigation under the Competition Act 1980 in place of a report by the DGFT. These provisions will take effect on 3 January 1995.

Competition under EC law

The framework for regulation within the EC is provided by Articles 85 and 86 of the EEC Treaty (the Treaty of Rome). Detailed rules for enforcement are found in secondary legislation. Articles 85 and 86 are 'directly effective' which means that they can be applied directly by the national courts of the member states without the need for further legislation. The principles of Articles 85 and 86 are extended to public undertakings by Article 90. Articles 92 to 94 ban the giving of state aids except in certain circumstances to enterprises. This mechanism makes it illegal for member states to distort competition by subsidizing ailing industries.

The principle of competition at Community level also governs tendering for public works and supply contracts above a certain value. Invitations to tender must be placed in the Official Journal, which contains notices about EC matters and proposed legislation.

Managers should be aware of the need to devise a strategy to comply with both domestic and EC competition rules. The implications of a breach of the rules are serious. The Commission has substantial powers to enforce competition law and may impose a fine of up to 10 per cent of the turnover of the enterprises concerned. When the enterprise forms part of a group the fine may be calculated on the basis of the world–wide turnover of the group. In July 1991 the biggest fine so far (£52 million) was imposed on *Tetra Pak plc* for breach of Article 86.[7] The Commission also possesses the power to investigate alleged breaches, to enter premises and to seize documents. Such enforcement tasks are often delegated to the national competition authorities.

Agreements which are illegal under Article 85

Article 85 prohibits agreements and concerted practices which have as their object or effect the prevention, restriction or distortion of competition within the common market and which may affect trade between member states. Examples of prohibited agreements include agreements to fix prices and to limit production or markets. Agreements or concerted practices which infringe Article 85 are void unless they are exempted by the Commission.

Three basic elements must be present for an infringement of Article 85:

- an agreement between enterprises, or a decision by an association of enterprises or a concerted practice;
- an effect on trade between member states;
- an object or effect of the agreement is to prevent, restrict or distort competition within the EC.

'Agreement' is interpreted liberally to include agreements which are not legally binding. A 'concerted practice' may involve an informal arrangement to exchange advance information on prices (as under UK law). In the *Net Book Agreements* case the Court of First Instance (CFI) considered that it was not necessary to establish that the agreements had an effect on trade between member states.[8] It was enough that an influence on inter-member trade could be foreseen. This influence need not be actual. A potential effect would suffice. The facts showed that about 80 per cent of books imported into Ireland came from the UK, about 75 per cent of which were marketed as net books. UK produced books amounted to about 50 per cent of books sold in Ireland. Scope existed for both an actual and potential effect on trade between member states.

Enterprises based outside the EU may be caught if the effects of their agreement are felt within the EU. In one case the enterprises responsible for supplying two-thirds of the EU requirement for wood-pulp were situated outside the EU. Despite their location they were fined for a breach of Article 85. An agreement which intends to distort competition but is unsuccessful is covered, as is the converse, i.e., an agreement which does not so intend but has the effect of distorting competition.

There have been many instances of agreements and activities which have been found to be in breach of Article 85. The following examples give some idea of the scope of prohibited agreements:

- price-fixing agreements, not only cartels but also joint discount and profit-pooling schemes
- agreements to share markets or sources of supply
- agreements which discriminate between trading partners by applying different terms to equivalent transactions, placing some parties at a competitive disadvantage
- unnecessary, supplementary terms in contracts.

Although many agreements may be seen to infringe Article 85, they may be considered desirable in commercial and consumer terms. A procedure exists under Article 85 (elaborated in Regulation 17/62)[9] which enables the Commission to grant exemption or negative clearance to an agreement which has been notified. Negative clearance is a declaration by the Commission that the agreement does not infringe Article 85. Exemption is appropriate where the agreement does infringe the Article but is considered to be beneficial.

Four conditions must be satisfied if the Commission is to grant an exemption to an agreement:

- it must contribute to improving production or distribution of goods or to promoting technical or economic progress (for example, through the discovery and application of new technology)
- it must allow customers a fair share of the resulting benefit (for example, by passing on lower prices)
- there must be no unnecessary restrictions
- there must be no elimination of competition.

An enterprise need not notify the Commission in all cases to gain exemption. Block exemptions have been granted by the Commission to cover agreements including franchising, exclusive dealing, specialization, research and development, and patent licensing. Provided the conditions (covering matters such as turnover limits) in the relevant regulation are satisfied, there is no need to notify the Commission. In other circumstances exemption is only available following individual notification.

Managers should seek legal advice before embarking on a commercial venture which may infringe Article 85. It may be possible to plan the venture so that it falls within the limits of a block exemption. Otherwise notification may be necessary. Agreements between small enterprises may be considered sufficiently minor not to require notification. Informal letters of reassurance of the competition rules known as 'comfort letters' may be issued by the Commission. They are *not* legally binding.

Abuse of a dominant position under Article 86

Article 86 prohibits any abuse by one or more enterprises within the Common Market or in a substantial part of it where it may affect trade between member states. Three key elements must be present to establish a breach:

- a dominant position in the EC or part of it
- an abuse of that position
- an effect on trade between member states.

A dominant position exists where an enterprise can, acting independently, influence the market significantly and is aware of its power. This may, sometimes, be shown by the ability to eliminate or weaken competitors, or deter competitors from entering the market. It is necessary to carry out an economic analysis to determine whether an enterprise is dominant. Such analysis will focus on two main areas: the product market and the geographical market. In some cases the temporal market is also examined where there is a seasonal factor, for example, in the supply of fresh fruits.

The product market

The relevant product market is one in which the products are regarded by consumers as readily interchangeable. The smaller and more specialized the market, the more likely it will be that dominance may be established. In one action under Article 86 the producers (who were also the importers) of bananas argued that the relevant product market was fresh fruit. The European Court of Justice rejected the argument, ruling that there was a separate market for bananas which were not regarded by consumers as interchangeable with apples or pears.[10]

Factors usually considered when identifying the product market include:

- market share; a market share below 30 per cent is unlikely to show dominance
- the length of time that the undertaking has held its position in the market
- financial and technical resources
- access to raw materials and markets.

Examples of product markets identified by the European Court of Justice include:

- advance weekly listings of programmes given in television guides in the UK and Ireland; weekly listings were distinguished from daily listings available in newspapers (regarded as a separate product market)
- spare parts for cash registers made by one producer who refused to supply competitors.

The geographical market

The geographical market is calculated by reference to the costs and feasibility of transportation and to consumer preferences. The market may be global where competition is on a world scale. The UK has been found to be a substantial part of the common market. The territory of some member states (Luxembourg, for example) may be too small to be regarded as 'substantial'.

Examples of abuses of dominant positions include:

- limiting production, markets (e.g., by refusing to supply a long-established customer) or technical development (e.g., a requirement by British Telecom (BT) that third parties could not undercharge BT)
- 'tying', that is, imposition of unnecessary additional requirements (e.g.,

the linking of tyre dealers through a system of refunds which prevented them from changing suppliers)
- imposing unfair prices or conditions, that is, prices which are either excessively high or unrealistically low (predatory pricing)
- acquisition and exercise of intellectual property rights (see Chapter 7); whether or not intellectual property rights contravene EC law depends on how they are exercised. There may be a breach of Article 30 (free movement of goods) or of Articles 85 or 86. In the Television Guide case the refusal of the copyright holder to license weekly lists of television programmes was an abuse of a dominant position.

EC merger control

Mergers have long been held to be subject to Article 86. The Mergers Control Regulation which was adopted in 1989[11] governs all mergers and takeovers (known as 'concentrations') and applies when the undertakings involved have:

- a combined world-wide turnover of ECU 5,000 million (£3,500 million) or above; or
- an EC-wide turnover of at least ECU 250 million (£175 million).

The turnover limits are likely to be lowered in the future. If each of the undertakings derives two-thirds of its business from one member state the merger will not be subject to EC control.

All concentrations covered by the regulation must be notified to the Commission which may grant an exemption (not otherwise available under Article 86). Failure to notify renders the agreement void and the undertakings liable to penalties.

Where a merger lacks an EC dimension (because it is confined to the UK or involves the UK and a country which does not belong to the EU, or where it is below the thresholds of the regulation) it is regulated by UK law. In theory, there should be no need to notify mergers covered by the regulation to the UK authorities, but uncertainty over the relationship between the two systems of merger control has led to the notification of such agreements to both national and EC authorities.

FREE MOVEMENT AND THE SINGLE MARKET

One of the fundamental principles underpinning the European Community is that of the single market. This means among other things that no member state should impose any restriction on goods which has the effect of limiting imports to that state. Such a restriction is viewed as limiting competition.

Case study 2

In the former West Germany the importation and sale of alcoholic drinks was regulated by the state as a monopoly. *Rewe-Zentral AG*, a German company, applied for a licence to import a fruit liqueur known as 'Cassis de Dijon' from France. Under German law fruit liqueurs could only be sold if they had a minimum alcohol content of 25 per cent, whereas French law required only a 15 to 20 per cent alcohol content. An import licence was refused. *Rewe* challenged the requirement in the German courts on the grounds that it contravened Article 30 of the EEC Treaty which bans measures restricting the free movement of goods within the Community. Although the legislation did not state that only German liqueurs could be sold in Germany, the indirect effect of the legislation was to safeguard the German market from foreign competition.[12]

The Court of Justice ruled that the prohibition in Article 30 covered the fixing of a minimum alcohol content by a member state in relation to the importation of alcoholic drinks lawfully produced and marketed in another member state. It followed that Germany had to admit the French liqueur, Cassis, to the German market.

Box 8.2 Cassis de Dijon (1979)

The single market and the free movement of goods

The single market is an extension of the original idea in the EEC Treaty that there should be an area within which goods, persons, services and capital may circulate freely without barriers. The Single European Act (SEA) was signed in 1986 to provide a deadline, 31 December 1992, for the removal of remaining barriers. This task has largely been achieved. The territory of the single market was extended in 1994 to cover the EFTA member states (excluding Switzerland) in a new arrangement known as the European Economic Area (EEA).

Article 30

This Article prohibits member states from applying quantitative restrictions, and all measures having equivalent effect on imports. This means that the UK, for example, cannot attach a quota (that is a measure restricting access to the UK market of a particular type of goods by number or value) to the goods of any other member state. Other member states may not attach such a quota on goods entering their territory from the UK. No state may not seek to defeat Article 30 by a measure which indirectly produces the same effect, as the *Cassis* decision shows. Article 34 imposes a similar prohibition in relation to exports.

Examples of infringements of Article 30 under the *Cassis* formula include:

- the origin-marking of certain products
- the hall-marking of silver
- a requirement to sell margarine in cube-shaped packets
- a requirement to sell wine in specially shaped bottles
- laws on the purity of beer which prohibited certain additives or preservatives
- a requirement that vinegar be made from wine (preventing the importation of vinegar made from cider).

It is difficult to etablish that a restriction is justified. Recent decisions indicate that protection of the environment and, possibly, cultural policy may justify restrictions on trade between member states.

The European Court considered that the restriction in *Cassis* was excessive since consumer protection could have been achieved by clear labelling, which would enable consumers to make up their own minds on matters such as alcohol content, preservatives and additives. The Court rejected the German government's argument that the minimum alcohol content was justified on grounds of both public health and the protection of consumers against unfair commercial practices. However, the Court did accept that restrictions applying to both imported and domestic goods might be justified where they are 'necessary' to satisfy mandatory requirements for tax purposes, or for the protection of public health, or to ensure the fairness of consumer transactions, or for the defence of the consumer.

A requirement must not exceed what is necessary. This principle, known as 'proportionality', has been widely applied in EC law, particularly in relation to the single market.

Principle of ' recognition'

In 1980 the EC Commission made an important statement about the *Cassis* decision, declaring that any products which have been lawfully produced within any of the member states must be admitted into the territories of the other member states. This principle, sometimes called the principle of 'recognition', can be seen as the basis of the single market programme and has been applied to many areas beyond the free movement of goods, such as the recognition of professional qualifications.

Uniform standards

In order to achieve uniform standards throughout the EU, two bodies have been established: CEN, dealing with general standards and CENELEC, with electrical standards. A programme of directives has been drawn up as part of the 1992 programme in relation to health, safety, consumer protection and the environment. The Toy Safety Directive, which typifies the new EU approach to technical harmonization and standards, provides that any goods bearing the 'CE' mark indicating conformity with the EU or national standard may circulate freely throughout the EU.

Article 30 and Sunday trading

The proportionality principle has been invoked in the context of Sunday trading. In the UK retailers have been prosecuted under the Shops Act 1947 for trading on Sundays. The defendants have invoked Article 30 as a defence, arguing that the UK legislation contravenes Article 30 by restricting the movement of goods between member states. Similar issues have arisen in France and Belgium out of bans on the employment of labour on Sundays.

The Court of Justice has taken the view that such legislation forms a legitimate part of national economic or social policy. Article 30 is not infringed unless the legislation exceeds what is necessary to achieve its aims. In other words, it was a matter for the UK Parliament to decide whether or not to ban Sunday trading. (The recently lifted ban did not apply to Scotland where Sunday trading was already permitted.) Now that the Sunday Trading Act 1994 is, in the main, in force, the legal position on Sunday trading in England and Wales is less restrictive, permitting shops of less than 280 square metres to be open at any time on Sunday. Other shops may open for a continuous six-hour period between 10 a.m. and 6 p.m.

In *Keck*[13] the ECJ limited the application of Article 30. The decision has widespread implications and should enable member states to exercise greater discretion in regulating trading arrangements such as Sunday trading. It is important to appreciate that while restrictions which apply equally to both domestic or imported goods may be justified if they are 'necessary' according to the *Cassis* decision, measures applying only to imported goods are illegal unless they are justified under Article 36.

The 'escape clause'

Article 36 provides an 'escape clause' enabling restrictions on imports and exports to be applied on specific circumstances, provided the restrictions do not amount to arbitrary discrimination or a disguised restriction on trade. The grounds are:

- public morality, public policy or public security
- protection of health and life of humans, animals and plants

- protection of national treasures of artistic, historic or archaeological value
- the protection of industrial or commercial property.

Article 36 was successfully invoked as a justification for restricting free movement in the following examples:

- UK legislation prohibiting the importation of pornographic materials, defined as indecent or obscene (public morality)
- a UK restriction on the import and export of gold collectors' coins (public policy)
- an Irish law requiring importers of petroleum products to buy 35 per cent of needs from the Irish National Petroleum Company at fixed prices (public security)
- the requirement for a plant health inspection to keep out a plant pest not affecting domestically produced goods (health of plants)
- a restriction arising out of a registered trademark preventing the importation of goods under another name which appeared sufficiently similar to cause confusion (industrial or commercial property).

It should be noted that in many cases involving foodstuffs the Court has been unwilling to accept restrictions unless forming part of a seriously considered health policy. Such a justification was found to apply to a UK licensing system for heat treating milk, but not to a requirement for repackaging before the milk could be sold in the UK (another application of the *Cassis* principle: the milk had already been packaged to a satisfactory standard in another member state).

The single market and the free movement of people

Under English law

Contracts which restrict the freedom of individuals to work or carry on a business have long been subject to the control of the courts in English law. Such contracts under the doctrine of 'restraint of trade' are contrary to public policy and void, unless they can be justified as reasonable. The current position is that:

- the doctrine does not apply to restrictions forming part of normal commercial or contractual relations
- if a contract is covered by the doctrine, it will only be valid if it is reasonable from the point of view of the parties and in the public interest.
- only legitimate interests of the parties may be protected
- the restriction must not be excessive in area, length of time of operation, or of prohibited trades.

Two areas in which restraints are often found in English law are in contracts of employment and in contracts for the sale of a business.

Restraints in a contract of employment

Restraints placed upon an employee in a contract of employment are only reasonable where there is a proprietary interest of the employer requiring protection. Typical restraints would be a prohibition on setting up in business within a certain distance or period of time. A 'proprietary interest' has been identified by the courts as either:

- trade secrets such as confidential information; or
- business connections such as goodwill (that is, reputation and established customers).

Restraints in a contract for the sale of a business

As with contracts of employment, restrictions in a contract for the sale of a business are only valid if they are connected with a proprietary interest which has been purchased. The courts are more willing to uphold restrictive clauses when a business is being sold (in the interests of business mobility) than in contracts of employment.

Other restrictive agreements are also of interest to the manager, and may be upheld if they are reasonable. Examples are 'solus' trading agreements between oil companies and garage owners under which an oil company lends the garage owner money to buy the garage, or offers some other advantageous terms, in return for an undertaking to sell only fuel products supplied by the company. Similar arrangements exist in the supply of other goods and services.

It is important for managers to note that the approach of the courts to contracts in restraint of trade is subject to both UK legislation (mainly the RTPA 1976) and the EEC Treaty, Articles 85 and 86.

Under EC law

The EC Treaty, as may be expected in a treaty which is essentially economic, provides for the free movement of EU nationals holding the status of 'worker' or 'provider of services' and their families. A general right of residence for European citizens independent of economic status was not recognized until the Maastricht Treaty.[14]

The free movement of workers

Article 48 of the EEC Treaty provides for the free movement of workers. Discrimination based on nationality in relation to employment, remuneration and other conditions of employment is prohibited. As with goods, this right may be restricted on grounds of public policy, public health and public security. Restrictions may not be imposed on purely economic grounds, for example to protect the employment of the state's own nationals during a recession.

A worker, defined by the European Court of Justice as someone who provides services for remuneration under the direction of another for a period of time, is entitled:

- to enter the territory of another member state to accept offers of employment
- to move freely throughout the territories of the member state for this purpose
- to stay for the purpose of employment; and
- to remain in the territory after employment.

Similar rights extend to the spouse or members of the worker's family.

Once working in a member state other than the home state, the EU worker and his family are entitled to equal treatment on a par with nationals of the state concerned.

The right of establishment and the freedom to provide services

Article 52 of the EEC Treaty provides for the abolition of restrictions on the establishment of nationals of one member state in the territory of another. This enables both individuals and enterprises (that is, companies registered in one of the member states) to set up in business in another member state, and to create agencies, branches or subsidiaries there. A new form of business organization, the European Economic Interest Group (EEIG) enables undertakings in the EU to co-operate across national boundaries for non-profit-making purposes (see Chapter 2).

Once established, EU nationals may provide services under Article 59 throughout the EU, the right of residence being restricted to the duration of the services. Only services provided for remuneration qualify. Professional people and the self-employed should be particularly aware of the opportunities for setting up in business in another member state or of providing services across national boundaries. Managers of enterprises seeking to expand or relocate the basis of their operations, should be assisted by the entitlement to establish a branch or subsidiary in another member state.

Recognition of qualifications

To speed up the harmonization of professional qualifications, a Directive was issued in 1989 based on the *Cassis de Dijon* principle of recognition of standards.[15] The Directive provides for the mutual recognition of qualifications throughout the EU of higher education diplomas requiring education or training of three years or more. Qualifications will be recognized where education or training is substantially the same in the member states. Where it is not, the same recognition may be gained by completing an adaptation period or passing an aptitude test.

A second Directive was adopted in 1992, with a two year implementation period, extending recognition to professions requiring less than three years' training provided they are regulated by the state.[16]

The two Directives on recognition of qualifications are of considerable importance to managers, making it easier to set up in business or to provide services in other member states. The removal of remaining barriers on qualifications should make it easier to achieve professional mobility where there is a skills surplus in one member state and a shortage in another.

The single market and the free movement of capital

Articles 67 to 73 of the EEC Treaty provided for the free movement of capital, but many barriers to movement remained until the completion of the internal market. A Directive (1988)[17] removing controls from the movement of capital within the EU was implemented for all member states, with the exception of Greece which had an extension until June 1994. The market in financial services has been completed by directives on banking, insurance and investment.

The EC Treaty (after amendment by the Maastricht Treaty) provides that the free movement of capital and payments will extend to transactions between the EC member states and non-member states, with some exceptions.

Managers should be aware of the improved opportunities for investment in other member states resulting from the free movement of capital, for example, in setting up a factory or opening a bank or building society account outside the UK without restriction. Inward investment into the UK may also be encouraged as member states may no longer require prior authorization before permitting its residents to open a bank account in the UK. Borrowers will also be able to 'shop around' between the member states for the best source of finance.

STRATEGIES FOR MANAGERS

Managers should identify any agreements or practices which their enterprise has adopted which potentially or actually restrict competition in the market in which the enterprise operates. The market also needs to be identified, so that the relevant law can be identified. Similarly it may be worth obtaining information about the agreements and practices followed by competing enterprises if there is any suspicion that these may be illegal under UK or EC law, since the enterprise can challenge their validity.

If an enterprise is considering entering an agreement or adopting a practice which may restrict competition, then legal advice should be sought as to whether it is necessary to notify the national or EC authorities of a proposed agreement. It may be possible to draft the agreement in such a way that it is covered by a block exemption. Care should be taken that agreements drawn up now in the UK comply with the proposed approach in the White Paper.[18]

Managers should ensure that their products meet the relevant UK and EC technical standards. If they do, these products may circulate freely within the EC. Barriers to free movement within the EC may be reported to the Commission or challenged before the national courts. It is most important to remember that goods should be clearly labelled particularly if they are to be exported to another EC member state.

Considerable export opportunities are offered not only by the single market but also by the European Economic Area which opens up such potential markets as Austria and Scandinavia. The counter-risk is that products from the rest of EC and the EEA gain access to the UK market. To compete successfully UK goods must be produced to a sufficiently high standard in quality and price.

Managers should ensure that their enterprise's recruitment practices reflect the availability of skilled workers and professionals throughout the EC. This may involve reference to adaptation periods or aptitude tests. Managers should also ensure that they are in a position to take advantage of the possibilities of setting up branches or agencies in other member states and of providing services across national boundaries.

KEY LEARNING POINTS

- **Anti-competitive agreements made in the UK or another EC member state may contravene EC law where there is a potential effect on trade between member states.**
- **Competition in UK law is currently regulated by a number of statutes, notably the Restrictive Trade Practices Act 1976 which concentrates on the form of the agreement. If the recommendations**

of the White Paper[19] are adopted, competition law in the UK will be reformed along the lines of EC competition law.

● Article 85 of the EC Treaty prohibits agreements and concerted practices which restrict competition in the EC. Such agreements are void unless exempted by the Commission.

● Article 86 prohibits abuse of a dominant position. To determine whether Article 86 has been infringed, an economic analysis of the product market and the geographical market should be carried out. Mergers with an EC dimension which are covered by the Merger Regulation may be notified to the Commission for the purpose of exemption.

● *The Cassis de Dijon* decision has been interpreted to mean that goods which satisfy the standards of one member state may circulate freely within the EC as a whole. This principle has underpinned the single market programme.

● Articles 30 to 36 provide for free movement of goods within the EC. Movement may only be restricted under Article 36 in limited circumstances.

● UK law severely limits the ability of employers or purchasers of a business to restrict the subsequent business activities of former employees or sellers of the business.

● Articles 48 and 59 provide for the free movement of people within the EC, either as workers, or those exercising the right of establishment (a right which may also be exercised by an enterprise) or the freedom to provide services. There is no general right of residence until Article 8 of the EC Treaty (providing for European citizenship) is implemented.

EXERCISES

1   Find out whether there are any agreements or practices by which your enterprise restricts the availability of goods or services or information to other enterprises. If there are, consider whether they are lawful. If they are not, what should the enterprise do to protect its position?

2   Does your enterprise have any difficulty in obtaining goods or services or information because of restrictions placed on their availability by other enterprises? If yes, are the restrictions lawful?

3   Find out whether there are any restrictions on the price at which you buy or sell goods or services. If there are, consider whether they are lawful. If they are unlawful, what should the enterprise do about them?

4   Find out whether your enterprise has a policy on the labelling of its

products. If it has, is the policy effective to ensure compliance with UK and EC law. If it is not, draft such a policy.

5   Consider the legal implications for staff recruitment if your enterprise wishes to recruit personnel from EU member states or wishes to transfer UK personnel to a European base.

NOTES: CASE REFERENCES ETC

1 *Re Net Book Agreement 1957* [1962] 1 WLR 1347; [1962] 3 All ER 751.
2 Case T-66/89 *Publishers' Association* v *EC Commission (re the Net Book Agreements)* [1992] 5 CMLR 120; [1992] 4 All ER 70. On appeal to the ECJ as Case C-360/92P *Publishers' Association* v *EC Commission* (pending).
3 As footnote 2 above.
4 As footnote 1 above.
5 Council Regulation 4064/89/EEC on the control of concentrations between undertakings.
6 *Opening Markets: New Policies on Restrictive Trade Practices*, Cm 727, 1 July 1989.
7 Case T-51/89 *Tetra Pak Rausing SA* v *EC Commission* [1990] ECR II-309; [1991] 4 CMLR 334.
8 As footnote 2 above.
9 Regulation 17/62, the First Regulation implementing Arts. 85 and 86 of the Treaty.
10 Case 27/76 *United Brands* v *EC Commission* [1978] 1 CMLR 429; [1978] ECR 207.
11 Regulation 4064/89.
12 Case 120/78 *Rewe-Zentral AG* v *Bundesmonopolverwaltung für Branntwein ('Cassis de Dijon')* [1979] ECR 649; [1979] 3 CMLR 494.
13 *'Keck and another'*, The Times, 25 November 1993.
14 See Articles 8 and 8a of the EC Treaty (Maastricht version) which are not yet implemented.
15 Directive 89/48/EEC on a general system for the recognition of higher education diplomas awarded on completion of professional education and training of at least three years' duration.
16 Directive 92/51/EEC.
17 Directive 88/361/EEC.
18 See footnote 6 above.
19 See footnote 6 above.

JOURNALS AND DATABASES

Common Market Law Review.
European Law Review.
European Business Law Review.
Journal of Common Market Studies.
Databases: *CELEX* (official EC database); *JUSTIS* (provides gateway to *CELEX*); *SPEARHEAD* (DTI database; provides gateway to *CELEX*); *LEXIS* (commercial legal database).

FURTHER READING

DTI publications on the single market and the EEA.
European Commission background reports and weekly briefing.
White Paper *Opening Markets: New Policies on Restrictive Trade Practices*, Cm 727, 1 July 1989.
Dinan, D. (1994) *Ever Closer Union? An Introduction to the European Community*, London: Macmillan.
Green, N., Hartley, T.C. and Usher, J.A. (1991) *The Legal Foundations of the Single European Market*, Oxford: Oxford University Press.
Kent, P. (1991) *European Community Law*, London: Pitman Publishing.
Rotherley, B. (1993) *What Maastricht Means for Business*, London: Gower.
Singleton, E.S. (1992) *Introduction to Competition Law*, London: Pitman Publishing.
Weatherill, S. (1994) *Cases and Materials on EC Law*, London: Blackstone Press.
Weatherill, S. and Beaumont, P. (1993) *EC Law*, Harmondsworth: Penguin.
Whish, R. (1993) *Competition Law*, London: Butterworths.

USEFUL ADDRESSES

European Commission Information Office
8 Storey's Gate
London SW1P 3AT   Tel. no. 0171 973 1992

European Parliament Information Office
2 Queen Anne's Gate
London SW1H 9AA   Tel. no. 0171 222 0411

Department of Trade and Industry telephone 'hotline'   01272 444 888.

Chapter 9

Future developments

Edited by Anne Ruff

Law is not a fixed, immutable body of rules. Aspects of the law are always changing. Successful managers need to keep themselves informed about changes in those areas of law which are of particular relevance to their enterprise.

This chapter makes some suggestions about how a manager can keep up to date with legal change, as well as highlighting areas of likely reform or change in the context of Chapters 2–8. Finally there will be a discussion of general strategies which managers could adopt to make their enterprise 'litigation resistant', if not 'litigation proof'.

KEEPING UP TO DATE

Cases are decided both in the English courts and in the European Court of Justice. The important decisions are normally to be found in the Law Reports. In addition, and usually of more profound significance, there are changes in the law introduced by English or EC legislation. Managers generally will not have the time or the desire to plough through recent cases and legislation. An enterprise needs to ensure that it has up-to-date legal information. It should obtain on a regular basis information about changes in the law in a straightforward and practical form. This can be done by:

- obtaining leaflets and brochures from, for example, the Office of Fair Trading, the Department of Trade and Industry, or the Department of Employment, or the European Commission Information Office
- being put on the mailing list of organizations which have a regular newsletter, such as the Health and Safety Commission
- subscribing to trade journals or even legal/industrial relations journals, such as the *Equal Opportunities Review*, or the *New Law Journal*
- purchasing relevant books, particularly loose-leaf volumes which have an up-dating service such as Tolley's *Employment Law*.
- enabling employees to attend relevant seminars and conferences.

LIKELY DEVELOPMENTS

This section highlights areas of likely reform or change in the context of Chapters 2–8. As will be seen, many of the proposed reforms have been suggested by the various bodies of the EU. The EU, itself is currently in the process of major change, and the implications of this are also discussed.

Enterprise structures, finance and the law

The main developments are likely to be in company law rather than in the law relating to partnerships and sole traders.

As in the past, future developments of company law will predominantly be influenced by the harmonization programme of the European Commission in Brussels and to a lesser degree by changes on a purely national level.

Several EC Directives and a regulation of great significance for the management of companies are presently still at the proposal or draft stage.

Board structure and worker participation

The Fifth Draft Directive, dating back to 1972, concerns the board structure of public limited companies employing more than 1,000 workers within the EU and worker participation in corporate decision-making. According to the latest draft of 1989 the member states may choose:

● a two-tier board of directors, one with a managerial function and one with a supervisory function, as found in Germany, or
● a one-tier board of directors, as exists in the UK.

If a one-tier board of directors is adopted, it must be composed of solely managing, executive directors and solely supervising, non-executive directors.

Worker participation may be achieved by:

● representation on the one-tier or two-tier board at supervisory level
● a works council
● a collective agreement between the company and a body representing the employees, allowing either board representation or rights to consultation.

The Commission has also proposed a Directive, known as the 'Vredeling' Directive, applicable to organizations with a work force of more than 1,000 persons within the EU. This proposal deals with the procedures for informing and consulting employee representatives at least once a year.

Both these Directives still await approval by the member states and are not very popular in the UK. The Conservative government favours voluntary, rather than mandatory consultation and participation of workers.

Furthermore the United Kingdom is the only member state to have opted out of the Social Chapter. This provides for more involvement of employees in their enterprise's decision-making process.

Draft regulation for a 'European company'

A 1989 draft regulation proposed that two or more public limited companies from different member states should be able to merge or form a joint holding company or subsidiary, known as 'Societa Europa'. This company would be governed by the provisions of the European Commission's draft company statute and the national law of the country where it was registered.

The Department of Trade and Industry has issued a consultative document on these proposals. They are not favoured by the current government, because they also provide for employee participation and consultation. A Labour government may well have different views on the issue of employee participation.

The relationship between the holding company and a subsidiary company

The Ninth Draft Directive, first proposed in 1984, deals with the relationship between dominant (or holding) companies and their subsidiaries. It aims for a 'unified management' of a public limited company and any other enterprise with a controlling interest in it, whether or not that enterprise is a company. The Directive intends to establish to what extent a dominant company is bound to consider the interests of its subsidiaries and the members of these subsidiaries, and also to what extent the dominant company should be liable for the debts of its subsidiaries. English law at present does not provide a satisfactory answer to these issues. The dominant company will only be liable if it has given a formal guarantee for its subsidiary.

Proposed Directives

These include:

- a *Tenth Directive* dealing with mergers based on share exchange
- a *Thirteenth Directive* dealing with takeovers and disclosure of information by the parties involved in the takeovers, and the equal treatment of shareholders.

Other directives are pending on matters such as:

- disclosure of major shareholdings in listed companies
- co-ordinating regulations on insider dealing
- consolidated accounts of certain partnerships and unlimited companies.

The Cadbury Code

The law still needs to address the issue of the accountability of large public companies to their shareholders. The courts are not usually willing to support litigation by shareholders against companies. However, the Department of Trade and Industry and the Securities and Investments Board are now empowered by law to act as watchdogs on behalf of the shareholders. In 1993 the Committee on the Financial Aspects of Corporate Governance issued the 'Cadbury Code' giving guidelines on aspects of corporate governance, such as the composition of the board of directors of executive and independent non-executive directors, conduct at board meetings, requirement of shareholders' approval for directors' service contracts for more than three years, financial reporting by companies to give a fair and true assessment of their position. These recommendations are to be implemented by companies on a voluntary basis.

The enterprise and its workforce

There are a variety of changes put forward which would affect the rights of employees.

Anti-discrimination laws

It has been argued that the scope of the Race Relations Act 1976 should be extended to cover religious discrimination. At present protection is afforded to religious groups who have common ethnic origins, for example Sikhs and Jews, but not otherwise. It has also been suggested that in cases of indirect discrimination, attention should focus less on the existence of a requirement or condition which causes disadvantage and more on the discriminatory result. Thus a finding that collective bargaining was conducted in a non-discriminatory way may not be sufficient in itself to justify a difference in pay for work of equal value carried out for the same employer. Given the Employment Appeal Tribunal's endorsement of the view that the time it takes for an equal value case to be completed is wholly unacceptable, some alteration to procedures in this area is anticipated. Despite considerable pressure being exerted, including several Private Members' Bills in Parliament, there is still little prospect of legislation outlawing age discrimination. However, legislation in 1995 is likely, affording greater employment rights to disabled persons.

Industrial tribunal practice and procedure

The government has recently used its powers to give these tribunals jurisdiction to hear claims for breach of contract which are outstanding on termination of employment. Such a reform was long overdue, even though it will add to the heavy caseload of both the tribunals and the EAT. These institutions are already overburdened and the problems of delay in obtaining both an initial and an appeal hearing will have to be addressed in the very near future if the system is to be maintained.

The enterprise and its environment: occupational health and safety

The major changes in occupational health and safety now come from the EU. The Framework Directive and five subordinate directives were introduced into English law by a form of subordinate legislation called regulations. These came into effect on 1 January 1993. The implementation of these regulations at the workplace is likely to be a major concern for employers for the foreseeable future.

The Management of Health and Safety at Work Regulations 1992

These implement the Framework Directive and are particularly challenging because of their requirement that every employer make a risk assessment and respond to it by setting up and maintaining a system to control the hazards identified. Now that these regulations are in force, managers will need to watch for guidance in case law or literature as to how these obligations can best be discharged. The requirement within these regulations that employers appoint competent persons to assist them in complying with safety law is also a new concept with which English management will have to grapple and it may be expected that the evolving system of National Vocational Qualifications (NVQs) will result in the identification of standards of competence in safety management.

Subordinate regulations

Of the subordinate regulations the Health and Safety (Display Screen Equipment) Regulations 1992, SI 1992 No. 2792, have attracted most attention, but a systematic response to the Manual Handling Operations Regulations 1992, SI 1992 No. 2051, might actually do more to maintain the health of persons at work.

Other developments

A controversial question remains as to whether the United Kingdom sufficiently complies with EC requirements for worker participation with management in determining workplace safety standards. It is possible therefore that there may be further United Kingdom regulations to amend or supplement the existing Safety Representatives and Safety Committees

Regulations 1978 in order to introduce a system of safety representatives and safety committees to non-unionized workplaces. Meanwhile the Trade Union Reform and Employment Rights Act 1993 has given employees the right not to suffer detriment or dismissal as a result of activities in connection with preventing or reducing health and safety risks at the workplace.

It is likely that future developments in English law on occupational health and safety will be the introduction of further sets of regulations to comply with the ongoing activities of the European Community in adopting Directives to harmonize the laws of the Community in relation to particular hazards. One example is the Construction (Design and Management) Regulations which after much debate will be implemented during 1995, to ensure that effective direction and co-ordination of health and safety matters takes place throughout the duration of a construction project. For the most part, however, any further sets of regulations are likely to concern hazardous substances whose dangers are made apparent as the development of scientific knowledge both identifies the risks and the means of controlling them.

The enterprise and its environment: planning and pollution controls

As in the previous sections the EC has had a major impact on this area of law. This impact will increase with the implementation of the Maastricht Treaty.

Action programmes

There have been four Action Programmes in this field of law, and the fifth was agreed in 1993. It is planned to run for longer than normal, i.e. from 1993–2000. It is much wider than previous programmes and emphasizes amongst other things the need to reduce waste and damage to the environment caused not just by industry but also by agriculture, tourism and transport. Fiscal measures will be more important ('polluter pays') as will more freedom of information, education and cost/benefit analysis.

Integration of environmental issues

In 1987 the Single European Act made changes to the Treaty of Rome which among other things required that a high level of environmental protection should be achieved in the internal market, and introduced a formal legal basis for EC action in relation to the environment. In addition it is clear from the Action Programmes and policy proposals that the EC aims more and more to integrate environmental issues into its other activities. An illustration is the emphasis on 'sustainable' development and the importance attached to the 'precautionary' principle in the Fifth Action Programme.

Other EC initiatives include the establishment of a European Environment Agency in Denmark and draft Directives on Integrated Pollution Control and on Civil Liability for Harm to the Environment. These Directives, if passed, would have a major impact on UK enterprises. There is also a draft Packaging Directive (see p. 211) which is close to final agreement.

Other developments

On the international front, although much cynicism has been expressed about the United Nations Rio Conference in 1992, there seem to be some moves by the EC, the USA and others to begin to give effect to some of the agreements contained in e.g., the climate change Convention, and the concept of 'sustainability', with implementation through the Agenda 21 action programme. All of this may seem somewhat distant, but it could eventually emerge as new law in this country.

On the national front, there are a number of points to note. First, the government will be under increasing pressure to bring UK law into line with a number of EC Directives, e.g. Impact Assessment. Equally, there are a number of Directives which will have to be implemented in the near future, e.g., relating to water quality. Second, the categories and implementation of IPC and APC are under review. Third, a new integrated Environmental Protection Agency designed to replace the majority of separate bodies involved in environmental and pollution control is again on the political agenda. Fourth, the introduction of a new Urban Regeneration Agency in England and Wales, with its remit to target disused land for development, could have an impact on the planning regime as it will be able to override the normal planning process. Fifth, the EC emphasis on sustainable development is being reflected in UK planning controls, particularly in Policy Guidances. For example, out of town developments should be restricted and proposals which discourage use of the car and encourage inner city developments are to be favoured.

Finally, there have been a number of calls for some kind of Environment Court, which indicates some of the problems which have arisen in relation to the enforcement of the wide range of criminal and civil liabilities.

The enterprise and its product

There are three areas of potential development in English law, as well as one EC proposal of importance.

Consumer guarantees

Recent years have seen several law reform proposals, and in 1992 the DTI published a Consultation Document on consumer guarantees, inviting views on the following proposals, viz:

1 The manufacturer should be civilly liable under statute for the performance of his guarantee to the consumer. In cases where the manufacturer is outside the UK, the manufacturer's guarantee would be enforceable against the importer.
2 The retailer should be jointly and severally liable with the manufacturer for the manufacturer's guarantee to a consumer.
3 Manufacturers or, in the case of imported goods, importers, should be liable with the seller for the satisfactory quality of goods under the Sale of Goods Act.

Meanwhile, November 1993 saw publication of the *European Commission's Green Paper on Guarantees and After-Sales Services* (COM(93) 509). The Green Paper deals with legal (i.e. consumer) guarantees, commercial guarantees and also after-sales services. National legislation will have to await the outcome of this consultation process.

Privity of contract

The English Law Commission has proposed a change to the principle of privity of contract which as a general rule only allows parties to a contract to sue and be sued on the contract (see pp. 18 and 149). The tort of negligence and the Consumer Protection Act 1987 would sometimes provide a remedy where a third party suffers physical injury or damage to property, but not where the only loss was economic such as loss of profits. Another area where privity causes difficulty is where work is subcontracted and there is a chain of contracts. The main contractor cannot usually sue a sub-contractor for breach of contract. The Law Commission has proposed that the law should be reformed to allow third parties to enforce contractual provisions made in their favour. However, it should be noted that similar proposals were also put forward over fifty years ago.

New remedies

Certain developments have considerable potential as the basis for new remedies. These developments have mainly been in the field of services. It is not uncommon for providers of services to form organizations which then regulate the activities of their members. One example is ABTA (Association of British Travel Agents.) Such organizations often provide arbitration or conciliation as a method of resolving a dispute between, for example in the case of ABTA, a dissatisfied holidaymaker and the tour operator. Usually an aggrieved individual can also take the organization to court. In a limited number of situations the individual may be able to make a complaint to an Ombudsman who can investigate it and recommend how the dispute should be resolved.

Packaging

The EC issued in 1993 an amended draft Directive aimed at encouraging manufacturers to reduce the amount of packaging used and to recycle more of that packaging. The final version will soon be agreed. Manufacturers and retailers are likely to be required to recover initially 25–40 per cent of their packaging waste. The percentage will be increased to 50–65 per cent within five years. Products will have to state how much of the packaging is recycled. A Packaging Standards Council was established in the United Kingdom in 1992, which applies a code of practice and deals with complaints about packaging.

The enterprise and its intellectual property

Not surprisingly, most of the likely developments in intellectual property law come from the European Community.

Patent recognition

Potentially the most important development is the Community Patent Convention. The Convention would provide a system whereby a patent obtained in one member state would be recognized in all others. This, however, will not come into force until ratified by all member states. Given that the Convention dates from 1975 and is still subject to national concerns and political horse trading, it may still be some time before it comes into law. One of the concerns some member states have is in relation to the patentability of biotechnological inventions. An EC directive on the legal protection of biotechnological inventions is due by 1995 which aims to harmonize the exclusion of subject matter from patentability on moral grounds. This moral and political issue will continue to be a matter of dispute generally.

Trade marks

The Trade Marks Act to implement the EC Trade Marks Directive passed through Parliament in 1994 receiving the Royal Assent on 21 July 1994. The Act widens the definition of trade marks to include any sign capable of distinguishing goods and extends protection against lookalike products. In addition there are long term proposals for the introduction of a unified Community trade mark.

Decompilation of computer programs

The EC Computer Programs Directive has been incorporated into UK law by the Copyright (Computer Programs) Regulations 1992, Sl 1992 No. 3233. The most important effect of this is to allow decompilation of computer programs where it is necessary to achieve interoperability. This has been, and will continue to be, a hotly disputed area in Europe and America. Difficult political and judicial decisions will have to be made to draw a line between protection of computer program authors' rights and the prevention of monopolies.

Other developments

The 1992 EC Directive on rental and lending rights gives copyright owners the exclusive right to authorize or prohibit the rental or lending of their material. It also gives performers and broadcasters similar rights in relation to re-production. The Directive should be implemented by 1995.

Draft EC proposals on design law seem to be a long way from even draft legislation. So far proposals have foundered on the conflicting interests of differing manufacturing industries.

Draft Directives have been issued on the co-ordination of copyright regarding satellite broadcasting and cable re-transmission, data protection and harmonizing protection of copyright. Such moves reflect the desire of the EU to move towards a harmonized intellectual property regime and the need for the law to keep up with rapidly developing technology.

The enterprise and competition

It is clear that the strongest impetus for change from the EC whose approach is likely to dominate competition law and policy in the UK in the future. The government published a White Paper in 1989, *Opening Markets: New Policies in Restrictive Trade Practices*, Cm 727, which proposed reforming UK competition law to bring it into line with EC law. The Deregulation and Contracting Out Act 1994 introduced some piecemeal changes to this area of the law, rather than wholesale reform. In addition legislation reforming the Sunday trading laws was passed in 1994.

Agreements which restrict or distort competition in the UK

The White Paper proposed that UK law should adapt the principle in Article 85 of the EC Treaty so that it is no longer only applicable to agreements which affect trade between member states. It will in effect be applicable to agreements which have the object or the effect of restricting or distorting competition in the UK unless the agreement does not have an appreciable effect. If the total turnover of the parties to the agreement is not more than £5 million then it is unlikely that the legislation will apply.

However, all resale price maintenance agreements will be regulated by the proposed legislation. It is uncertain to what extent the grant of licences of intellectual property rights, such as the right to use a patent or know-how, will be regulated under the new provisions.

Individual and block exemptions from the provisions will be available. The latter are likely to include agreements between a supplier or manufacturer and a retailer which give a retailer the exclusive right to obtain goods from the supplier or manufacturer or to sell the goods in a particular area.

Any agreements made in breach of the legislation will be void unless exempt. Enterprises entering into such an agreement will be liable to pay a heavy fine which is likely to have a maximum figure of £1,000,000. Directors and managers can incur personal liability of up to £100,000. In addition enterprises will also be liable to pay damages to any third party who can establish that their business was damaged by the agreement.

Newspaper sales

The Monopolies and Mergers Commission published a report in 1993 on newspaper sales which made various recommendations including a proposal that the supply and distribution of newspapers needed to be reformed. This was because under the present system wholesalers will not supply new retail outlets if they consider that a particular area has an adequate number of such outlets. The MMC concluded that this system amounted to a monopoly which was not in the public interest and proposed that retailers should be able to supply other outlets.

The enterprise and the European Union

The EC Treaty (see Chapter 1) set out the basic economic and social aims of what was originally known as the European Community, which included the idea of a common or single market.

The Single European Act 1985

The Single European Act 1985 gave impetus to the single market by aiming to get rid of existing internal barriers to trade and to achieve harmonization and centralization of the rules which apply to the market, by 31 December 1992. In particular, the Act had certain specific goals including health and safety of workers, research and technological development, as well as environmental and consumer protection. Most of the 282 proposals for the implementation of the single market have been approved by the EC and have become part of the national law of the member states.

The introduction of the single market is having a far-reaching and general impact on business in the United Kingdom, because all enterprises, even small local ones, are in reality operating in a European not a UK market. This market now accounts for more than one-third of all world import and export trade.

The rationale for the single market is economic and political, not legal. Nevertheless, the law is one of the mechanisms which helps to establish the single market. As can be seen by looking at all the chapters in this book, EC law has had and will continue to have a considerable impact on enterprises.

The major changes which came into effect on 1 January 1993 were the abolition of border controls and formalities for traders. This has, for example, made life much easier for international trucking enterprises which no longer have to queue for hours to obtain customs clearance. In addition a new system for administering VAT for intra-EC trade was introduced which effectively shifted VAT obligations from shippers and forwarders to an enterprise's own accounting system. Collection of intra-EC trade statistics now falls on importers and exporters. Banking and insurance became part of the single market for the first time. Finally many technical changes were introduced, mostly relating to standards and to health and safety regulations.

One factor still remains a major obstacle to a complete single market. Divergent product standards in different member states in practice mean that manufacturers often have to manufacture different products for different countries. However, under the *Cassis de Dijon* principle (see Chapter 8), goods which have been produced to the standard required by one member state cannot be excluded by any of the other states. In 1987 the EC introduced ISO 9000, a quality assurance system applying to all aspects of manufacturing. ISO 9000 provides a purchaser with proof that a product has been manufactured to satisfactory standards of design, production and inspection.

The Maastricht Treaty

The Maastricht Treaty, formally known as the Treaty on European Union (TEU), was ratified in November 1993. This treaty built upon the foundations of the Single European Act. It is chiefly concerned with achieving economic and monetary union, as well as political union in the EU. The Treaty deals with many matters beyond the scope of this book, but it is worth noting that:

- its goals include full economic and monetary union (supposedly by 1999) and a common currency called the ECU (European Currency Unit), which is at present used as the unit of account within the EU and increasingly used in international accounting
- it adopts policies relating to the environment and to consumer protection
- it has introduced the concept of European citizenship which, when fully implemented, will allow nationals of the European Union to settle anywhere in the member states' territory
- its Social Chapter has been adopted by eleven member states but not by the United Kingdom. The Social Chapter is concerned with improving living and working conditions, terms of employment, employee consultation and social security. UK enterprises which operate both in the UK and in other EC states need to be aware that different requirements may be applicable in those states
- it adopts the principle of 'subsidiarity' which recognizes the right of member states to implement the aims of the EC through legislation. The EC should only take action where that is necessary to achieve the objectives of the treaty
- the European Parliament has an increased legislative role in certain areas including trans-European networks in transport, telecommunications and energy, training, consumer affairs and the environment.

Expansion of the European Union

There are two routes for widening membership of the EU in the future. The first is by extending membership to member states of the European Free Trade Association. Six of the seven member states (Austria, Finland, Iceland, Liechtenstein, Norway and Sweden) have agreed to create a European Economic Area (EEA) which in effect extends the operation of the single market to these states. The EEA came into effect in 1994 and should open up additional valuable export markets. Sweden, Finland and Austria became full members of the EU on 1 January 1995.

The second route for extending membership is by admitting as members east European states which were members of the former Soviet bloc. These states have only recently moved to free market economies and have levels of prosperity well below those of current EU members. As a result full membership is not an immediate prospect.

STRATEGIES FOR MANAGERS

The overall conclusion must be that enterprises should aim to avoid legal disputes. Managers should try to have systems and procedures in place which minimize the risk of legal liability and which if legal liability arises, reduce the extent of that liability.

Each of the preceding chapters, apart from Chapter 1, suggests strategies in relation to the subject-matter of the particular chapter. Some common themes arise which are worth emphasizing.

Enterprises should have a system which provides for the obtaining, holding and distribution of legal information to relevant personnel.

Enterprises should ensure that their processes and procedures meet current legal and technical standards.

Employees should receive regular training and up-dating sessions about relevant new techniques and legal requirements. A system should be in place for incorporating such changes into the day to day operation of the enterprise.

Enterprises should have clear lines of responsibility, with such responsibilities specifically allocated to particular individuals.

Enterprises should keep accurate, precise and confidential records.

Enterprises should adopt a European marketing and production strategy.

Index